Foreign Policy, Domestic Politics and International Relations

This book offers a re-examination of foreign policy in relation to domestic politics and international relations.

Bringing together a vast body of literature from International Relations, Foreign Policy Analysis, Comparative Politics and Public Policy, this book systematically reconceptualises foreign policy as a dialectic produced by the interplay of context, strategy and discourse. It argues that foreign policy defies easy understandings and necessitates a complex framework of analysis. It therefore introduces the 'strategic-relational model', as conceptualised in critical realism, to the field of Foreign Policy Analysis for the first time. Combining a comprehensive investigation of Italian foreign policy over the last century with an exploration of a key theoretical issue within the field of Foreign Policy Analysis and International Relations, this book analyses key episodes within Italian foreign policy, including Italy's Cold War alliance politics, colonial interventions, fascist foreign policy and participation in the wars of Kosovo, Iraq and Afghanistan. It provides a comprehensive and up-to-date account of the long-term historical trajectory of Italian foreign policy, from the Liberal age to the 'Second Republic', including all four governments of Silvio Berlusconi.

Foreign Policy, Domestic Politics and International Relations will be of interest to students and scholars of International Relations, Foreign Policy Analysis and Italian politics.

Elisabetta Brighi is a Lecturer in International Relations at the Department of Politics and International Studies at the University of Cambridge, UK.

Routledge Advances in International Relations and Global Politics

1 **Foreign Policy and Discourse Analysis**
France, Britain and Europe
Henrik Larsen

2 **Agency, Structure and International Politics**
From ontology to empirical enquiry
Gil Friedman and Harvey Starr

3 **The Political Economy of Regional Co-operation in the Middle East**
Ali Carkoglu, Mine Eder and Kemal Kirisci

4 **Peace Maintenance**
The evolution of international political authority
Jarat Chopra

5 **International Relations and Historical Sociology**
Breaking down boundaries
Stephen Hobden

6 **Equivalence in Comparative Politics**
Edited by Jan W. van Deth

7 **The Politics of Central Banks**
Robert Elgie and Helen Thompson

8 **Politics and Globalisation**
Knowledge, ethics and agency
Martin Shaw

9 **History and International Relations**
Thomas W. Smith

10 **Idealism and Realism in International Relations**
Robert M. A. Crawford

11 **National and International Conflicts, 1945–1995**
New empirical and theoretical approaches.
Frank Pfetsch and Christoph Rohloff

12 **Party Systems and Voter Alignments Revisited**
Edited by Lauri Karvonen and Stein Kuhnle

13 **Ethics, Justice and International Relations**
Constructing an international community
Peter Sutch

14 **Capturing Globalization**
Edited by James H. Mittelman and Norani Othman

15 **Uncertain Europe**
Building a new European security order?
Edited by Martin A. Smith and Graham Timmins

16 **Power, Postcolonialism and International Relations**
Reading race, gender and class
Edited by Geeta Chowdhry and Sheila Nair

17 **Constituting Human Rights**
Global civil society and the society of democratic states
Mervyn Frost

18 **US Economic Statecraft for Survival 1933–1991**
Of sanctions, embargoes and economic warfare
Alan P. Dobson

19 **The EU and NATO Enlargement**
Richard McAllister and Roland Dannreuther

20 **Spatializing International Politics**
Analysing activism on the internet
Jayne Rodgers

21 **Ethnonationalism in the Contemporary World**
Walker Connor and the study of nationalism
Edited by Daniele Conversi

22 **Meaning and International Relations**
Edited by Peter Mandaville and Andrew Williams

23 **Political Loyalty and the Nation-State**
Edited by Michael Waller and Andrew Linklater

24 **Russian Foreign Policy and the CIS**
Theories, debates and actions
Nicole J. Jackson

25 **Asia and Europe**
Development and different dimensions of ASEM
Yeo Lay Hwee

26 **Global Instability and Strategic Crisis**
Neville Brown

27 **Africa in International Politics**
External involvement on the continent
Edited by Ian Taylor and Paul Williams

28 **Global Governmentality**
Governing international spaces
Edited by Wendy Larner and William Walters

29 **Political Learning and Citizenship Education Under Conflict**
The political socialization of Israeli and Palestinian youngsters
Orit Ichilov

30 **Gender and Civil Society**
Transcending boundaries
Edited by Jude Howell and Diane Mulligan

31 **State Crises, Globalisation and National Movements in North-East Africa**
The Horn's dilemma
Edited by Asafa Jalata

32 **Diplomacy and Developing Nations**
Post-cold war foreign policy-making structures and processes
Edited by Justin Robertson and Maurice A. East

33 **Autonomy, Self-governance and Conflict Resolution**
Innovative approaches to institutional design in divided societies
Edited by Marc Weller and Stefan Wolff

34 **Mediating International Crises**
Jonathan Wilkenfeld, Kathleen J. Young, David M. Quinn and Victor Asal

35 **Postcolonial Politics, the Internet and Everyday Life**
Pacific traversals online
M. I. Franklin

36 **Reconstituting the Global Liberal Order**
Legitimacy and regulation
Kanishka Jayasuriya

37 **International Relations, Security and Jeremy Bentham**
Gunhild Hoogensen

38 **Interregionalism and International Relations**
Edited by Heiner Hänggi, Ralf Roloff and Jürgen Rüland

39 **The International Criminal Court**
A global civil society achievement
Marlies Glasius

40 **A Human Security Doctrine for Europe**
Project, principles, practicalities
Edited by Marlies Glasius and Mary Kaldor

41 **The History and Politics of UN Security Council Reform**
Dimitris Bourantonis

42 **Russia and NATO Since 1991**
From cold war through cold peace to partnership?
Martin A. Smith

43 **The Politics of Protection**
Sites of insecurity and political agency
Edited by Jef Huysmans, Andrew Dobson and Raia Prokhovnik

44 **International Relations in Europe**
Traditions, perspectives and destinations
Edited by Knud Erik Jørgensen and Tonny Brems Knudsen

45 **The Empire of Security and the Safety of the People**
Edited by William Bain

46 **Globalization and Religious Nationalism in India**
The search for ontological security
Catrina Kinnvall

47 **Culture and International Relations**
Narratives, natives and tourists
Julie Reeves

48 **Global Civil Society**
Contested futures
Edited by Gideon Baker and David Chandler

49 **Rethinking Ethical Foreign Policy**
Pitfalls, possibilities and paradoxes
Edited by David Chandler and Volker Heins

50 **International Cooperation and Arctic Governance**
Regime effectiveness and northern region building
Edited by Olav Schram Stokke and Geir Hønneland

51 **Human Security**
Concepts and implications
Shahrbanou Tadjbakhsh and Anuradha Chenoy

52 **International Relations and Security in the Digital Age**
Edited by Johan Eriksson and Giampiero Giacomello

53 **State-Building**
Theory and practice
Edited by Aidan Hehir and Neil Robinson

54 **Violence and Non-Violence in Africa**
Edited by Pal Ahluwalia, Louise Bethlehem and Ruth Ginio

55 **Developing Countries and Global Trade Negotiations**
Edited by Larry Crump and S. Javed Maswood

56 **Civil Society, Religion and Global Governance**
Paradigms of power and persuasion
Edited by Helen James

57 **War, Peace and Hegemony in a Globalized World**
The changing balance of power in the 21st century
Edited by Chandra Chari

58 **Economic Globalisation as Religious War**
Tragic convergence
Michael McKinley

59 **Globalization, Prostitution and Sex-trafficking**
Corporeal politics
Elina Penttinen

60 **Peacebuilding**
Women in international perspective
Elisabeth Porter

61 **Ethics, Liberalism and Realism in International Relations**
Mark D. Gismondi

62 **Law and Legalization in Transnational Relations**
Edited by Christian Brütsch and Dirk Lehmkuhl

63 **Fighting Terrorism and Drugs**
Europe and international police cooperation
Jörg Friedrichs

64 **Identity Politics in the Age of Genocide**
The holocaust and historical representation
David B. MacDonald

65 **Globalisation, Public Opinion and the State**
Western Europe and East and Southeast Asia
Edited by Takashi Inoguchi and Ian Marsh

66 **Urbicide**
The politics of urban destruction
Martin Coward

67 **Transnational Activism in the UN and the EU**
A comparative study
Jutta Joachim and Birgit Locher

68 **Gender Inclusive**
Essays on violence, men and feminist international relations
Adam Jones

69 **Capitalism, Democracy and the Prevention of War and Poverty**
Edited by Peter Graeff and Guido Mehlkop

70 **Environmental Change and Foreign Policy**
Theory and practice
Edited by Paul G. Harris

71 **Climate Change and Foreign Policy**
Case studies from East to West
Edited by Paul G. Harris

72 **Securitizations of Citizenship**
Edited by Peter Nyers

73 **The Power of Ideology**
From the Roman Empire to Al-Qaeda
Alex Roberto Hybel

74 **The Securitization of Humanitarian Migration**
Digging moats and sinking boats
Scott D. Watson

75 **Mediation in the Asia-Pacific Region**
Transforming conflicts and building peace
Edited by Dale Bagshaw and Elisabeth Porter

76 **United Nations Reform**
Heading North or South?
Spencer Zifcak

77 **New Norms and Knowledge in World Politics**
Protecting people, intellectual property and the environment
Preslava Stoeva

78 **Power, Resistance and Conflict in the Contemporary World**
Social movements, networks and hierarchies
Athina Karatzogianni and Andrew Robinson

79 **World-Regional Social Policy and Global Governance**
New research and policy agendas in Africa, Asia, Europe and Latin America
Edited by Bob Deacon, Maria Cristina Macovei, Luk Van Langenhove and Nicola Yeates

80 **International Relations Theory and Philosophy**
Interpretive dialogues
Edited by Cerwyn Moore and Chris Farrands

81 **Superpower Rivalry and Conflict**
The long shadow of the Cold War on the twenty-first century
Edited by Chandra Chari

82 **Coping and Conformity in World Politics**
Hugh C. Dyer

83 **Defining and Defying Organized Crime**
Discourse, perception and reality
Edited by Felia Allum, Francesca Longo, Daniela Irrera and Panos A. Kostakos

84 **Federalism in Asia**
India, Pakistan and Malaysia
Harihar Bhattacharyya

85 **The World Bank and HIV/AIDS**
Setting a global agenda
Sophie Harman

86 **The "War on Terror" and the Growth of Executive Power?**
A comparative analysis
Edited by John E. Owens and Riccardo Pelizzo

87 **The Contested Politics of Mobility**
Borderzones and irregularity
Edited by Vicki Squires

88 **Human Security, Law and the Prevention of Terrorism**
Andrej Zwitter

89 **Multilayered Migration Governance**
The promise of partnership
Edited by Rahel Kunz, Sandra Lavenex and Marion Panizzon

90 **Role Theory in International Relations**
Approaches and analyses
Edited by Sebastian Harnisch, Cornelia Frank and Hanns W. Maull

91 **Issue Salience in International Relations**
Edited by Kai Oppermann and Henrike Viehrig

92 **Corporate Risk and National Security Redefined**
Karen Lund Petersen

93 **Interrogating Democracy in World Politics**
Edited by Joe Hoover, Meera Sabaratnam and Laust Schouenborg

94 **Globalizing Resistance against War**
Theories of resistance and the new anti-war movement
Tiina Seppälä

95 **The Politics of Self-Determination**
Beyond the decolonisation process
Kristina Roepstorff

96 **Sovereignty and the Responsibility to Protect**
The power of norms and the norms of the powerful
Theresa Reinold

97 **Anglo-American Relations**
Contemporary perspectives
Edited by Alan P. Dobson and Steve Marsh

98 **The Emerging Politics of Antarctica**
Edited by Anne-Marie Brady

99 **Genocide, Ethnonationalism, and the United Nations**
Exploring the causes of mass killing since 1945
Hannibal Travis

100 **Caribbean Sovereignty, Development and Democracy in an Age of Globalization**
Edited by Linden Lewis

101 **Rethinking Foreign Policy**
Edited by Fredrik Bynander and Stefano Guzzini

102 The Promise and Perils of Transnationalization
NGO activism and the socialization of women's human rights in Egypt and Iran
Benjamin Stachursky

103 Peacebuilding and International Administration
The cases of Bosnia and Herzegovina and Kosovo
Niels van Willigen

104 The Politics of the Globalization of Law
Getting from rights to justice
Edited by Alison Brysk

105 The Arctic in International Politics
Coming in from the cold
Peter Hough

106 Understanding Transatlantic Relations
Whither the West?
Serena Simoni

107 India in South Asia
Domestic identity politics and foreign policy from Nehru to the BJP
Sinderpal Singh

108 A Strategic Understanding of UN Economic Sanctions
International relations, law and development
Golnoosh Hakimdavar

109 Politics and the Bomb
The role of experts in the creation of cooperative nuclear non-proliferation agreements
Sara Z. Kutchesfahani

110 Interpreting Global Security
Mark Bevir, Oliver Daddow and Ian Hall

111 Foreign Policy, Domestic Politics and International Relations
The case of Italy
Elisabetta Brighi

Foreign Policy, Domestic Politics and International Relations

The case of Italy

Elisabetta Brighi

Routledge
Taylor & Francis Group
LONDON AND NEW YORK

First published 2013
by Routledge
2 Park Square, Milton Park, Abingdon, Oxfordshire OX14 4RN

and by Routledge
711 Third Avenue, New York, NY 10017

First issued in paperback 2015

Routledge is an imprint of the Taylor & Francis Group, an informa business

British Library Cataloguing in Publication Data
A catalogue record for this book is available from the British Library

Library of Congress Cataloging-in-Publication Data
A catalog record has been requested for this book

ISBN 13: 978-1-138-94620-0 (pbk)
ISBN 13: 978-0-415-83512-1 (hbk)

Typeset in Times New Roman
by Wearset Ltd, Boldon, Tyne and Wear

To my parents
and their land

Contents

Figures

Acknowledgements

It is a pleasure to acknowledge the individuals and institutions that have been crucial in the making of this book. First, thanks to my alma mater in Italy, the University of Bologna, for giving me formidable teachers such as Angelo Panebianco, Marco Cesa, and Filippo Andreatta. They sparked my interest in the subject of foreign policy and set me on the path that led to where I am today. Second, thanks to my alma mater in the UK, the London School of Economics and Political Science, where I spent many wonderful years as a student. William Wallace was the most enthusiastic of tutors, and Amnon Aran and Alexander Bukh were fun colleagues and are now good friends. Christopher Hill supervised the PhD dissertation on which the book is based with rigour, commitment and *simpatia*. As a mentor he has been simply indispensable. Walter Carlsnaes and Roger Morgan were the best examiners I could have hoped for. Their feedback was invaluable in revising this manuscript and understanding my own arguments better. Brunello Vigezzi and Fulvio Cammarano engaged with my work generously, contributing a much needed historical and critical perspective. At Routledge two anonymous reviewers offered insightful comments and Alexander Quayle provided solid and kind editorial guidance.

Since my time at LSE I have also incurred debts of gratitude towards a number of institutions and places where I have worked, lived and grown intellectually and personally – especially Exeter College, Oxford, Central Saint Martin, London, and Loyola Hall, Liverpool. A number of people have been with me on this journey and I would like to thank them in no particular order: Elizabeth De Michelis, Alan F., Michele Chiaruzzi, Alessandra Pigni, Fabio Petito, Rafal S. and, especially, A.S. My family has seen me through years of hard academic work, and always knew how to put things in perspective: to Beatrice, Davide, Daniele, Pietro, Andrea and Simone I wish to say 'thank you' a million times. Michael W. shares a special place with me called home, for which I am very grateful. Finally, I wish to dedicate this book to my parents and to the land of my childhood, twelve acres of unspoilt 'English countryside' beautifully set in central Italy, among the rolling hills of Bertinoro.

Abbreviations

AN	*Alleanza Nazionale*
CCD	*Centro Cristiano Democratico*
CdL	*Casa delle Libertà*
CIA	Central Intelligence Agency
CLN	*Comitati di Liberazione Nazionale*
CSCE	Conference on Security and Cooperation in Europe
CSCM	Conference on Security and Cooperation in the Mediterranean
DC	*Democrazia Cristiana*
ECSC	European Coal and Steel Community
EDC	European Defence Community
EEC	European Economic Community
EMU	European Monetary Union
EPC	European Political Cooperation
ERM	European Exchange Rate Mechanism
EU	European Union
EURATOM	European Atomic Energy Community
EUROFOR	European Operational Rapid Force
EUROMARFOR	European Maritime Force
FI	*Forza Italia*
FPA	Foreign Policy Analysis
GDP	Gross Domestic Product
IdV	*Italia dei Valori*
IGC	Intergovernmental Conference
INF	Intermediate-range Nuclear Force
IR	International Relations
LN	*Lega Nord per l'Indipendenza della Padania*
MEP	Member of European Parliament
MPF	Multinational Protection Force
MSI	*Movimento Sociale Italiano*
NATO	North Atlantic Treaty Organisation
PCI	*Partito Comunista Italiano*
PdCI	*Partito dei Comunisti Italiani*
PDS	*Partito dei Democratici di Sinistra*

PKK	*Partiya Karkerên Kurdistan*
PLI	*Partito Liberale Italiano*
PLO	Palestinian Liberation Organization
PPI	*Partito Popolare Italiano*
PRC	*Partito della Rifondazione Comunista*
PRI	*Partito Rebupplicano Italiano*
PSDI	*Partito Socialdemocratico Italiano*
PSI	*Partito Socialista Italiano*
QMV	Qualified Majority Voting
SISMI	*Servizio per le Informazioni e la Sicurezza Militare*
START	Strategic Arms Reduction Treaty
UDC	*Unione Democratica Cristiana*
UN	United Nations
UNHCR	United Nations High Commission for Refugees
UNIFIL II	United Nations Interim Force in Lebanon II
UNOSOM	United Nations Operation in Somalia I
UNOSOM II	United Nations Operation in Somalia II
UNPROFOR	United Nations Protection Force
US	United States
USSR	Union of Soviet Socialist Republics
WEU	Western European Union

Introduction

Despite being at the heart of foreign policy empirically, conceptually and theoretically, the issue of how foreign policy develops on the shifting boundary between, and in constant interaction with, domestic politics and international relations has been subject to scanty theorising and limited agreement in the field of Foreign Policy Analysis (FPA). Antipathy for theory and metatheory within this subfield is certainly to blame for the current interpretative impasse, where traditional theories about the 'primacy of the domestic' and of the 'international' are often still pitted against each other, while attempts to devise more complex conceptual frameworks flounder in the absence of scholarly debate and/or empirical research.

An understanding of how foreign policy meets politics at the domestic and international level, however, could hardly be more urgent. The end of the Cold War has given way to an international order in which political cleavages at the domestic and international level are no less profound than they were prior to 1989. Rather than ushering the world into an era of liberal peace radiating from the inside to the outside of states, the fall of the Berlin Wall has restructured politics at home and abroad according to new – but by no means less divisive – fault-lines. Italy is an emblematic example of this larger trend (Andreatta 2001, 2008c). Two decades of extreme domestic political turbulence have characterised the *ventennio* of the 'Second Republic' now at the twilight (Urbinati 2012) and left the country struggling to cope with a conflict-ridden and ever-demanding external environment. Needless to say, foreign policy has absorbed blows from both sides, oftentimes landing on the boxing canvas as a casualty.

In this book I take issue with the way FPA as a subfield of International Relations (IR) has so far dealt (or not dealt) with the question of how to account for foreign policy in its relations with domestic and international politics. My aim is twofold: theoretical and empirical. First, I wish to evaluate the conceptual and theoretical tools currently at our disposal, as well as the particular framing of the problem-field from which these derive. Drawing on critical realism, I suggest that this needs to be systematically reconceptualised by redrawing its ontological and epistemological perimeter around a tripartite distinction between monocausal, dualist and dialectical models. By way of a contribution to the debate, I flesh out the contours of a dialectical, strategic-relational approach to foreign policy. Because of the way in which this model solves the tension between domestic and international determinants of foreign policy, and between naturalistic and intepretativist epistemology, the strategic-relational model bears particular promise when applied to the study of the relations between foreign policy, domestic politics and international relations. Grounded in an understanding of foreign policy as a dialectic, this model provides a plausible path out of the interpretative impasse currently characterising the debate on causation in FPA.

Second, in this book I wish to advance our empirical understanding of the subject matter. By focusing on the case of Italy, I offer an example – and not too unique a one, at that – of how foreign policy has resulted from and interacted with the domestic politics and international relations of the country. Further, I argue that the analysis of how these patterns have evolved through four main eras of Italian foreign policy – namely the liberal period, the fascist era, the 'First Republic' and the 'Second Republic'– not only provides a privileged angle of investigation into the political development of the country, but also defies all too common interpretations. Neither monologues nor dualisms are helpful in decoding the complex ways in which Italian foreign policy has encountered domestic and international politics through those four eras. Complex, dialectical conceptualisations are needed in order to more critically engage foreign policy in its fundamentally political nature.

Foreign policy, domestic politics and international relations: (re-)defining the terms of the question

To posit foreign policy as a process constituted by the interaction of domestic and international phenomena does not, of course, come without problems. The neat geometry of the inside/outside, international/domestic distinctions typically tends to hide a number of not-so-clear-cut questions, relying as it does upon a number of ethical, if not metaphysical and phenomenological, assumptions (Walker 1993; Bachelard 1964). The issue of the inherently contestable and porous nature of borders between 'home' and 'abroad', domestic and international – as well as, more generally, between different domains of social life – is something that cannot be simply done away with by definitional fiat (Hill 2000). Yet, definition is inevitable and, indeed, necessary for the task at hand.

To start with, in this book I understand foreign policy to be

> not a residual category to be associated with a dwindling number of diplomatic 'issues'. [...] It is the sum of official external relations conducted by an independent actor (usually a state) in international relations. [...] It is, in short, the focal point of an actor's external relations.
>
> (Hill 2003: 3, 5)

Within this broad definition of foreign policy, in what follows I especially concentrate upon a particular subset of 'external relations', namely political relations. While conscious of the problematic nature of the distinction at the analytical (let alone empirical) level, when analysing the foreign policy of Italy over the last century I will not deal with the purely economic, administrative, or cultural relations which Italy entertained with the outside world, except when and if these acquired a highly political relevance for foreign policy. Besides the need to limit the universe of data, this choice also responds to a more specific concern relevant to the country at hand. Italy has often experienced a high degree of fragmentation in its external relations. In the history of Italian foreign policy, especially post-Second World War, political relations and economic relations exhibited a very low degree of coherence, were carried out by different actors and institutions, and often followed a different logic, hence the need to privilege the subset of political external relations, while remaining aware that this category is far from water-tight.

If this is how I understand foreign policy, what about foreign policy actorness? What actor do I identify as the producer of a particular foreign policy? What is the 'Italy' to which I refer? The position which I put forward here builds on the rejection of two common 'solutions' to the problem of actorness in foreign policy. On the one hand, I reject the notion that 'the state' is a sufficiently clear label to identify a foreign policy actor. Failure to do so leads us back to the strictures of 'black box' realism (ironically, even from a constructivist route; see Wendt 1999: 215 and cf. Jackson 2004). On the other, the decision to focus exclusively on foreign policy makers, on the grounds that it is only they who ultimately act, is logically and empirically impeccable. However, this easily falls into the kind of 'psychologism' which has vitiated so much of traditional FPA scholarship, and which has failed to account for the larger societal, institutional and political forces at play. Hence, the unit of analysis that I take to be the foreign policy actor is *the foreign policy political process*, intended as a subset of the domestic political process, and defined as that broad political site where 'a community thinks collectively' about its foreign policy and foreign policy decisions come to be taken (cf. Hill 2000). Thus, rather than physical or anthropomorphic, I privilege a *processual* notion of actorness, i.e. a notion which is able to encompass a plurality of actors and processes and which, at the same time, has the merit of resisting the temptation to reify entities such as the state or the body-politic.

The aim of the book is to focus on the area of influence, confluence and interference that develops between foreign policy, domestic politics and international relations and explore patterns of efficient and systemic causality from the theoretical and empirical point of view. In doing so, I intend to keep the nature and consequences of this interplay for foreign policy open. Indeed, the empirical investigation which follows also provides material for an analysis of the degrees of proximity or distance that the 'international' and the 'domestic' have enjoyed over the last century, and the varying impact this has had on foreign policy.

A definition of the elements of this interplay other than foreign policy, i.e. of the 'international' and the 'domestic', must also be attempted. Although acknowledging that these form 'two ends of a continuum rather than being sharply demarcated' (Hill 2003: 38), the issue of how to operationalise them cannot be simply evaded. Hence, in what follows I treat the 'international' as that domain of political relations among actors (generally states) which is influenced by, and only analytically distinct from, a variety of global geopolitical, normative, military, social, institutional, and economic factors (Sørensen 2001; Halliday 1994; Strange 1988; Smith and Light 2001; Hill 2003: 159–215). As will become clear in the empirical investigation of the case of Italy, however, the 'balance of forces' (broadly defined) has been different in different historical periods, hence the need to have a definition of the 'international' broad enough to capture this variance.

As for the 'domestic', the book will resist equating this with the state and will adopt a pluralist view of the society and, ultimately, of the community around which domestic political life revolves. Despite the empirical focus on the political aspects of the 'domestic', I shall take into broad account the cultural, institutional, economic and societal factors that have historically impinged upon it in the specific case of Italy.

At a time when narratives of globalisation reign almost unchallenged, many have preferred to altogether dismiss the idea that foreign policy bridges the inside and outside of states. As a recent book has famously put it, 'there is no more outside' (Hardt and Negri 2000: 186), hence there is precious little need for bridges. Quite aside from empirical considerations regarding the breadth or limits of political globalisation, in this book I resist this solution on a number of analytical grounds. First, the domestic/international boundary has functioned as a major line of division within the field of FPA and IR. For a study that seeks to problematise the state of the art, this boundary is thus an indispensable point of departure. Second, though porous and nebulous, the boundary is still critical in defining foreign policy vis-à-vis other public policies. After all, foreign policy is that type of domestic or public policy that is explicitly aimed at the 'outside' of political actors and thus depends, rather existentially, on the existence of an environment and of an 'other'. Third, positing a boundary between the 'domestic' and the 'international' does not imply subscribing to an ontological dualism, nor to the reification of the institutional and historically contingent boundaries of sovereignty. Rather, its problematisation is a necessary and natural step in the re-conceptualisation of the field that this book contributes to the debate, towards a richer and more complex understanding of the dialectic between foreign policy, domestic politics and international relations (see also Aran 2009).

Last, this book starts from the commitment that it is still possible to envisage roles for theory, concepts and models in FPA without buying into their caricatured positivist forms nor yielding to a common anti-theoretical reflex. In fact, the 'new wave' of recent FPA theorising in a long-dormant discipline must be greeted as a particularly welcome and long-awaited development (Smith *et al.* 2012; Manners and Whitman 2000; Eun 2012; White 1999; Carlsnaes 1992; Hill 2003). This book subscribes to a Weberian understanding of theory whereby to conceptualise does not mean to conceal the fact that reality is much more complex than our representations of it; nor that every concept possesses a normative significance; nor, finally, that every model is constitutive, and not merely descriptive, of reality. Concepts, rather, should be understood for what they are, namely heuristic devices able to highlight patterns or phenomena to which we attach a particular interest or meaning – that are, in other words, 'relevant' to the inquirer (Weber 1949, 1968).

Further, if our theories are to account for foreign policy intended as purposive behaviour, it is necessary that our frameworks embrace a deeper and broader understanding of causality (Kurki 2008), able to accommodate efficient and intentional elements. In other words, the dichotomy between explanation and understanding and the accompanying statement by Hollis and Smith that 'there are always two stories to tell' (Hollis and Smith 1991: 7, 211, 213–4) is firmly rejected here, in line with what Hidemi Suganami (cf. Weber 1968: 11–12; Bryant 1985: 89) has submitted:

> It would be impossible to explain anything to someone who understood nothing. [...] 'Explanation' and 'understanding' can [...] be conceived of as two sides of the same narrative coin [...] – not incompatible as Hollis and Smith insist, but inseparable.
>
> (Suganami 1999: 372)

In fact, the aim of this book is precisely to escape this harsh logic and chart a critical realist path towards a single integrative conceptual framework in which to analyse the interactions of foreign policy, domestic politics and international relations (cf. Carlsnaes 1994: 280). This should not be mistaken for yet another episode of the unfruitful quest for absolute knowledge. The 'optimism' inherent in the exercise needs to be balanced against the acknowledgement that what we can aspire to is at best 'local' and 'partial' theories (Boudon 1984), i.e. constructs able to provide intelligible narratives that acknowledge the open-endedness of all social systems and the role of contingency (Suganami 1999; Bernstein *et al.* 2000).

Why Italian foreign policy: five reasons and a prologue

The decision to focus on the case of Italy was spurred by five reasons. Three of these are case-specific, while the remaining two have to do with Italy as a heuristically fecund case in which to study foreign policy in its relations with domestic and international politics.

In terms of the former group of reasons, the first relates to a fundamental 'given' of this country's foreign policy. Since the unification of the country in 1861, and partly because of its status as 'late-comer', foreign policy constituted one of Italy's fundamental means of survival on the international scene, to the point that 'United Italy (as a state) could exist only while it had a foreign policy' (Bosworth 1996: 19). Suffice it to mention here that both the unification of the country in 1861 and the eventual establishment of its capital in Rome in 1871 resulted mainly from a successful diplomatic manoeuvring played out in rather favourable diplomatic conjunctures.[1] Literally overburdened with expectations and aspirations – 'Rome is never without cosmopolitan projects', the German historian Theodore Mommsen once noted (quoted in Croce 1929: 4) – for much of its trajectory, however, Italy's foreign policy was challenged and often frustrated by the country's internal weakness, by the pace of a modernity it could not equal, and by its vulnerable external position.

The tension deriving from the persistent gap between ambitions and achievements, expectations and circumstances thus provides a first clue for engagement in a detailed study of Italy's foreign policy. In only a few other countries does foreign policy stand for such a critical yet inherently flawed – or systematically frustrated – enterprise. That this deserves attention is only amplified by the rather barren landscape of studies available, especially to a non-Italian audience.

The second reason justifying the choice of Italy is that since the end of the Cold War this country has seen the slow but progressive emergence of a distinctive and assertive foreign policy. While Italy may still be seen as oscillating between the category of small and middle power, there is little doubt that since the 1990s the country has raised its profile in European affairs, in transatlantic relations and in various other arenas of the globe, with its troops, interests and resources (let alone diaspora communities) in the Mediterranean, the Balkans and the Middle East. Though never an easy or straightforward partner, Italy is a necessary and inescapable one – a country that simply cannot be taken for granted in contemporary international affairs.

The third reason for pursuing an in-depth analysis of Italy's foreign policy is that although this country is unique in more than a few respects, it is arguably also a representative case of middle-sized, relatively prosperous European democracy caught between decline and defeat on the one hand, and reinvention and multilateralism on the other. Italy, in other words, shares many of the predicaments of middle powers such as Germany and France – or Canada and Japan (Samuels 2003), in different continents. An investigation into how its foreign policy has been affected by the confluence and interference of domestic and international politics, therefore, is useful and relevant to these countries too. Paradoxically, however, this acknowledgement is most beneficial to Italy itself. Emphasising similarities, rather than differences, with these countries is a crucial therapeutic step in curing Italy's long-standing inferiority complex vis-à-vis great powers that no longer are: the more Italy perceives itself to be a normal country, the more it is so.

Heuristically, Italy provides a particularly fruitful case for the subject of this book. First, Italy has experienced a dramatic evolution of both its domestic politics and its international relations over the last century, the combination of which has generated its rather peculiar foreign policy course. Domestically, the country has lived through at least three forms of government over the last century – including an authoritarian regime – and has experienced powerful (and at times disruptive) political dynamics. Internationally, it has at different times both suffered and benefited from its positioning in the international system: from the struggle to be acknowledged as the 'least' of the great powers in the early twentieth century, to the asset (and curse) of its key geopolitical positioning during the Cold War, to the recent espousal of an active yet contradictory multilateralism. The degree of interpenetration of the domains has often also been remarkably high. Suffice it to mention the way in which Italy's nineteenth century political life was completely penetrated by the external influence of great powers such as France or Austria, or how Italy's post-1945 political system came to parallel in almost exact terms the Cold War confrontation between the US and the USSR.

Methodologically, therefore, the way in which the changing domestic politics and international relations of Italy combined to generate its foreign policy makes for a particularly good case in which to 'stimulate the imagination toward discerning important general problems and possible theoretical solutions' at the heuristic level (Eckstein 1975: 104).

This alone stands in stark contrast to the rather dire state of extant works on Italian foreign policy. To start with, the analysis of foreign policy as an academic subfield is practically non-existent, with the result that its study is left to jurists and historians, when not to journalists or (former) diplomats themselves. Two consequences follow directly from this state of affairs. On the one hand, the tone of much of the debate is often descriptive and its contributions inevitably fail to draw on the FPA or IR toolkit. On the other, there is almost a default reliance on an arch-materialist, 'matter-of-fact' proto-realism that discourages any critical, or creative, engagement with the subject matter (Brighi and Petito 2012; Lucarelli and Menotti 2002).

Historically, the body of reflections on Italy's foreign policy has tended to advance two rather polarised, if not totally reified, views: either Italy as the small country prey to overwhelming environmental constraints, or Italy as the political system in eternal turmoil, whose foreign policy eternally suffers from the ebbs and flows of its shaky domestic institutions. Either the country with no freedom of action and indeed no foreign policy, or the country whose foreign policy reflects intricate patterns of political, societal and ideological dynamics. The former arch-Machiavellian, the latter inward-looking, these two narratives advance two monologic readings that have rarely engaged with one another. This has so far impeded an assessment of the actual margins of freedom and forms of necessities through which foreign policy has been generated over the decades.

Plan of the book

The book develops its theoretical and empirical argument in five chapters. In the first I concentrate on concepts and theory. Bringing together and critiquing a vast body of literature from IR, FPA, Comparative Politics, and Public Policy, here I survey and systematically re-examine the ways in which the relationship between domestic politics, foreign policy and international relations has been explained and understood in academe. In particular, by drawing on critical realism, I reconceptualise the perimeter of the problem-field around a tripartition of monocausal, dualistic and dialectical models. This reconceptualisation usefully sidesteps and transcends – without collapsing – the set of unnecessarily rigid ontological and epistemological cleavages which inform current approaches.

Drawing on the work of Colin Hay and Bob Jessop, I then introduce the strategic-relational model to FPA and illustrate its comparative advantage via a close engagement with competing theoretical approaches – from Putnam's 'two-level games' to Carlsnaes' 'tripartite approach', from Wolfers' 'pendulum approach' to the neoclassical realist approach of 'nested games'. Grounded in an understanding of foreign policy as a dialectic of strategy, context and discourse – and on the strength of its solution to the tension between domestic and international determinants of foreign policy, and between naturalistic and intepretativist epistemology – I argue that the strategic-relational model provides a plausible path out of the interpretative impasse currently characterising the debate on causation in FPA.

Chapter 1 concludes by spelling out the research questions derived from this theoretical inquiry and to be addressed in the empirical investigation of Italy's foreign policy. These questions reflect three different concerns: first, the issue of whether international or domestic factors have ever enjoyed a 'primacy' over Italian foreign policy; second, the question of the different combinations, or relative weight, of international/domestic influences, and whether and how this has changed over time; and third, the issue of foreign policy adaptation and change, in its domestic and international determinants.

Against this conceptual backdrop, Chapters 2 to 5 pursue the country-study examination of Italian foreign policy in the liberal period (1901–1922), the fascist *ventennio* (1922–1943), the 'First Republic' (1943–1992), and the 'Second Republic' (1992–2011), respectively.[2] For each of these periods I develop my analysis in four steps.

First, I offer a brief historical narrative to set the stage.[3] Second, I investigate the politics of Italian foreign policy at the time, with particular reference to the competing foreign policy paradigms articulated in the domestic political debate, especially by political parties. Drawing on Hay (2005) I define policy paradigms as those intersubjectively agreed-upon narratives that provide templates for interpreting foreign policy and international relations. In each chapter I identify these paradigms as the foreign policy 'visions', ideas and traditions used by the political community to think collectively about its foreign policy and the international environment.

Third, I review and critically evaluate the historical and theoretical approaches available in order to argue that the domestic/international cleavage provides the most frequent, and often exhaustive, interpretative fault-line. Last, through plausibility probes (George 1979: 57–58) and counterfactuals (Tetlock and Belkin 1996; Hawthorn 1991; Snyder 1991: 307) I interrogate the conceptual frameworks advanced in Chapter 1. A number of alternative explanations are generated and assessed in terms of their plausibility and consistency with the empirical record. On the one hand this liberates space to move beyond the current interpretative impasse and towards more complex accounts of Italy's foreign policy and, on the other, it helps in adjudicating the validity of the competing frameworks.

The Conclusions serve the purpose of weaving together my theoretical and empirical arguments, presenting my main findings and exploring their theoretical, normative and policy implications. Monocausal approaches are largely unsatisfactory when applied to the case of Italy. Dualist and dialectical models, on the other hand, prove to be more promising and have different domains of applicability. Grounded in the dialectical interplay of context, strategy and discourse, the strategic-relational model, in particular, seems best equipped to account for the interrelations between foreign policy, domestic politics and international relations. When applied to the case of Italy, this model helps to liberate some interpretative space for a more critical engagement with foreign policy. Through its lens, foreign policy emerges as a wholly political, discursively mediated activity, one that takes place at the ever-changing interface of domestic politics and international relations, and in which choice and agency are always just as critical as interests and power.

1 Foreign policy, domestic politics and international relations

A strategic-relational analysis

It is widely agreed that foreign policy occupies a critical, interstitial space in world politics, produced as it is at the porous interface of domestic politics and international relations. Four generations of foreign policy scholars, often from radically different standpoints, have converged around the idea that foreign policy is a 'boundary' activity, straddling disciplinary fields as well as the inside and outside of political actors, generally states. Thus, in 1966 Robert B. Farrell characterised the study of foreign policy as a 'no man's land' at the intersection of Political Science and IR (Farrell 1966: vi). Similarly, in the early 1970s William Wallace argued that 'the study of foreign policy is a boundary problem' for both the foreign policy student and practitioner (Wallace 1971: 7). A decade later, James Rosenau famously used the metaphor of a 'bridge' to identify the location of foreign policy between the 'domestic' and the 'international' (Rosenau 1987: 1). In the 1990s David Campbell gave vast popularity to Richard Ashley's notion of foreign policy as a 'specific sort of boundary-producing political performance' separating inside from outside, identity from alterity (Campbell 1998: 62). Most recently, analysts have reiterated the call for a multi-causal analysis of foreign policy able to accommodate sources placed on the inside and outside of states (Eun 2012).

Despite this broad agreement, the twin questions of how to conceptualise foreign policy as produced at the cusp of the 'domestic' and the 'international' and how to couch this conceptualisation into a larger understanding of causation in foreign policy have been subject to a less sustained and self-conscious debate than one may think.[1] Attempts have floundered, arguably not just due to the complexity of the task, but also due to the poor propensity towards theory and metatheory within FPA and, in particular, to the conflation and reification of a number of relevant epistemological and ontological issues, only a few of which have been properly understood in terms of their foreign policy implications. However, in so far as foreign policy is understood as a form of action (Carlsnaes 1986: 27; Hill 2003: 283–307), and as a process oriented to some – albeit multiple, contrasting and collectively defined – goals and aims, the issue of how to explain foreign policy can hardly be avoided. Indeed, it echoes a classic question in the analysis of politics.

This chapter seeks to advance our understanding of causation in FPA by providing an overview of the state of affairs, formulating a diagnosis and proposing a way forward. It does so in four steps. First, it surveys and unpacks the ontological, epistemological and conceptual questions at stake in a causal analysis of foreign policy. Second, it offers a taxonomy of empirical theories employed by scholars in FPA and IR to account for the patterns of causation between foreign policy, domestic politics, and international relations, exposing their limitations. Third, drawing on the critical realism of Colin Hay and Bob Jessop, it suggests a way to systematically reconceptualise the problem and redraw the boundaries of the field around a tripartite distinction between monocausal, dualist and dialectical models. Fourth, and last, the chapter fleshes out the contours of the strategic-relational model, a dialectical approach to foreign policy that bears particular promise. Because of the way in which it solves the tension between domestic and international determinants of foreign policy, and between naturalistic and intepretativist epistemology, the strategic-relational model manages to transcend without conflating the unnecessarily rigid cleavages informing alternative approaches. Grounded in an understanding of foreign policy as a dialectic interplay of context, strategy and discourse, the model avoids the limits of monocausal accounts by integrating factors placed at different levels, moves beyond dualist views by highlighting the dynamic interaction among variables, reconciles causal and systemic analysis while foregrounding contingency and complexity, and provides a plausible path out of the interpretative impasse currently characterising the debate on causation in FPA.

Mapping the problem-field

The issue of how foreign policy is predicated on the shifting nexus between international relations and domestic politics has been approached from a variety of angles within contemporary FPA as a subfield of IR. The behavioural revolution which played such a large part in launching FPA as a 'scientific' enterprise, however, can hardly claim to have started a debate which has long roots in the history of political thought. By the seventeenth century, the tradition of thought variously inspired by the writings of Niccolò Machiavelli and Giovanni Botero and known as *Raison d'Ètat* had already initiated a conservative, state-centric turn in historical scholarship – away from its previous focus on peoples, ethnicities and nations – that relied on a specific, prescriptive understanding of the relation between foreign policy, domestic politics and international relations (Butterfield 1975). In the words of one of its most eminent followers, Leopold von Ranke, 'the degree of independence determines a state's position in the world, and requires that the state mobilize all its inner resources for the goal of self-preservation. This is its supreme law' (von Ranke 1950: 169; see also Simms 2003; Smith 1999: 13–17).

This law came to be known as *Primat der Aussenpolitik* – the primacy of foreign policy (Czempiel 1963; Schulin 1987) – a model which was to inspire generations of historians as well as political scientists to produce sweeping accounts of modern European and international history in terms of the international dynamics of security and power politics (see, for instance, Hintze 1962 [1906] and Tilly 1975; and, in IR, Kennedy 1986; Kennedy 1988; Gourevitch 1978). It was not until the 1930s, but especially from the 1960s, that the traditional primacy of foreign policy in historical scholarship was challenged from 'below', as it were, by its very mirror image. Eckart Kehr initiated a 'revisionist' strand of scholarship centred around the *Primat der Innenpolitik* (the primacy of domestic politics) which foregrounded the crucial role of economic interests and élites, instead of supposed international necessities, to explain German foreign policy during the Wilhelmine period and in the run-up to the First World War (Kehr 1977). Drawing on Kehr, Hans Ulrich Wehler explicitly used the category of imperialism to explain Bismarck's foreign policy, thus openly calling on Marxist and critical theory (Wehler 1984, 1973; Hillgruber 1987). But it was Fritz Fischer's 1961 book on the causes of the First World War which, finally, gave the greatest popularity to a domestic- and economic-based analysis of foreign policy (Fischer 1975 [1961]), thus igniting a controversy which was to divide scholars across Europe, and then across the Atlantic, in two opposing camps: 'orthodox' vs. 'revisionists' (Stephanson 1994).

At the heart of this historical debate was arguably an antithetical understanding of the sources of foreign policy behaviour, namely a distinction between international and domestic causes, as well as the espousal of opposite traditions in international political theory. On the one hand, the 'Rankean' penchant for political Realism – stretching from Thucydides to Rousseau through Machiavelli and Hobbes – and its international accounts of foreign policy, its typical cross-historical generalisations and its privileged focus on power and security. On the other, the appeal of Marxism and Liberalism to Kehr's followers, interested in uncovering the domestic sources of foreign policy, and concerned about issues of political responsibility and the possibility of change.

If this is arguably the pre-history of contemporary attempts to arrive at satisfactory conceptualisations of foreign policy in its international and domestic determinants, a lot more layers have calcified around the issue since then. These need bringing into sharper focus in order to gain a clear picture of what is at stake in an account of foreign policy from the point of view of international and domestic politics. Of ontological, epistemological and disciplinary kind, these layers have been often understood as coterminous and confluent – if not wholly blurred – in contemporary FPA. For my argument, however, it is important to consider them separately.

The first and most notorious question revolves around the issue of levels of analysis. Originally conceptualised by David Singer, anticipated by Kenneth Waltz and revisited by Martin Hollis and Steve Smith, the level-of-analysis debate addressed the issue of which level to choose in order to explain events in world politics (Singer 1961; Waltz 1959; Hollis and Smith 1990, 1991, 1992; Buzan 1985; Wendt 1991, 1992). Arguably, the focus of this debate was never foreign policy, but rather the outcomes of interaction among states, i.e. the aggregate effects of interaction. In fact, in the level-of-analysis framework foreign policy was simply bypassed, with the three levels of the individual, the state and the system said to exhaust the universe of world politics. While Waltz and Singer raised and solved the question of how to explain aggregate outcomes by choosing the third level (that of the international system), this solution never had much purchase in FPA (for an exception, see Hollis and Smith 1986). The mission of the then emerging discipline was to unpack notions (such as that of the state) that the levels of analysis approach used precisely as assumptions. The levels of analysis framework was hugely influential and certainly helpful in explaining 'outside in' or 'inside out' dynamics, i.e. how systemic events shape unit-level attributes (also called 'second image-reversed' perspectives), or how unit-level attributes influence the nature/characteristics of the system ('second image') (Gourevitch 1978). However, it was virtually silent on how these dynamics were mediated by foreign policy – in fact, it was silent about foreign policy *tout court*.

Although primarily concerned with ontology, the level-of-analysis framework re-ignited the classic epistemological issue of causation and explanation in IR and, to a lesser extent, FPA. This is a classic debate in the social sciences, with roots that extend as far back as the sociological diatribe between the holism of Emile Durkheim to the methodological individualism of Max Weber (Taylor 1985; Dallmayr and McCarthy 1977; Hollis and Smith 1990). Since the advent of the so-called post-positivist turn the debate has become familiar to the IR or FPA scholar (Wight 2012; Waever 1996), especially in its incarnation as 'agency-structure' debate (Giddens 1984; Wendt 1987, 1999; Dessler 1989; Hollis and Smith 1990; Doty 1997; Wight 1999, 2006; Bieler and Morton 2001;

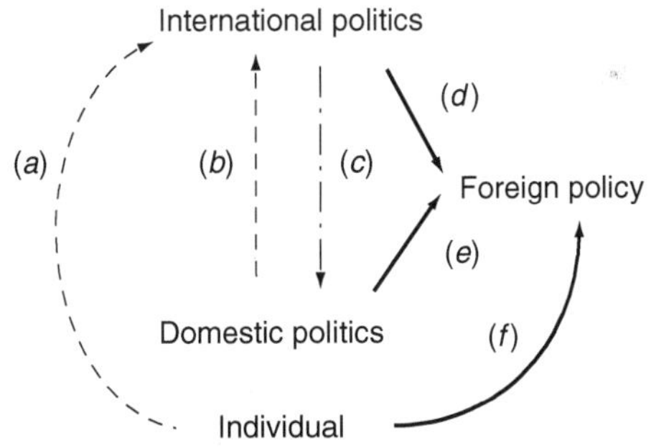

Figure 1.1 Foreign policy, images and levels of analysis. While arrow *a* represents how international political events are influenced by individual-level properties, arrow *b* represents how domestic politics influences international politics: these are the only two causal arrows analysed in the original level-of-analysis discussion by Singer ('images' *à la* Waltz). Arrow *c* represents 'second-image-reversed' influences, studied by Gourevitch, *inter alia*. Arrows *d*, *e* and *f*, on the other hand, represent international, domestic and individual influences on foreign policy. It is only the latter that are of concern here.

Suganami 1999; Carlsnaes 1992, 1994, 2013). At its most basic level, the debate focused on the question of how to account for action, whether in terms of the environment (system, structure) in which a particular actor is embedded, or in terms of the properties of the actor (motives, beliefs, intentions, aims, etc.). In so far as they deal with action, and to the extent that they are interested in looking for its causes, all social sciences need to grapple with this question – foreign policy included.

As some scholars have pointed out, the application of this frame of analysis to issues of foreign policy is intuitively fitting and heuristically fruitful, albeit not entirely straightforward (Hill 2003: 25–30; Carlsnaes 2013). After all, isn't foreign policy caught between the Scylla of structural, environmental forces and the Charibdes of agential, unit attributes? Naturally, depending upon the unit of analysis considered (e.g. the state, the government, the individual foreign policy maker, etc.), structures will be of different kinds (e.g. the international environment, the bureaucracy, the Cabinet, etc.), as will the unit's attributes (e.g. the domestic political process, group dynamics, the individual's psychology, etc.). Thus, the 'agency-structure' framework can be applied at each step of the foreign policy-making ladder, from the individual level to the aggregate level of the state, and vice versa (cf. Hollis and Smith 1990: 1–10 and 196–216; see also Wendt 1991: 384).

However, whether we settle questions of ontology in terms of levels of analysis or agency and structure, the epistemological choice about how we actually treat the *explanans* and construct an explanation of foreign policy necessarily remains a separate one. This epistemological choice has often been subsumed, erroneously, in peremptory decisions about the alleged primacy of structure or agency. Such a move, however, is obfuscating in so far as it forecloses epistemological questions of four different kinds.

First, there is the issue of whether to adopt a naturalistic or interpretative approach. With Gabriel Almond, this is often framed in terms of the choice between an external, naturalistic, 'clock-like' type of inquiry and an internal, interpretative, 'cloud-like' approach (Almond with Genco 1990). Or, in the Weberian terms utilised by Hollis and Smith, the two 'stories' of 'explaining' or 'understanding' (Hollis and Smith 1990). This choice evidently presents itself at every level of analysis, for both agents and structures, as all of these ontological elements are open to a naturalistic or interpretative treatment.[2]

Second, there is the question of what time frame our account is supposed to accommodate, and what strategies we utilise to conceptualise change. The opposition of Jean Braudel's *longue durée* with the *conjuncture* comes to mind here as a particularly relevant example of the tension between diachronic and synchronic modes of investigation (Braudel 1972; Aron 1964). From this perspective, it has often been concluded that the structural level is not just the realm of 'inevitability' and structural laws, as already said, but also the domain of general, long-term developments, of those 'vast impersonal forces' that run their course through decades, if not centuries. On the other hand, analyses placed at the level of agency are supposed to offer snapshots of more short-term, conjunctural developments whose effects may be exhausted in a very brief span of time. This confluence of ontological and epistemological strategies is, however, far from inevitable or necessary.

Third, there is the fundamental question of what passes or counts for cause in FPA and IR – a question which is implicit in much of the literature, yet is hardly ever discussed explicitly (Suganami 1996; Kurki 2008). Essentially, the choice is whether a cause is only to be understood as identifying empirically observable, objective and efficient entities that bring about change directly, mechanically and predictably, or whether we accept that 'many different things can all be causes … not, however, causes in the same way' (Aristotle quoted in Kurki 2008: 12). Beyond a narrow conception of cause lies the possibility of different causes operating in different ways – conditioning, predisposing, influencing, 'pushing and shoving', rather than simply via straight determination – well beyond the simplistic confrontation between 'causal' and 'constitutive' accounts. As Kurki has demonstrated, naturalistic explanations have often utilised a narrow Humean conception of cause, and, paradoxically, some interpretative approaches have ended up subscribing to the same model too, despite their rhetorical commitments (Kurki 2006, 2008).

Fourth and finally, there is the issue of how to relate and/or integrate different causes in our explanation – whether our aim is to disentangle different causal strands so as to 'control' and observe causality in isolation; whether, instead, our aim is to construct 'stories' able to map events and provide a narrative of their sequence and outcome; or whether, finally, our aim is to arrive at an integrative framework able to accommodate different causes and, even more importantly, the complex interactions among causes and how these impact upon foreign policy. Ultimately this presents a choice between a causal and a systemic account of foreign policy.

The peculiar location of foreign policy – on the boundary between the inside and outside of states – has traditionally reinforced die-hard dichotomies: 'top-down' or 'bottom-up', *Primat der Aussenpolitik* or *Primat der Innenpolitik*, structure or agency. However, just as the debates reviewed above have different *foci*, there are no inevitable and catch-all solutions. The epistemological and ontological questions raised above cannot be reduced to or conflated into a single puzzle. Rather, they are different aspects of the problem of causality when applied to foreign policy. As a matter of fact, it is their intersection – and ultimately their boundaries – which are worth highlighting.

This is particularly useful if the aim is to provide a taxonomy of domestic and international theories of foreign policy and the international/domestic nexus developed in FPA and IR in order to expose a few gaps and problems. One caveat is necessary, however, before proceeding with this exercise. While the issue of how to explain foreign policy, whether in international terms or domestic terms (or both) is a classic analytical issue in FPA and beyond, its *theorisation* has been far less common. In fact, the theorisation of foreign policy as such has been typically scanty in a field that has privileged, as the name itself suggests, analysis over theory (Zakaria 1998: 13).

In what follows I consider explanations of foreign policy in terms of their domestic and international 'causes' from two distinct viewpoints: as an ontological problem (vertical axis) and as an epistemological issue (horizontal axis) (cf. Buzan 1985; Carlsnaes 2013: 306–7; Wendt 1991: 384, 184–5). The taxonomy resulting from their intersection (Figure 1.2) is able to map a number of competing approaches to foreign policy according to their most important 'pre-theoretical' choices relating to a) their ontological referent along the international/domestic dimension and b) their mode of investigation in terms of the distinction between naturalistic and interpretative epistemologies.

In the next section, I offer an overview of the approaches placed in different parts of the matrix. I then move on to argue that this static two-by-two matrix, though helpful in mapping first-order approaches and empirical theories, needs moving beyond if we want to arrive at second-order models of foreign policy, domestic politics and international relations. This will open up the space for a reconceptualisation of the field.

1 International/naturalistic theories of foreign policy

Geopolitics

Generations of scholars have insisted on the importance of the geographical external environment to the formulation of foreign policy. After all, geopolitics was born primarily as a foreign policy doctrine. The essential insight of

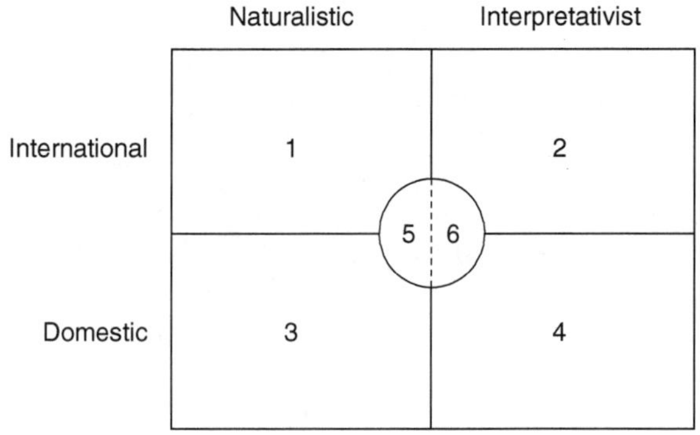

Figure 1.2 Domestic and international theories of foreign policy: a taxonomy. The matrix represents six sets of first-order, theoretical perspectives on foreign policy. Position no. 1 represents international and naturalistic explanations; no. 2 international and intepretativist explanations; position no. 3 domestic explanations, understood naturalistically; position no. 4 domestic accounts of foreign policy drawing on interpretativism. Finally, positions 5 and 6 indicate approaches that exhibit a 'mixed' ontology, tentatively combining domestic and international elements, while subscribing respectively to either naturalistic or interpretative modes of investigations.

geopolitical thought is that the external environment, in its geographical features, poses constraints that foreign policy makers cannot ignore (Dodds and Atkinson 2000; Parker 1998; Gray 1988). The distribution of natural resources, the geographical configuration of lands and seas, climatic conditions and the existence of natural borders act as multiplier of opportunities and limits to the foreign policies of states. Advancing a case for geographical determinism, figures such as Harold Mackinder, Alfred T. Mahan, and Klaus Haushofer all espoused radical forms of geopolitical thought as they conceptualised foreign policy as being determined naturalistically and mechanically by environmental pressures (hence their location in box 1, Figure 1.2). Geographical features, i.e. material and empirically observable data, explained the regularity and periodicity of certain patterns in the foreign policy of nations – from Great Britain's location as an island and its foreign policy of 'splendid isolation' to landlocked or 'encircled' states, such as Germany according to Haushofer, and their 'natural' desire to expand.

More sophisticated accounts of geopolitics and foreign policy have allowed for a greater role for a number of domestic factors, often compromising the naturalistic epistemology of geopolitical determinism and mixing in interpretative motives. Harold and Margaret Sprout's environmental possibilism is one classic case in point. According to the Sprouts, if one seeks to explain foreign policy actions, then the geographical environment can

> be perceived, reacted to, and taken into account by the human individual or individuals under consideration. In this way, *and in this way alone* [...], environmental factors can be said to 'influence, or to 'condition', or to otherwise 'affect' human values and preferences, moods and attitudes, choices and decisions.
>
> (Sprout and Sprout 1965: 11, emphasis added)

Influenced by the broader movement of social constructivism in IR, the recent wave of critical geopolitical studies has re-issued the Sprouts' original intuition to stress the role of the intersubjective, social interpretation of geographical features in explaining the environment's impact upon foreign policy (O'Tuathail 1996; Tunander *et al.* 1997; Guzzini 2012). With reference to Figure 1.2, then, in so far as these works allow for the mediation of geopolitical stimuli by elements of domestic politics, these approaches tend to the centre of the matrix and should be placed in box 5, while originating in box 1. In so far as they also mix epistemological strategies, these approaches also try to transcend the boundary between boxes 5 and 6.

Neorealism

The most traditional representation of the 'international' after geopolitics is that which develops around the element of war and the dynamics of international security. As with geopolitics, structural explanations of foreign policy have been the rule in much of IR scholarship, especially in the neo-realist tradition *à la* Waltz (Waltz 1979). The primacy of anarchy leaves little space for any domestic influences on foreign policy, as states are compelled to make necessary moves on the international scene, lest they 'fall by the wayside' (Waltz 1979: 118). Interestingly, neorealists have long claimed that outcomes at the international level – war, peace, the balance of power – can be studied without recurring to foreign policy, and that for this reason neorealism is not a theory of foreign policy (Elman 1996a; Waltz 1996; Elman 1996b). However, this position has been shown to be problematic, if not untenable (Mouritzen 1996; Baumann *et al.* 2001; Lebow 2001; and, *ante-litteram*, Hoffmann 1968: 12). It has also been progressively abandoned by many self-confessed neorealists interested in moving away from a teleological and functional view of the international system. In so far as it relies upon a modern day version of the 'Primat der Aussenpolitik' and understands international politics in 'objectivist' terms, neorealism *à la Waltz* presents a conceptualisation of foreign policy that belongs squarely to box 1 (Figure 1.2).[3]

The constant attacks upon neo-realist theories since the end of the Cold War stimulated a number of neo-realist scholars to reconsider some of their basic assumptions vis-à-vis foreign policy (Rose 1998; Nexon 2009). While so-called 'offensive' realists re-confirmed the primacy of anarchy and the relatively unimportant role of domestic politics in shaping foreign policy and international relations (Mearsheimer 1990), 'defensive' realists such as Jack Snyder (who coined the offensive-defensive terminology) tried to incorporate domestic politics into their explanations of foreign policy (Snyder 1991; Rosecrance and Stein 1993; but see also Milner 1998; Caporaso 1997). Parallel to this, 'neoclassical realists' such as Fareed Zakaria and Randall Schweller have similarly argued for an understanding of foreign policy where the 'international' (structurally conceived) determines the *grandes lignes* of foreign policy, while domestic politics functions as a – usually imperfect, indirect and problematic, 'rough and capricious' – 'transmission belt' (Rose 1998: 158; Zakaria 1992, 1998; Schweller 1994, 1998, 2006; Labs 1992; Kaufman 1992). In terms of Figure 1.2, then, these contributions have attempted to move from the margins of box 1 towards the centre of the matrix, though retaining a fairly narrow objectivist epistemological understanding of explanation and causation and an ontological frame skewed in favour of international factors.

2 International/interpretativist theories of foreign policy

Social, normative and institutional theory

A different perspective is provided by those analyses which focus on the social, normative and institutional international environment and their influence upon foreign policy. Two perspectives are especially noteworthy here: the English School and constructivism.

The English School has tended to advance a view of international relations as an essentially social and institutional construct, with states belonging to an anarchical, international society (Dunne 1998; Linklater and Suganami 2006). Despite the centrality of such a tradition in IR, however, the English School has typically failed to engage directly with the analysis of foreign policy (Hill 2003: 159–60). Still, the position that could be derived from this tradition of scholarship concerning foreign policy is that states respond not just to considerations of power, but, more importantly, to a set of normative standards. For their emphasis on the social nature of the 'international' and for the interpretative strategies they adopt, these approaches should be placed in quadrant 2 of Figure 1.2.

Similarly to the English School, constructivism initially claimed to be equally uninterested in matters of foreign policy. As Alexander Wendt himself stated:

> Theories of international politics are distinguished from those that have as their object explaining the behaviour of individual states, or 'theories of foreign policy' [...] Like Waltz, I am interested in international politics, not foreign policy.
>
> (Wendt 1999: 11)

Wendtian constructivism has thus advanced a view of international relations as a social domain in which states' moves need not be explicitly conceptualised (although see Wendt 1992: 365). Other constructivists have tried to redress this state of affairs and formulate constructivist theories of foreign policy, arriving at divergent results, however (cf. Checkel 2012; Kubálková 2001; Boekle *et al.* 2001; Waever 1994). Although a coherent constructivist theory of foreign policy in its relations with domestic and international politics is yet to be advanced, constructivism can be said to belong to that group of approaches that privilege the social, normative and institutional aspect of international relations treated in interpretative terms – hence they should be placed in box 2 of Figure 1.2.

3 *Domestic/naturalistic theories of foreign policy*

Domestic regime and institutions

A classic strand of theorising in IR and FPA causally connects the structure of domestic institutions and forms of government (i.e. 'regime') to foreign policy. Scholars have investigated the link between domestic institutional arrangements and foreign policy, focusing on three areas in particular. First, and most traditionally, many authors have examined the link between authoritarian, conservative or revisionist domestic polities and their foreign policy, usually in counterpoint with studies of democratic foreign policy and often with a view towards assessing their relative performance or war-proneness (Kissinger 1968; Waltz 1968; Auerswald 1999, 2000). A second area attracting vast attention in FPA has dealt with the impact of bureaucracies on foreign policy: the bureaucratic model elaborated by Graham Allison in response to another naturalistic and domestic-based view of foreign policy, namely the rational-actor model, is probably the best known FPA work and has given way to a rich tradition of scholarship (Allison and Zelikow 1999). Third, a host of different approaches drawing on the pluralist and Liberal traditions have focused on the role of the domestic economic institutions (Moravcsik 1993a, 1993b, 2003), in particular, 'domestic structure' (Evangelista 1997) and state 'strength' (Katzenstein 1978; Krasner 1978), in directing and deciding upon the contents of foreign policy. In so far as these approaches tend to posit a causal link between foreign policy and key domestic political elements, structurally and objectively understood, they should be placed in box 3 of Figure 1.2.

Democratic peace theory

Arguably, the democratic peace theory is one strand within the larger study of the impact of domestic political institutions upon foreign policy. Initiating a revival of Kant's theses about the peaceful nature of democracies, Michael Doyle most notably focused on the spread of peace among Western states, arguing that its cause must be found in the spread of democratic institutions inside these states (Doyle 1983; Brown 1996). In his version, the democratic peace theory is a naturalistic theory of foreign policy, i.e. democracy is defined in terms of its 'objective', observable processes and structures, rather than understood interpretatively in terms of its meanings, ideals and values.

Interestingly, Doyle's theory was initially presented as yet another 'systemic' theory that did not include an explicit account of foreign policy. Peace among democracies would thus materialise without necessarily involving the need for *democratic* foreign policies. However, other scholars after Doyle have redressed this state of affairs and made the link between foreign policy and democracy explicit in their work (Kahler 1997; Milner 1996). In their emphasis upon the domestic side of the domestic/international equation, all of these scholars have in different ways reasserted a *Primat der Innenpolitik*. Their representation of foreign policy appears to be skewed in favour of domestic factors and an explanatory, naturalistic epistemology (box 4, Figure 1.2).

3 Domestic/interpretativist theories of foreign policy

'Middle-range theories' on cognitive and idiosyncratic factors

These are probably FPA's most classic approach to foreign policy and that strand of 'middle-range' theorising which has formed the backbone of the discipline over the decades (George 1969; Brecher 1972; Janis 1972; Greenstein 1969; Allison and Zelikow 1999; Jervis 1970, 1976). In so far as these approaches tend to posit foreign policy as primarily influenced by individuals and their cognitive processes, these approaches tend to ignore not only the international dimension, but also parts of the domestic environment as well. In so doing, they thus reduce the relation between foreign policy, domestic politics and international relations to a primacy of individual factors. In some cases, individual and cognitive factors are approached from the point of 'understanding', i.e. stressing beliefs, motives, and cognitive idiosyncrasies understood in broadly interpretative terms (thus, they feature in box 4, Figure 1.2). However, in some other cases (certainly most frequent in the mainstream camp), cognitive/individual factors are treated objectively – as an application of rational choice to foreign policy would lead to – with these theories ultimately ending up in box 3 of Figure 1.2.

National identity

Amongst the approaches in IR and FPA that hold domestic variables to have a primacy over foreign policy and approach these 'from the inside' of individual or collective agency, particular mention must be made of the burgeoning literature on national identity and foreign policy. Over the last few years, a variety of approaches have stressed the crucial link between national identity – and, more generally, norms, beliefs and values – and a state's external projection. These approaches, however, have arguably pursued different strategies of inquiry.

Mainstream positivist accounts have generally posited a straightforward causal link between identity and foreign policy, with the former affecting the latter from the 'inside out', i.e. treating 'culture' as simply yet another variable, arguably at the risk of reifying or essentialising the notion of identity altogether (Gordon 1993; Katzenstein 1996; Ruggie 1997). Post-positivist works, instead, have typically offered a more sophisticated account of this link, stressing above all the nature of identity as a social construction and adopting epistemological strategies geared to the interpretativist principles of discourse analysis (Neumann 1998; Larsen 1997; Campbell 1998). These approaches have nonetheless converged around the idea that identity develops first and foremost around the nation-state: identity, in other words, tends to separate 'inside' from 'outside', the domestic from the international (cf Larsen 1997: 168; Wendt 1999: 215; and note Campbell 1998: 219).

In so far as identity is conceived of as a domestic variable resulting from a process of social construction, this position on foreign policy is to be placed in box 4 of Figure 1.2. On the other hand, the kind of structural understanding of national identity advanced by positivists tends to yield theories of foreign policy based on identity that should properly be placed in box 3, under the heading of domestic-based and objectivist, naturalistic theories of foreign policy. Arguably, however, the complex issue of identity is an apt example of how necessary it may be to transcend the very cleavage between domestic and international on the one hand, and explaining and understanding, on the other, to move our understanding further.

5 and 6 'Complex' theories of foreign policy

Each quadrant of the matrix contains alternative conceptualisations of foreign policy in its domestic and international determinants. However, as illustrated above, from each quadrant also originate approaches that seek to integrate international and domestic variables and, albeit less frequently, different epistemological strategies. There is, in other words, a centripetal pull towards the centre of the matrix.[4]

This is unsurprising if one considers how, in the last twenty years, a good number of scholars have agreed on the need to develop a complex theory of foreign policy able to acknowledge that foreign policy is indeed affected by both domestic and international variables. As Harald Müller and Thomas Risse-Kappen argued,

> A complex model [...] has to be conceptualized which integrates the three levels of analysis: society, political system, and international environment. [...] Several authors [...] over the last twenty years have come to surprisingly similar conclusions.
>
> (Müller and Risse-Kappen 1993: 31)

Yet scholars have disagreed on just *how* to achieve such a result. James Rosenau, Wolfram Hanrieder, Walter Carlsnaes and Robert Putnam have offered alternative attempts at constructing 'complex' theories of foreign policy. While different, these have similarly failed to question the framing of the issue and the diagnosis of the problem, which I argue is a necessary move to open up space for its reconceptualisation.

James Rosenau's linkage theory

In the mid-1960's, the pioneer of the behaviouralist revolution in the study of foreign policy, James Rosenau, first introduced the concept of 'linkage politics'. Starting from the distinction between systemic variables and domestic variables, Rosenau emphasised how recurrent events that 'originated on one side of the boundary [...] became linked to phenomena on the other side in the process of unfolding [...] thus connecting domestic and international politics' (in Rosenau 1971: 318; see also Rosenau 1969). Following this intuition, Rosenau produced a number of typologies able to discriminate between different kinds of 'linkage' – the penetrative, the reactive, and the emulative linkage – and combine them with different strategies of adaptation pursued by states. The concept of linkage was a thoroughly objective one, to be studied scientifically (hence the positioning of his theory in box 5, Figure 1.2).

Rosenau's main concern in advancing the concept of linkage, however, was not just to combine variables and factors from the international and domestic spheres of foreign policy, but also to interrogate the distinction between the two spheres. Responding to what was perceived as an increased blurring of boundaries between domestic politics and international relations, Rosenau theorised the emergence of a transnational level, whose cornerstone was precisely the category of linkage and which to some extent bypassed states and their foreign policies. His linkage theory therefore assumed and theorised the dissolution rather than the solution of the international/domestic nexus. Rosenau's conceptualisation of foreign policy ultimately suffered from a very high degree of abstraction – something which in his intention was perfectly understandable, considering the task of developing 'pre-theories' of foreign policy, which were intended merely to pave the way for a more rigorous theorising (Rosenau 1971). His legacy, however, was to be more durable and lasting in the then burgeoning transnationalism (and then globalisation) literature than in FPA (Bloomfield 1982; Senghass 1992; Caporaso 1997; Müller and Risse-Kappen 1993: 28).

Wolfram Hanrieder's 'compatibility-consensus' formula

More or less contemporary to Rosenau's conceptualisation is Wolfram Hanrieder's 'compatibility-consensus' formula (Hanrieder 1971). According to this construct, foreign policy had to be considered as 'a continuous process bridging the analytical barriers between the international and the domestic political system' (Hanrieder 1971: 253). However, Hanrieder did not follow Rosenau in espousing a view of foreign policy as linkage politics. Rather, he maintained that foreign policy could be conceptualised as unfolding necessarily within a 'double constraint'. States need to pursue a foreign policy that is compatible with the international system; moreover, this policy has to be supported by a reasonable degree of agreement inside the state. Instead of dissolving the boundary between domestic and international politics, Hanrieder treated them as almost discrete spheres of politics that could be perfectly and objectively explained from the 'outside', and viewed foreign policy as a balancing act between the two (box 5, Figure 1.2).

Despite its inspiring formulation of the question, Hanrieder's approach also failed to go beyond very broad generalisations, and it was not successful in opening up a research agenda able to build on his initial efforts (Smith 1981: 6–39). The extensive empirical research that Hanrieder himself carried out into comparative foreign policy also failed to apply his theoretical construct to specific foreign policy case studies, except for the case of West Germany (Hanrieder 1980). For these reasons, his approach left a limited legacy.

Robert Putnam's 'two-level games'

An influential approach to the issue emerged in the late 1980s following Robert Putnam's metaphor of 'two-level games' (Putnam 1988; Evans *et al.* 1993). Using this metaphor, Putnam focused on the issue of how democratic foreign policy tends to be internationally and domestically constrained in the context of multilateral economic bargaining.

Admittedly, Putnam merely reformulated a concept – that of a double constraint to foreign policy making – that was already clear in Rosenau's but especially in Hanrieder's metaphor of the 'compatibility-consensus' formula. In theoretical terms his approach added little to these earlier theorisations, least of all in terms of an epistemology which remained grounded in a narrow, naturalistic understanding of causation and explanation. Putnam's model was also highly influenced by game theory and deprived foreign policy of much political content. While Rosenau's pre-theories might be criticised for their complexity and ambiguity, Putnam's work encounters exactly the opposite problem, i.e. providing a dry and simplistic account of foreign policy. His conceptualisation tended to assume a lack of distinctiveness between domestic and international politics, treating all sources of influence as homogeneously belonging to the same 'game' of politics. Finally, Putnam's focus on the entanglements between international and domestic politics cannot help in problematising the lines of causation that go from one realm to the other, while at the same time it is not complex enough to yield a truly systemic account of the relations between foreign policy, domestic politics and international relations.

Walter Carlsnaes' tripartite approach

Addressing the broad issue of how to explain foreign policy as action, in his book *Ideology and Foreign Policy* Walter Carlsnaes advanced an original three-dimensional framework with the aim of integrating the 'intentional, dispositional and situational dimension of [foreign policy] explanation' (Carlsnaes 1986: 84; see also Carlsnaes 1992, 2013). Although not completely overlapping with the issue of the domestic and international origin of foreign policy, this approach ultimately deals with the issue of how to integrate variables placed at different levels of analysis, as do the other 'solutions' grouped in box 5, Figure 1.2. However, differently to those approaches, Carlsnaes' conceptualisation does not buy into a naturalistic, objectivist epistemological strategy, but privileges instead a complex version of interpretation and understanding. This approach belongs thus to box 6, Figure 1.2, although it tends towards the centre of the matrix, where the ontological and epistemological axes intersect, offering a valuable mediation of many earlier positions.

According to Carlsnaes, the explanation of any foreign policy action ought to start from a (teleological) examination of the motivations/preferences of those who actually decide foreign policy (Carlsnaes 1986: 81–116). On the other hand, intentional explanation can – although, according to Carlsnaes, need not necessarily – be 'deepened', or complemented, by a (causal) analysis of the dispositional dimension of the decision, namely an analysis of those values and perceptions that have made the decision-maker's preference possible in the first place. Last, one can trace the origins of the dispositional determinants of any foreign policy action to those 'objective conditions' and 'institutional/organisational settings' that make up the situational dimension of any foreign policy action, with the proviso that this should not be carried out in causal terms, but should rather be understood as a relation of cognitively mediated constraint (Carlsnaes 1986: 84; cf. however slightly different positions on causality in Carlsnaes 1992: 254, 255n19; 1993: 20).

Carlsnaes' tripartite framework is a sophisticated account of how one can not only attempt to combine domestic and international factors, but also of how to use an expansive notion of causality that does not collapse the category of cause into that of 'efficient' cause. While the epistemological balance of the model remains tilted towards interpretation and teleological accounts, the approach is capacious enough to include ideas of causality closer to the naturalistic understanding, though qualified as illustrated above.

The framework, however, is by and large silent on the issue of the international and domestic causes of foreign policy. Most probably this is because the standpoint adopted is markedly different, i.e. that of the single decision-maker/the government (which in turn is logically justifiable from the characterisation of foreign policy as essentially purposive behaviour). If one sought nevertheless to delineate the location of the boundary between the 'domestic' and the 'international' in the framework, one would probably find it somewhere inside the 'situational/structural' dimension of foreign policy. Presumably, that is, part of the situational/structural conditions of any foreign policy decision will be domestic (e.g. bureaucracy, domestic regime, economic institutions) while another part will be international in kind (i.e. conditions originating in features of international relations, e.g. alliances, international/supranational organisations, international society).

If this is the case, however, a first weakness of the framework when applied to the theme of this book emerges. The 'situational/structural' dimension seems to constitute a rather big residual category in which everything not immediately pertaining to the motivations of the decision-maker (albeit broadly defined) is lumped together. When applied to the question of how foreign policy relates to domestic politics and international relations this weakness can vitiate the clarity of the model.

Second, largely missing from the framework is an account of classic elements such as interests and power. The individual standpoint around which the approach revolves does in fact do justice to the premise that it is only individuals who *act* in foreign policy (as in any other policy); yet, it inevitably falls short of providing an account of the larger *political* process in which decisions and actions come to be taken (Knudsen 1989: 100).

Last, as the author himself conceded, this framework is only helpful in providing snapshots of foreign policy behaviour as it reconstructs its structural, dispositional and intentional conditions. However, it needs to be modified to account for foreign policy change. Just as with Newtonian physics, three dimensions are not enough to capture the development of foreign policy; in order to account for foreign policy as an evolving process, one needs to accommodate Albert Einstein's insights and include a 'fourth dimension' – that of time.

Beyond the matrix: a critical realist reconceptualisation

The approaches reviewed above differ in terms of epistemology and ontology, but not in their overall acceptance of the framing of problems, as illustrated pictorially in Figure 1.2. Paraphrasing Colin Wight, however, the two-by-two matrix is clearly inadequate to deal with the level of detail and complexity demanded of it. Ultimately it is unable to 'contain the weight [it is] being asked to bear' because the theoretical cleavages on which it relies are not only unnecessarily rigid but, more importantly, to some extent distortive of the real gamut of theoretical possibilities (Wight 2012: 30).

To move beyond this state of affairs I propose a reconceptualisation around which to construct alternative and more fruitful theoretical positions. I argue that overall there are three different ways to conceptualise the relations between foreign policy, domestic politics and international politics – monocausal, dualist and dialectical (Figure 1.3). Monocausal positions are the crudest ones: they deny the very need to combine domestic and international variables since they rely on one or another form of primacy. Dualist conceptualisations are slightly more sophisticated, in that they acknowledge the necessity to integrate variables placed at different levels, although they typically operate this integration in rather simple terms. Dialectical conceptualisations are the most complex ones of all since they not only acknowledge the interaction between domestic and international variables in generating foreign policy, but they employ complex epistemological strategies to account for it.

While monocausal and dualist conceptualisations have frequently been employed in the field, dialectical accounts have, with a few notable exceptions, been entirely overlooked. In particular, I outline the features of a strategic-relational model to foreign policy – a type of systems approach – that rejects the peremptory logic of the naturalistic/interpretative cleavage as well as the notion that foreign policy can be reduced to either external constraints or internal preferences. Instead, it conceptualises foreign policy behaviour as a product of a dialectic interplay between actor and context, as mediated by the role of ideas.

The tripartition of monocausal, dualist and dialectical accounts presented here draws on similar tripartition elaborated by a strand of scholarship recently

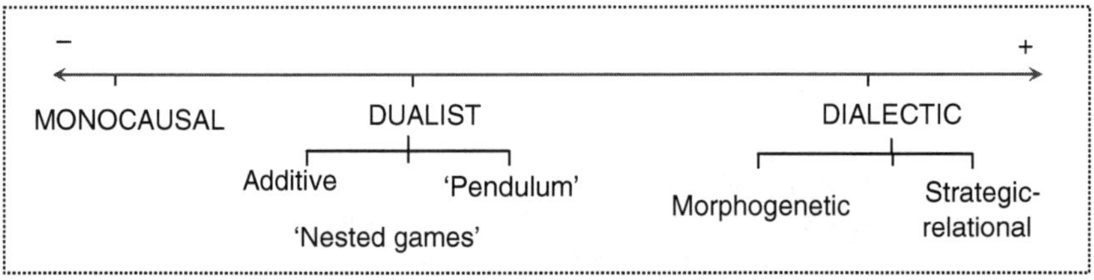

Figure 1.3 Foreign policy, domestic politics and international relations: a critical realist reconceptualisation.

developed in cognate fields of inquiry (such as sociology, anthropology and political science) from the epistemological tradition of critical realism (Bhaskar 1979, 1986, 1989; Archer *et al.* 1998; Collier 1994; Sayer 2000; Joseph and Wight 2010). In particular, it is inspired by the writings of Bob Jessop, David Marsh and Colin Hay and their response to the stalemate reached by the 'agency-structure' debate. Their contributions have sketched out the features of a strategic-relational approach which, as I show below, can fruitfully be applied to foreign policy.

1 Monocausal approaches

Monocausal approaches offer the crudest conceptualisation of foreign policy in its relation to domestic and international politics, as they tend to reduce this complex interplay to a straightforward and reductionist primacy of either one of the two sides of the equation – the 'international' or the 'domestic' – defined in interpretativist but more often naturalistic, structural terms. In terms of the map of approaches presented in the first half of this chapter, all theories placed in boxes 1, 2, 3 and 4 (i.e. excluding those tending to the centre of the matrix and those in boxes 5 or 6) correspond to this position. Although rather unsophisticated, these approaches have been the most common in FPA and IR. As stated in Chapter 1, the way in which the discipline has traditionally treated the issue of the interplay between foreign policy, on the one hand, and domestic politics and international politics, on the other, has often boiled down to the confrontation between '*Primat der Aussenpolitik*' and '*Primat der Innenpolitik*' and their more recent versions. A simple graphic representation of these two models can be found in Figure 1.4:

The limits and inadequacies of both models, when applied to foreign policy, are rather straightforward. Theories of foreign policy that focus on international

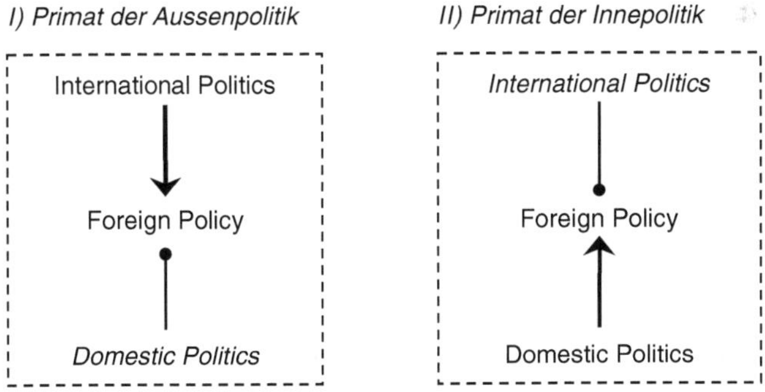

Figure 1.4 Monocausal approaches. I) corresponds to boxes 1 and 2 of Figure 1.2; II) corresponds to boxes 3 and 4. Each of the two models defines the other away.

factors typically dismiss domestic and individual influences on foreign policy, either because they posit the international as a structure to which states respond in seemingly functional and non-purposeful terms, or because they assume the uncontested primacy of a socially constructed sphere over states' domestic processes or, indeed, over individual preferences. Conversely, domestic-based theories neglect the broader environmental setting in which foreign policy is generated, in terms of either the material or the ideational set of constraints in relation to which foreign policy is articulated: they are, in other words, dismissive of context. Taken in isolation, then, monocausal theories are the least plausible and their empirical applicability seems to be limited to very few and extreme cases – something which will be discussed later.

2 *Dualist interpretations: middle ground or dead end?*

In contrast to monocausal conceptualisations, dualist accounts start from the assumption that foreign policy cannot be reduced to either domestic politics or international relations. Rather, it is their often uneven combination that produces foreign policy actions, with domestic influences adding to international trends (and vice versa) in the determination of foreign policy.

Adhering to a neat separation between the 'international' and the 'domestic', these accounts deal with the catch-22 question of whether the domestic or the international determines foreign policy by adopting the unsophisticated (but commonsensical) answer: 'both'. If this characterises all dualist positions, there are at least three different ways in which these solve the issue of the relative weight to be assigned to international and domestic factors: a simple additive view, a model resembling that of 'nested games', and a 'pendulum' approach.

'Additive' conceptualisations

The simple, additive approach the least complicated of all dualist conceptualisations. It posits foreign policy as being the result of a simple, straightforward 'addition' of pressures and influences placed at the domestic and international level (see Figure 1.5):

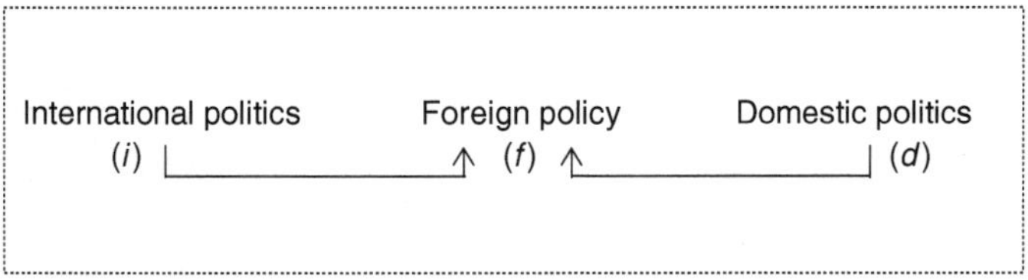

Figure 1.5 Dualist/additive conceptualisations. In simple, *additive* dualist models, domestic and international politics equally influence foreign policy, and the latter results from the summation of the former ($f = i + d$). International politics, domestic politics and foreign policy are placed at the same level, with no necessary hierarchy among the levels.

Because of their empirical appeal, these accounts have in fact been used quite often, especially in historical research, often providing the only real alternative to the traditional 'primacies' (see, for instance, Kissinger 1957: 28). In FPA, both the 'compatibility-consensus' formula articulated by Wolfram Hanrieder and the 'two-level games' of Robert D. Putnam (despite its brief discussion of synergies and entanglements) can be considered dualist/additive accounts.

In these accounts, the nature of the dual constraint to foreign policy-making is not hierarchical, but, rather, symmetrical. There is no implicit or necessary hierarchy between international politics, domestic politics and foreign policy, in contrast to, for instance, monocausal accounts (for example, see Putnam 1988: 434). Given the balancing function it performs, foreign policy often ceases to be conceptualised in terms of the projection of some shared goals among a community of people. Instead, in these models it seems to be permanently caught in a balancing act between domestic politics and international relations – with intentionality being lost in the bargaining (Putnam 1988: 442–8). Last, epistemologically these models leave a lot to be desired. To start with, their account of foreign policy does not lend itself to a complex view of causation, as they more pragmatically start from the assumption that foreign policy is *always* influenced by a combination of international and domestic political trends, primarily understood as 'efficient' causes narrowly defined in objectivist, naturalistic terms. The descriptive power of these accounts might be very high, but their explanatory value is diluted by a number of weaknesses and ambiguities. What influences the combination of international and domestic factors? Is this mediated by cognition at any level? Does it remain constant, or does it change over time? And if it does, according to what: size of the country, properties of the international or the domestic sphere, particular conjunctures?

'Nested games' conceptualisations[5]

A second dualist conceptualisation starts from assumptions similar to those underlying the 'additive' approach described above, except for one. While these approaches also share the idea of separateness of the two domains – the 'international' and the 'domestic' – and conceive of foreign policy as the addition of international and domestic influences, they differ in terms of how they understand the relation between these levels. While the additive model treats them as symmetrical, the nested games model considers them as hierarchical. Foreign policy results from a 'double constraint' in which one comes before and is more important than the other. Graphically, the dualist/'nested games' view of foreign policy can be represented as in Figure 1.6.

In this dualist conceptualisation there is thus a clear division of labour between international politics and domestic politics. In a logic resembling that of concentric circles, or 'successive filtering devices', the international system operates a first selection amongst all potential foreign policies by selecting the range of those compatible with the state's position in the system. Then, domestic

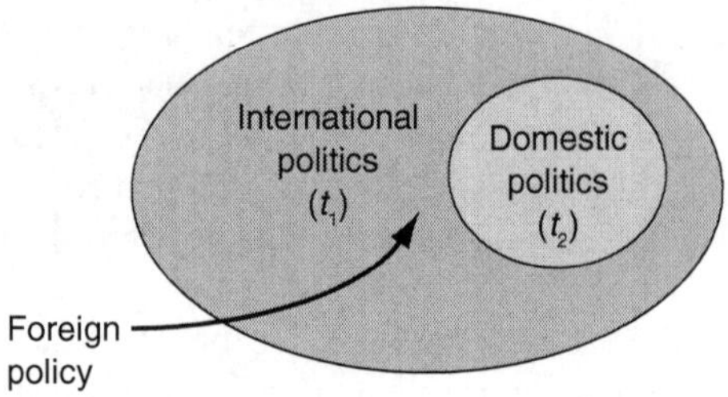

Figure 1.6 Dualist/'nested games' conceptualisations. Just as in the additive model, foreign policy results from the combination of international and domestic pressures. The way in which these constraints operate, however, is different in terms of their relative importance and sequencing: international politics operates at t_1 by 'fixing the contours' of foreign policy, while domestic politics impacts on foreign policy at t_2 and is responsible for its details.

politics operates a second selection by indicating those that are also compatible with the processes of domestic politics.[6]

In moving beyond the rigid monocausality of neo-realism, neoclassical realists such as Fareed Zakaria and Randall Schweller have proposed an understanding of the relation between foreign policy, domestic politics and international relations where the 'international' (structurally conceived) determines the *grandes lignes* of foreign policy, while domestic politics functions as a 'transmission belt' (Rose 1998: 158). According to Zakaria,

> A good theory [...] would first examine the effect of the international system on foreign policy, for the most important general characteristic of a state in international relation is its relative standing in the international system. [...However,] a theory of foreign policy must not ignore domestic politics, national culture, and individual decision makers [and] can be layered successively with additional variables [such as] domestic regime types, bureaucracies, and statesmen.
>
> (Zakaria 1998: 16 and 1992: 197)

The variables identified by Zakaria, including cognitive factors, are understood in fairly objectivist terms as his model still subscribes to a naturalistic understanding of causality. Both 'nests' impact upon foreign policy behaviour mechanically, as 'efficient' causes, and interactions between variables and feedback loops are conspicuously absent.

Despite its markedly different epistemology and focus, Carlsnaes' tripartite approach can also be understood as a 'nested games' approach – with the intentional dimension being nested in the dispositional dimension, and with both nested in a larger situational/structural dimension. Thence comes the characteristically 'layered' construction of the framework (Carlsnaes 1994: 281). In Carlsnaes' approach, however, the relations between 'nests' are not as straightforward as in the case of neo-realists à la Zakaria. They are not modelled after 'efficient' and objectivist kinds of causality, but rather after a mixed and complex epistemology.

The hierarchy at the heart of 'nested games' conceptualisations, however, is of course highly problematic. Where does the implicit order of constraints come from? And what about those foreign policies that 'defy the apparently irresistible pressures from the structure, or history [...] and delay the inevitable for a surprisingly long period' (Hill and Stavridis 1996: 10), for instance, or those that by virtue of their own determination 'manufacture' an international system that had previously not existed (Snyder 1991: 68)?

'Pendulum' model

Retaining a dualist perspective, other models have addressed the problem of the 'relative weights' to be assigned to domestic and international politics, advancing a third conceptualisation. Starting from the assumption that the relative weight of these sets of variables is not constant but is, rather, an empirical question, these approaches conceive of foreign policy as being determined relatively more by international relations or domestic politics, depending on which set of variables finds itself in a more 'acute' state.

This parallels Robert Jervis' argument about the relative importance of levels of analysis in analysing foreign policy.[7] Furthermore, it echoes Arnold Wolfers' well-known metaphor of the 'house on fire'. This he used in his 1962 *Discord and Collaboration* to describe how foreign policy mediates between and is influenced by international and domestic politics:

> Imagine a number of individuals [...] who find themselves in a house on fire. It would be realistic to expect that these individuals [...] would feel compelled to run towards the exit. Surely therefore, for an explanation of the rush for the exits, there is no need to analyse the individual decisions that produced it.
>
> (Wolfers 1962: 13)

Wolfers argued that just like the individuals in the metaphor, when states face overwhelming international pressures, foreign policy tends to adapt relatively more to international, rather than domestic, politics. The foreign policy analyst is, in these circumstances, excused from taking domestic politics into account, because its effects upon foreign policy will be only marginal. Conversely, domestic politics will be determinant in all those instances when international politics does not compel any particular action.

A similar position has been endorsed more recently by Jack Snyder, another neo-realist who defected from Waltz' strictly monocausal views of foreign policy. In his analysis of imperial foreign policies, Snyder focused on the question of what causes states to develop such foreign policies – whether it is international politics, domestic politics, or both. His answer is that domestic politics counts much more than neo-realism usually allows for. International politics alone, according to Snyder, is insufficient a cause for any foreign policy to be adopted: it creates opportunities, but never compels states. Both constraints are relevant to foreign policy, and their relative weight is variable (cf. also Waltz 1979: 48–9, 78, 87, 123 and 1986: 343):

> The state is a pivot between the domestic and international realms. [...] Is it to be considered [...] as governed by the exigencies of international competition? [...] Is it the captive of domestic interests [...]? The answer [...] is 'It depends'. At the most general level, it depends on whether international pressures are more threatening, insistent, and immediate than domestic pressures. Whether international or domestic woes are more pressing [...] is an empirical question.
>
> (Snyder 1991: 317)

As can be seen in Figure 1.7, when states face overwhelming international pressures, foreign policy tends to adapt relatively more to international, rather than domestic, politics. Conversely, when international politics is not compelling any particular action, domestic politics will greatly influence foreign policy, and the pendulum will lean towards domestic, not international, factors.

However simple and empirically significant, this conceptualisation has a number of limitations. First, it is not really clear when, to follow Wolfers' vivid metaphor, the house is 'on fire', i.e. what are the international conditions that

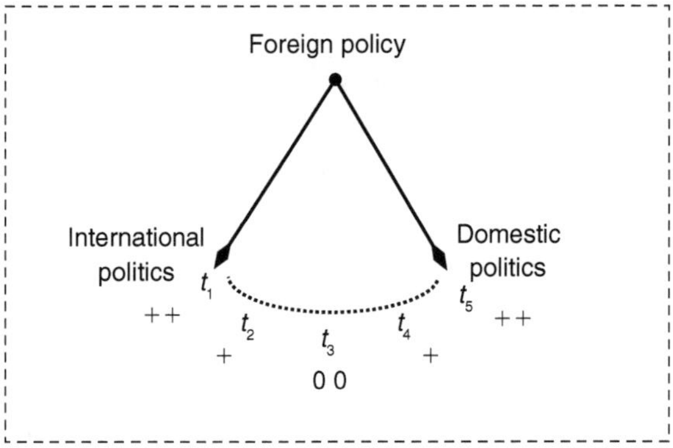

Figure 1.7 Dualist/'pendulum' conceptualisations. Following a *pendulum* trajectory, foreign policy swings between the two ends of domestic politics and international politics (t_1–t_5, and vice versa), and results from their changing combination. When international pressures are more acute (t_1), foreign policy will tend to reflect international politics relatively more; vice versa, when domestic politics is more pressing (t_5), foreign policy will swing towards that pole.

make the systemic constraint more compelling or, for that matter, what domestic conditions render this constraint acute. And, moreover, the assumption that foreign policy is always fire- (or crisis-) driven is indeed questionable: quite the opposite seems to be the case, most of the time.

Second, the model seems to assume that 'acute states' can be empirically observed and recognised unproblematically, an assumption that betrays a narrow understanding of causality and an exclusively naturalistic epistemology. Besides, what makes the pendulum swing in the first place? Foreign policy behaviour seems to result from an alternation of monocausal moments, but nothing in the model explains how one moves from one to the other (and whether this move has any relation to the actor's own foreign policy behaviour).

Third, and perhaps most importantly, what proves that when confronted by a conflictual international system, foreign policy tends to be unresponsive to domestic political stimuli? There are many historical examples, fascism and Nazism being two, that arguably offer a challenge to these theories: for example, was fascist foreign policy unrelated to domestic politics because the acute polarisation of the inter-war international system itself made fascism and its foreign policy inevitable? The implications of these models seem contestable.

3 Dialectical interpretations

Dialectical approaches differ from monocausal theories in that, applied to foreign policy, they analyse how both domestic and international variables participate in the articulation of foreign policy; but they also differ from dualistic approaches in that they reject any simple addition of these influences in favour of a more complex and dynamic account, with a particular focus on the interaction and feedback between levels. These approaches foreground the element of action and change, as well as the dialectic between structural and agential elements over time.[8] Of the two positions that can be singled out as dialectical, the first one has been only partially applied to foreign policy – with empirical research being in particularly short supply – while the second so far has not, in spite of its considerable potential.

Morphogenetic approach

The first dialectical approach was inspired by the critical realist scholarship of Roy Bhaskar, and was fully developed by the sociologist Margaret Archer in relation to the 'agency-structure' debate over the last 20 years or so (Archer 1988, 1995, 1998; McAnulla 1998, 2002).

According to this model, agents and structures are analytically and ontologically separate phenomena, and it is their sequential and dialectical interplay, rather than their mutual constitution, which provides a more accurate account of actions and their development over time (for variations and a critique, see King 1999). Structure and agency reside in different temporal domains, with the pre-existence of structure being a necessary condition for individual action. Action, in turn, can either reproduce or transform the structure, rather than creating it: if the structure is merely reproduced by agents, the result is *morphostasis*; if, on the other hand, the structure is changed and transformed by these actions, there is a process of *morphogenesis*. Rather than employing simple, efficient causality, the morphogenetic model relies, therefore, on a form of system theorising.

As Walter Carslnaes has noted, the implications of this model for foreign policy are extremely interesting (Carlsnaes 1992, 1993, 2004). Applied to the issue at hand, the model shows how foreign policy (understood as action) intervenes in an already set international environment, which necessarily pre-dates it. However, foreign policy is not merely the answer to a set of environmental stimuli (as structuralist positions would have it), but is in fact shaped by the states' 'emergent properties', i.e. domestic political dynamics, values, leaders, etc. The result is not so much an algebraic addition of different influences, but, rather, a sequential process. When a certain foreign policy is articulated, it can either restructure international affairs or reproduce the state of international relations. This, in turn, forms the precondition for another round of sequential interaction (see Figure 1.8).

When applied to foreign policy, domestic politics and international relations, the morphogenetic approach is quite illuminating in showing the dialectical and sequential interplay between international politics, domestic politics and foreign policy. However, it also presents a number of problems.

To start with, the analytical dualism which, according to some of Archer's critics, hardens into an ontological dualism between structure and agency, is inherently problematic. Structure (at t_1) tends to be conceived of as an entity in

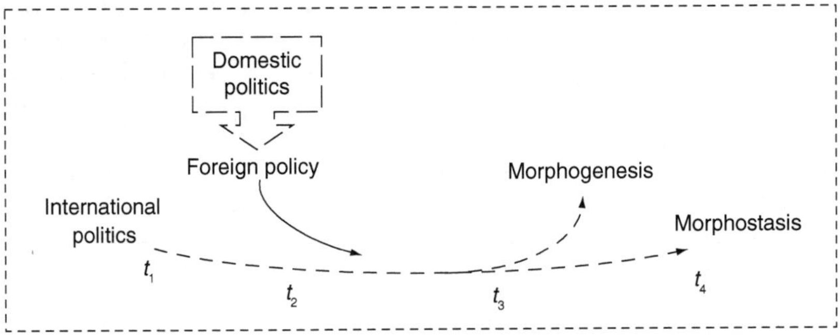

Figure 1.8 Dialectical/morphogenetic conceptualisations. In a morphogenetic sequence of structural conditioning and unit action applied to foreign policy, international politics provides the structural context of foreign policy action and predates foreign policy (t_1). Domestic politics corresponds to the 'emergent properties' of the actor: these shape the nature of foreign policy (t_2). Foreign policy action can (t_3) either leave the structure unaltered (morphostasis), or alter the structural constraint (morphogenesis). In either case, the result of this sequence produces (t_4) a new structure, which in turn provides the starting point for a new foreign policy, and a new cycle of sequential, dynamic interplay between domestic politics, foreign policy and international relations (cf. McAnulla 2002).

whose construction agency plays a limited (and temporally delayed) part. As Anthony King notes, however, this is not a particularly useful conceptualisation:

> the key error which Archer makes in her derivation of social structure is to draw the sociological conclusion of existence of a social structure from the perspective of a single individual [...] if she had de-centred her perspective to see that the constraint I face is other individuals – and no less serious for that – just as I form some of the social conditions which mutually constrain some others, she would not have fallen into ontological dualism.
>
> (King 1999: 217; cf. Hay 2002: 125–6)

The implication for foreign policy is that the morphogenetic model tends to see international relations as a remote and scarcely intelligible structure; this, however, ignores the fact that such a structure is (at least in part) the sum of relations between states, a context in whose construction each state plays a (different, yet equally indispensable) role.

Second, the morphogenetic model seems to rely upon an implicit division of labour between structure and agency. While structure appears to be a long-enduring, external and distant constraint, agency, which presumably lends itself to be studied causally, finds that its emergent properties and action are conceptualised to intervene as periodical, infrequent, ephemeral and contingent (e.g. in Figure 1.8, agency features only at t_2). In other words, there seems to be a certain bias in favour of the structural element in this conceptualisation, and a residual naturalism.

Thus, the harder the ontological dualism and the greater the residual structuralism, the more the morphogenetic approach tends to reproduce the logic of the dualist positions reviewed earlier, especially the 'nested games' position, instead of being truly dialectical.

Strategic-relational approach

The second dialectical approach was developed by Bob Jessop, Colin Hay and David Marsh as a response to Archer's contribution, and goes under the name of the 'strategic-relational' approach (Jessop 1990, 1996; Hay 1995, 1999, 2000, 2002, 2009; Hay and Marsh 1999; Hay and Rosamond 2002). Instead of Archer's view of structures as pre-existing agency, the strategic-relational model starts from the twin assumption that

> Structures can only be said to exist by virtue of their mediation of human conduct – structures constitute both the medium and the condition of human agency [...]. Structure and agency are best seen not so much (à la Giddens) as flip-sides of the same coin, but as metals in the alloy from which the coin is forged [...] though analytically separable, [they] are in practice completely interwoven.
>
> (Hay 1999)

> Neither agents nor structures are real, since neither has an existence in isolation from the other – their existence is *relational* (structure and agency are mutually constitutive) and *dialectical* (their interaction is not reducible to the sum of structural and agential factors treated separately).[9]
>
> (Hay 2002: 127, my emphasis)

The strategic-relational model places at the centre of this dialectical and relational dynamic a particular process that 'solves' the issue of structure and agency, which could be termed 'double internalisation'. On the one hand, through this process agency is brought into structure – to produce a structured context, an action setting for that particular actor. On the other, structure is brought into agency – to produce an actor-in-context, a situated agent. This process of double internalisation leads to the conceptual pairing upon which the strategic-relational model is framed: agency becomes a *strategic actor* operating within a structure turned a *strategically selective context.*

Actors are conceptualised as strategic in the sense that they are assumed to be aware of the context in which they act and are oriented by a sense of purpose to attain their goals, i.e. they are engaging in intentional conduct. However, this should not be taken to mean that their preferences are fixed, as in rational choice theory. Rather, these are always constructed and discursively mediated so that 'different actors in similar material circumstances (exposed, perhaps, to different influences and experiences) will construct their interests and preferences differently' and will reflexively revise them over time (Hay 2002: 131). Structures, on the other hand, are strategically selective environments, favouring certain strategies over others and presenting an unevenly distributed configuration of opportunity and constraint to actors. They are also spatially and temporally specific, i.e. the patterns of strategic selectivity are *always* contingent and specific to a particular actor at a particular time (Hay 1999).

As mentioned above, the dialectical interplay between strategic actors and strategically selective context is crucially mediated by discourse: '*ideas provide the point of mediation between actors and their environment*' (Hay 2002: 209–10, emphasis in original).[10] Thus, on the one hand, the actor's access to context is influenced by perceptions, interpretations and understandings of that context. On the other, structures too are discourse-selective environments in so far as they select the 'discourses through which [they] might be appropriated' (Hay 1999), 'selecting for and against particular ideas, narratives and constructions' (Hay 2002: 212). Particularly central to both processes of mediation are the so-called policy paradigms, i.e. intersubjectively agreed-upon narratives that provide 'cognitive templates' through which the world is interpreted (cf. Sprout and Sprout 1965: 28).

The strategic-relational model was introduced in political science in order to reject the view that (political) action could be reduced to either external constraints or internal preferences and that studying such action implied a stark choice between naturalism and interpretativism. The conceptualisation thus manages to give equal conceptual weight to both structure and agency, 'causal' and 'constitutive' mechanisms, material and ideational factors.

An application of the strategic-relational model to foreign policy and its relation with domestic and international politics yields particularly fruitful results (for earlier attempts, see Brighi 2007c and Brighi and Hill 2012). The intuition at the heart of the strategic-relational model is that foreign policy behaviour is produced via a dialectical interplay between the actor's own strategy, on the one hand, and context, on the other. The approach is strategic in that actors are conceptualised as oriented towards the attainment of stated goals. Preferences are constituted through a political process involving both domestic and international politics and are always 'constructed' politically and discursively (see Figure 1.9). The elaboration of foreign policy, in particular, involves an assessment of *both* the international context of action *and* the state's own domestic preferences. Furthermore, in the process of elaborating appropriate courses of action, actors inevitably have to take into account the strategies of all other players. The model is also relational because it assumes that actors and their behaviour only become intelligible when analysed in relation to their proper context.

Given its relational nature, international politics is conceived of as a selective constraint, one that favours certain foreign policies over others. As many states compose the international system, it is likely that their interaction and complex aggregation of interests will provide an uneven terrain for foreign policy: some actions, in other words, will be more successful than others, some will be severely sanctioned and considered unacceptable, etc.

The strategic-relational model thus manages to 'demystify' a structural understanding of international relations and avoids the fatalism usually associated with the term 'structure' in much IR literature by revealing its relational character. Context is not a monolithic and impenetrable entity which pre-exists actors, and against which actors stand virtually powerless. Rather, context is here intended mainly as other actors, no more and no less than the set of relations which they

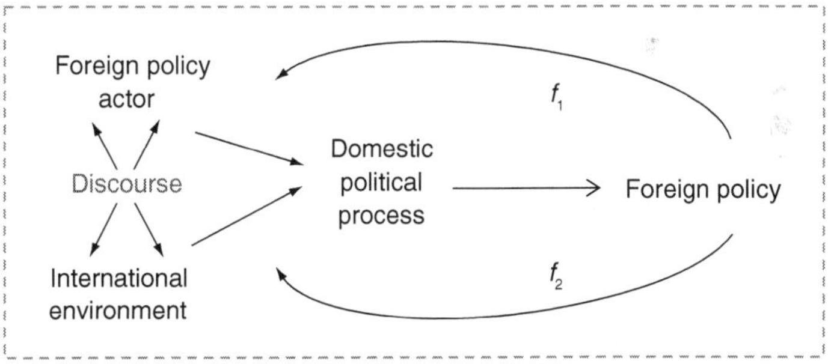

Figure 1.9 Dialectical/strategic-relational conceptualisations. In the strategic-relational model, foreign policy is elaborated through a discursively mediated political process which involves an assessment of both the international context and the actor's own preferences. Once articulated, foreign policy feeds back both into the international system, either restructuring the environment or leaving it unchanged (f_2), and into the actor – i.e. the state – (f_1), by making strategic adaptation possible (figure adapted from Hay 1995: 202, Hay 2002: 131, Brighi 2007c: 107; Brighi and Hill 2012: 150).

entertain and the patterns they have generated. Even the material environment, which is an important and arguably 'objective' part of the context, becomes fully meaningful only through the relations that actors establish with one another. The coexistence of different actors, their interaction and complex aggregation of interests, is what makes 'the international' an uneven terrain for foreign policy.

Moreover, context means different things to different actors, depending not only on where they are placed, but also on how they interpret the features of the terrain surrounding them. Context, in other words, only becomes truly 'real' when looked at from the perspective of the individual actor in question; it always exists in relation to something, or some other actor (cf. Michel 2012). As such, the strategic-relational model reinstates agency in a position central to the interplay between foreign policy, domestic politics and international relations.

The constant interplay between actors and context does not play itself out at the material level only, but is mediated by the role of ideas and language. Discourse features on both sides of the 'double internalisation' process and complements the dialectic of structure and agency with an ideational and reflexive dimension. Thus it is important not only to take into account the way the context responds to the actors' behaviour, but also the way such responses are filtered through perceptions, paradigms and narratives, eventually to be internalised in the political process. This dimension is crucially missing from dualist approaches and Archer's own dialectical framework. All of these tend to assume that domestic politics and international relations impact naturalistically and objectively upon foreign policy, with no discursive or ideational mediation.

Finally, by treating domestic politics and international relations as *temporally co-extensive* this conceptualisation does not fall in the trap of reifying a purely analytical distinction into an ontological one. In doing so, it goes beyond Archer's residual structuralism. Just as there is a constant interplay, so is there also a constant feedback from the actor to the context and vice versa. Once produced through an interactive process, foreign policy behaviour feeds back into the context, restructuring the environment or leaving it unchanged, and into the actor itself, by making adaptation possible.

Because of the way in which it solves the tension between domestic and international determinants of foreign policy, and between naturalistic and intepretativist epistemology, the strategic-relational model manages to offer a complex and fully systemic account of foreign policy in its relation with domestic and international politics, one which moves well beyond the stark dichotomies and cleavages that inform its competing approaches.

The strategic-relational model in foreign policy analysis: a comparative look

In sketching out the alternative conceptualisations of the section above, I have attempted to move up the ladder of abstraction to formulate specific and alternative models of how foreign policy, international relations and domestic politics interrelate. Aware that models (or ontological constructs) can never be falsified,[11] the exercise above has tried to derive specific propositions around foreign policy that can sustain an empirical test, which is a task that I pursue in the remainder of this book. Do these conceptualisations provide incommensurable frameworks for analysing foreign policy? Do they have different domains of empirical applicability? Can these be brought together in some way? And can they all be subsumed in the strategic-relational model?

In what follows I make three different but interrelated claims. First, I argue that each conceptualisation has a different domain of applicability. Thus, the less complex the framework elaborated to deal with foreign policy in its relation with domestic and international politics (as in Figure 1.3), the more limited its empirical applicability; conversely, the more complex the framework, the more general its empirical fit.

Second, on closer inspection these models also differ in terms of their explanatory focus or thrust. While monocausal and dualist models are for their most part content with studying foreign policy from the perspective of cause-effect relations (i.e. utilising a narrow, efficient causality), dialectical models are interested in explaining foreign policy from a more dynamic perspective able to include the interactions between variables. Ultimately, the continuum of Figure 1.3 spans the distance that separates the notion of efficient causality from that of systemic causality, causal theories from systemic ones.

Third, of all conceptualisations the strategic-relational model provides the most generally valid explanation of foreign policy in its relation with domestic and international politics – almost its default account. While other, less complex models have purchase only in specific circumstances, the strategic-relational model lends itself to be more widely applied.

As for my first claim, monocausal positions cannot help but have a limited applicability. *Ceteris paribus* and starting from monocausal theories of an international bent (of both interpretativist and naturalistic character), their applicability increases as the size of the state whose foreign policy we are analysing decreases (cf. Rosenau 1971: 132 n.45). Conversely, and all other things being equal, big states have a greater impact upon the 'international' and thus are subject to lesser pressures from this sphere. In turn, domestic politics is likely to influence foreign policy more in the case of big states and less in the case of small states. On the other hand, the applicability of monocausal approaches also varies according to the specific characteristics of the international or domestic political dynamic of the time. A high systemic connectivity (due to crisis/war, but also consolidated rules of behaviour, political integration, etc.) will increase the potency of the international constraint, whereas one can also hypothesise that a particularly demanding domestic political dynamic (e.g. democratic, pluralistic process) is likely to affect foreign policy relatively more, irrespective of the size of the state in question.

Dualist/pendulum accounts of foreign policy are also limited in two other respects. While they are able to provide a picture of foreign policy when this swings between extreme domestic and international pressures, they cannot account for what makes foreign policy swing in the first place, i.e. what ultimately causes relative weights to shift. This necessarily implies that there is nothing in the model that can account for foreign policy change, just as in their monocausal counterparts. Further, they cannot account for any non-linear non-additive interactions between the variables in question as they tend to see foreign policy as an 'either/or' affair. Just as dualist/pendulum models, dualist/additive models have trouble accounting for foreign policy change. In fact, they cannot go beyond the rather vague claim that foreign policy is always the result of a combination of forces.

Dualist/'nested games' approaches, on the other hand, have yet another domain of applicability: by relying on a hierarchical interpretation of the relation between the 'international' and the 'domestic', this approach limits the ability of states to go against the incentives of the environment around it and change the rules of the game. This, however, might be a more plausible assumption for small states than for big and powerful states, given that the latter are able to structure and restructure international relations precisely given their weight and influence. Further, as with all other dualist models, these approaches are unable to capture the interplay between foreign policy, domestic politics and international relations.

The last category of approaches, the dialectical approaches, have instead precisely this merit, but they differ in the applicability of their substantive claims. The morphogenetic model applied to foreign policy provides a manageable and useful construct for analysing foreign policy dynamically. Still, its emphasis on the pre-existence of structures and the ontological dualism upon which the model is predicated limits its application to cases where international influences are relatively more powerful, either because the state in question is small, or because of the particular characteristics of the environment surrounding it.

In contrast to the models above, the strategic-relational approach offers the most complex framework for analysing foreign policy. Because this approach is systemic and *inherently relational*, the model is able to capture all possible forms of interplay between foreign policy, international relations and domestic politics as it captures the relation between variables, rather than their absolute value (small states/big states, tense/relaxed international environment, etc.). Its particular solution to the relation between structure and agents, the conceptual pairing upon which the approach is framed (actor-in-context and action-setting), and the way it reconciles causal and systemic reasoning make this the most generalisable of the ones sketched out.

To sum up, in this section I have made three interrelated claims. First I have argued that the less complex the frameworks elaborated to deal with foreign policy in its relation with domestic and international politics, the more limited their applicability; conversely, the more complex the frameworks, the more general their empirical fit. Second, the different models seem to have different domains of applicability as well as different explanatory *foci*, and as such are suitable for different types of inquiry (causal vs. systemic). While monocausal and dualist approaches provide frameworks able to analyse foreign policy in terms of 'comparative static', dialectical models can also account for foreign policy change; while monocausal models perform best over a long time-scale, dialectical models are able to account for short-term discontinuities. Last, the strategic-relational model is able to provide the most general account of foreign policy in its relation with domestic and international politics, its default approach.

Foreign policy, domestic politics and international relations: a few questions on Italian foreign policy

Now that some considerations have been offered on the empirical applicability of the conceptualisations reviewed above, I shall move on to illustrate the research questions and hypotheses that will guide the empirical examination of Italian foreign policy (1901–2011) in the remainder of the book.

As a medium-sized state, Italy has historically experienced a startling variety of combinations of international relations and domestic politics, which in turn has influenced the development of a variegated foreign policy. Yet, the debate on the topic of Italian foreign policy has usually been framed around a confrontation between two narratives: those who favour an international and arch-structuralist reading of Italian foreign policy and, conversely, those who advance an inward-looking account of Italy's foreign policy.

Starting from this state of affairs, I intend to raise three groups of questions concerning Italian foreign policy over the four periods covered: first, the issue of the 'primacy' of either international or domestic factors; second, the issue of the different combinations of international/domestic influences upon foreign policy over time; third, the issue of foreign policy change. Needless to say, because the *foci* of these questions are different – some interrogating foreign policy causally (e.g. Q_1), some other systemically (e.g. Q_3) – different models will be particularly suitable to different questions, with the stretagic-relational model able to provide useful answers to both.

Thus, starting from the first group of questions:

> Q_1: Was Italian foreign policy *exclusively* a function of international relations? Or was it instead *exclusively* a function of domestic politics? In more theoretical terms, were monocausal theories (primacy of the international, primacy of the domestic) ever corroborated during each period? If so, under what conditions?

Naturally, this is a rather hard test for monocausal theories: few would really endorse the views that I intend to interrogate. Thus, the question could be seen as addressing a straw-man. Yet, by proving *a contrario* the limits of the two monocausal readings of Italian foreign policy for each period, the discussion serves to liberate some space for a more imaginative and less reified account of Italian foreign policy (cf. Snyder 1991: 307). Pointing out the specific limits of these two readings in each of the four periods covered is a preliminary step towards moving on to more complex explanations of Italian foreign policy.

Second, by moving up the ladder of complexity as illustrated in Figure 1.3, I examine what kind of combination of international and domestic influences have generated Italian foreign policy in each period. In doing so, I shall advance the following questions:

> Q_2: What was the 'relative weight' of international and domestic factors bearing on Italian foreign policy in each period? Are dualist conceptualisations able to capture such a combination?

Third, I shall move on to the last set of questions, those concerning foreign policy change. Here I investigate how Italian foreign policy has responded to changes in both the 'domestic' and the 'international', in particular asking the following questions:

> Q_3: What were the patterns of interaction between international relations, foreign policy and domestic politics during the period in question? How determining was this interplay in the construction of foreign policy? Can dialectical frameworks account for it?

With special reference to the strategic-relational model, in particular, I investigate how the discursively mediated interplay between strategy and the strategically-selective context has determined foreign policy in each period, thus asking the question:

> Q_4: Can the examination of the dialectic between strategy, context and discourse account for foreign policy change, as the strategic-relational model suggests?

Building on these questions, I will finally address the issue of Italian foreign policy in its relation to domestic and international politics over time, i.e. comparing the different periods together. After all, the periodisation followed in the book is not neutral. In fact, it aims to raise another research question pertaining to Italian foreign policy, namely:

> Q_5: Did Italian foreign policy change with each change of domestic regime, or did it stay the same despite it? What patterns of continuity or discontinuity can be traced in the relations between foreign policy, domestic politics and international relations in the Italian case over time?

Further, I shall address two questions concerning dualist frameworks, and ask whether they are able to provide an assessment of the overall trajectory of Italian foreign policy:

> Q_6: What was the relative weight of international and domestic factors bearing on Italian foreign policy over the four periods at hand? Did it vary or stay constant?

> Q_7: In theoretical terms, are dualist conceptualisations compatible with the way the relative weight of international and domestic factors have changed over time in the case of Italy? Can they provide a suitable account of it in terms of 'comparative static'?

Last, dialectical frameworks will also be interrogated as to their ability to capture the continuity/changes in Italian foreign policy over the last century:

> Q_8: What were the patterns of interaction between international relations, foreign policy and domestic politics over the four periods in question? How determining was this interplay in the overall construction of Italian foreign policy, and can dialectical approaches account for it?

> Q_9: Is the strategic-relational model able to provide a convincing account of the patterns of continuity and change in the foreign policy of Italy over the last century?

Conclusions

This chapter has advanced some conceptual tools for reflection upon the question of how foreign policy is produced at the intersection of domestic politics and international relations. In particular, it has advanced a number of alternative frameworks, offering a systematic investigation of their strengths and weaknesses. It is of course telling that the way in which FPA has thought about this subject has been largely confined to less than sophisticated monocausal, or, at best, dualist accounts. There is still much ground to cover in order to articulate more detailed and informed models. Despite the difficulty of the task at hand, however, some progress in this area is realistically within the discipline's reach.

This state of the art is also surprisingly similar to the state of reflection on Italian foreign policy. In the same way that FPA has so far failed to move beyond monocausal and dualist theories and towards more complex accounts, so has the literature on Italian foreign policy typically reinforced the confrontation between a structuralist, arch-realist interpretation of foreign policy and an inward-looking, ephemeral and often factionalist account of our diplomatic conduct.

In this confrontation one can again find many of the themes that this chapter has sought to expose and discuss, however briefly: to what extent is it possible to articulate accounts of foreign policy which are able to grasp the complex interaction of structural and agential elements? How is it possible to overcome monocausal narratives to gain a clearer and more complex picture of how Italian foreign policy has bridged the inside and outside of the country in the last century? The next four chapters will discuss these questions and analyse the trajectory of Italian foreign policy during four main periods: the liberal age (1901–1922), the fascist 'ventennio' (1922–1943), the 'First Republic' (1943–1992), and the 'Second Republic' (1992–2011).

2 Italian foreign policy

The liberal age (1901–1922)

To find a place in the world: the apogee and decline of Italy's liberal foreign policy

At the turn of the twentieth century the diplomatic horizon of Italian foreign policy revolved around three main poles of attraction: the Triple Alliance, Italy's relations with the *Entente* powers and, finally, its own colonial ambitions. As we will see, much of the complexity and ambiguity of the liberal foreign policy of Italy was caused by the desire to keep the country in an ambiguously close and yet eccentric orbit around all three poles (Lyttleton 2002; Bosworth 1979, 1996; Chabod 1998 [1951]; Salvemini 1970; Torre 1959; Aquarone 1981; Cammarano 1999).

By the turn of the century the Triple Alliance had become the cornerstone of Italian liberal foreign policy (Bosworth 1983a; Weitsman 2004). After much hesitation and against the wish of, on the one hand, many liberal statesmen and, on the other, the irredentist movement, the alliance with Austria-Hungary and Germany was signed in 1882, mainly for reasons of expediency. First, it provided an effective response against French expansion in the Mediterranean, an area in which Italy had colonial interests (Grange 1994; on the French occupation of Tunis, Petrignani 1987: 259–62; Bosworth 1996: 97–8). Second, Italy welcomed a partnership with Germany – its modernity and might were equally attractive for a weak state like Italy – in order to gain support for its own ambitions as great power. As a matter of fact, after so many decades of close relations with Britain and especially France during the glorious decades of Italy's Unification, Italy had come to recognise that the new situation on the continent of Europe (and especially but not exclusively the rise of Bismarck's Germany) required new diplomatic instruments. Hence, as Benedetto Croce laconically put it, it resolved to 'drink the bitter cup' and join the conservative powers following the quixotic dictum 'either allies or enemies' (Croce 1929: 109).

Third, the alliance with Austria-Hungary and Germany was strongly advocated by conservative institutions such as the Papacy and the King for domestic purposes, namely to contain the revamped republican and democratic elements in the country (Chabod 1951: 12; Torre 1959: 12, 230–1, 256–7; Croce 1929: 109).[1]

It was also supported by some sectors of the Left, who were eager to contain the French influence on Italian affairs and who had gained power only a few years back, in 1876. Finally, at the time of its signing, the Triple Alliance represented the only way to avoid what Italy feared most: a diplomatic isolation in Europe. Even moderate diplomats such as Emilio Visconti Venosta, who unremittingly voiced the need for Italy to concentrate on domestic reforms and give up too ambitious plans in foreign policy, supported the alliance as a means to stay 'indipendenti sempre, isolati mai' and more importantly preserve a European peace.[2]

The defensive alliance with Austria and Germany, however, was never intended to antagonise France, with whom relations had remained cordial, except through the late 1880s and early 1890s when Francesco Crispi's obstinate anti-French attitude had caused them to cool down considerably.[3] Thanks to the tireless work of mediation of first Visconti Venosta, and later Giulio Prinetti (Foreign Minister 1901–1903) and Tommaso Tittoni (Foreign Minister 1903–1905, 1906–1909, 1919–1920), however, an important *rapprochement* had been completed. In particular, the Prinetti-Barrère accords of 1902 finalised the terms of agreement over other African territories, namely Morocco and Libya: with these accords, France renounced any claims regarding Libya while gaining a free hand in Morocco.

Relations with Britain, on the other hand, remained a little more tenuous: 'as far as England is concerned there are no difficulties, but you may say there are also no relations' (Visconti Venosta quoted in Lowe and Marzari 1975: 85; see also Serra and Seton-Watson 1990; Rosselli 1954). If this was perhaps true on a strictly official level, on a more informal level contacts were amicable and cooperation assiduous, especially in the Mediterranean – so much so that an exchange of notes between Prinetti and Joseph Chamberlain confirmed in 1902 that Britain would not object should Italy decide to take possession of Libya.

The finalisation of these agreements was hailed, at that time, as a diplomatic masterpiece, and the diplomats involved considered it a personal success. Italy was now safer on the continent – thanks to the Triple Alliance – and in the Mediterranean – thanks to the agreements with the soon-to-be *Entente* nations.[4] Such triumphalism, however, was only partially warranted. The new, complex architecture of liberal foreign policy was to be harshly criticised, both from within and without, because of its ultimately contradictory nature: as it were, the current system of alliances was posited on peace, and crucially depended on the quality of Anglo-German relations, which in fact were rapidly changing for the worse. As the socialist Leonida Bissolati pointed out after the Algeciras confrontation between France (and the *Entente* powers) and Germany:

> The Triple Alliance is said to be essentially, exclusively peaceful. But these are just words. Suppose the Triple Alliance brought us to an armed conflict against England on the side of Germany, what formidable commitment would that become?
>
> (Bissolati quoted in Salvemini 1970: 368)

However, as Gaetano Salvemini polemically commented:

> But 'wise men' in Italy did not believe they should seriously consider these cries of alarm. In December 1906 the Foreign Minister Tittoni declared that it would be 'barely serious' to discuss the possibility of a war between England and Germany.
>
> (Salvemini 1970: 368)

The rivalry between Britain and Germany, and more generally between their two diplomatic blocs, was to escalate into the First World War only eight years later, as we now know. As to Italian foreign policy, the signing of agreements with France, Britain and Russia could have hardly been 'complementary' to the alliance with Austria-Hungary and Germany, as diplomats of that time insisted. In fact, just as the Anglo-German confrontation led to the progressive collapse of European peace, so did the contradictions at the heart of Italy's system of alliances result in the serious impasse of 1914.

Naturally, Germany and Austria-Hungary were fully aware of these contradictions, yet they proved more keen to have Italy as an ally than as an enemy. Thus, on 8 January 1902 the then Chancellor of Germany, von Bülow, had greeted the opening of Italy to France in the Reichstag with a telling metaphor, the *tour de valzer*.[5] In a nutshell, Germany was prepared to see Italy 'flirt' with France because it was Italy that was to lose the most in the case of a break-up of the alliance: to Germany, the alliance was useful but not necessary – certainly, it was less necessary than it was to Italy.

Despite such contradictions and ambiguities, Italy renewed the Triple Alliance in 1902 and again in 1912, and indeed stayed in it up to the summer of 1914, i.e. the outbreak of the First World War.[6] Still, phases of 'triplicist' foreign policy would alternate with phases of closer alignment with the *Entente* powers.[7] However, at almost no point would Italy think seriously about abandoning the Triple Alliance.

The contradictions of Italy's external relations stood in marked contrast with the apparent stability of the country's domestic political situation. The *età giolittiana* (1901–1914), named after the liberal leader Giovanni Giolitti, was one of relative reformism which aimed to push the social and economic conditions of the country towards modernisation through reforms such as the (near) universal male suffrage, the new legislation on labour and welfare, and the general improvement of infrastructures. Much of the promise of the *età giolittiana*, however, never really came to fruition – indeed, this period was later renamed one of 'reformism without reforms' (Salvemini 1955; see also Carocci 1963). However, differently from the nineteenth century liberalism, Giolitti's liberal platform had the undisputed merit of including some of the progressive elements (or at least concerns) of Italian society.

In the first ten years of the twentieth century liberal foreign policy kept a generally low profile and avoided any real assertiveness. Indeed, as one commentator claimed, 'until 1911 Giolitti paid almost no attention to foreign policy, unless, as in 1908–09, interest was forced on him by an international crisis' (in that case, the annexation of Bosnia by Austria-Hungary) (Bosworth 1979: 12). He too thought, without much enthusiasm, that the Triple Alliance was the only possible alliance for Italy, since any alternatives would have required Italy to build up its military forces – which was still impossible economically. On the other hand, abandoning the alliance to join the *Entente* was equally problematic, at least for the time being. Although hopeful that one day Italy would have the means for a high profile foreign policy, according to Giolitti in the current situation

> [Italian] foreign policy [had] to take into consideration events and situations which it [was] not in our power to modify, nor sometimes even to accelerate or retard.
>
> (Giolitti quoted in Lowe and Marzari 1975: 117)

In other words, Italy's best hope for international grandeur would be unforeseeable opportunities, if not chance.

The international opportunities which Giolitti was invoking were in fact to follow shortly, characterising the years of his fourth premiership (1911–1914) as the core years of the *età giolittiana*, and as a phase of newly found assertiveness in foreign policy. The intervention in Libya, the sudden collapse of European peace, Italy's participation in the First World War, and, finally, the collapse of the domestic base of Italy's liberal foreign policy would all follow in the span of just a few years, eventually marking the end of the liberal experiment in Italy.

In terms of Italy's colonial history, at Tunis in 1881 and at Adowa in 1896 Italy had not only suffered scorching diplomatic and/or military defeats, but it had realised its exclusion from the age of imperialism of the end of the nineteenth century. The Italian nationalist movement, which had fully institutionalised itself at the turn of the twentieth century, considered these episodes not only as epitomising the enduring ineptitude of Italy's liberal foreign policy élite, but also as exposing the contradiction between the ideal of a colonialist and imperial 'third Rome' and the reality of a 'maritime Switzerland', as Luigi Albertini's paper *Il Corriere della Sera* characterised Italy in 1911 (Lowe and Marzari 1975: 114; see also Albertini 1952–57; Petriccioli 1983).

Led by the strong economic interests of the then consolidating financial and industrial complex (Webster 1974; Adler 1995; Aruffo 2003; Vigezzi 1997a: 56–7; Zamagni 1990: 135–43), pushed by large sectors of the Parliament, press and society at large, the Italy of the 1910s was once again on the lookout for 'a place in the sun' – a colony able to transform the country into an Empire. As the then Foreign Minister Antonino di San Giuliano (1910–1914) aptly put it in one of his most 'Darwinian' parliamentary speeches, Italy urgently ought to join the 'great contest of peoples' in order to achieve a much longed-for 'relative place in world' (Bosworth 1979: 282).

The Agadir incident of July 1911 provided the opportunity. The crisis between Germany and France, which rapidly gave way to French occupation of

Morocco, presented Italy with the chance to invade Libya. In fact, the 1900 and 1902 agreements with France had 'linked' Libya with Morocco; now that France had occupied Morocco, Italy could do the same with Libya. Despite German and Austrian attempts to mediate between Italy and Turkey, on 27 September an ultimatum was handed to the Turkish government; two days later war was declared, and Italian warships sailed towards Tripolitania and Cirenaica.[8]

From the outset of the Libyan crisis to the end of the war, Italian foreign policy would assume very stark tones, unusual for a government keen to be identified with moderate and liberal reformism, but not entirely unprecedented in Italian history. The ultimatum given to the Turks, as Brunello Vigezzi notes, was 'one of the most drastic ever known', and Giolitti's diplomatic style throughout the crisis was more than assertive – it was 'brutal' (Vigezzi 1997a: 96). More than anything else, the Libyan intervention was rapid: on 18 October 1912 the treaty of Ouchy was signed, and the war ended a mere three weeks after it began. Turkey was defeated and Italy was formally in control of Libya.[9]

Despite the unexpectedly high economic costs of the war, Italy could finally assert that the country had its colony, with the nationalist public opinion and press rejoicing. However, the first cracks in the domestic coalition supporting Giolitti's government were also becoming apparent. The socialists were split between those who welcomed the newly found assertiveness in foreign policy – even a syndicalist like Arturo Labriola declared that 'a people that does not know how to make war, will never make a revolution' – while others, such as Salvemini and Turati, openly condemned the entire Libyan operation as a 'bourgeois war'. Among those socialists violently opposing the war was also Benito Mussolini, the newly appointed director of the socialist newspaper *Avanti!* (Seton-Watson 1967: 370–2, 81–7). Radicals and republicans were equally divided and in ferment.

Meanwhile, the orientation of Italy's international relations had once again changed: relations with France had worsened in the middle of the Libyan war, and at the same time the triplicist sentiments of di San Giuliano had won over the Consulta and Giolitti himself.[10] Just as European attention was progressively drawn to the Balkans, so was Italy's interest drawn to its continental allies. On 5 December 1912, the Triple Alliance was renewed – 19 months prematurely – while the first Balkan war was about to erupt.

1914 would eventually prove to be a fatal year not only for peace in Europe, but for Giolitti himself – and, with him, for the future of Italy's liberal foreign policy. As the months passed, it was clear that the Libyan war had both failed to appease the nationalists and managed to irritate the Socialists: in other words, Giolitti's domestic coalition was close to collapse. The general elections of 1913 only reinforced this trend: the socialist party, now in the hands of the 'maximalists', doubled its numbers in Parliament, while the liberals lost ground despite the electoral success of the secret pact they had struck with sectors of the Catholic movement, the so-called Patto Gentiloni (Spadolini 1960).[11] When the details of this operation were publicly revealed, this further alienated the support of the left, condemning Giolitti to more internal criticism, and eventually tearing apart the delicately balanced parliamentary majority upon which his government rested. Giolitti resigned on 7 March 1914, just three months away from the wave of civil unrest that would sweep across Italy in the *settimana rossa*, and four months before the July crisis and the outbreak of the First World War. In his place, Antonio Salandra formed a new government in which (after di San Giuliano's death in October 1914) the arch-conservative Sydney Sonnino served as Foreign Minister (Vigezzi 1969).

On the eve of war, Italy was probably at the highest point of pro-triplicism: the King Victor Emmanuel III, Sonnino and Salandra were all fervent supporters of the continental alliance. This position tied in well with their general contempt towards the democratic aspirations of the supporters of the *Entente*, as well as with their refusal of *giolittismo* in all its forms: as Sonnino himself stated, 'the alliance [with Austria] is for the present a necessity for Italy' (Lowe and Marzari 1975: 128).

How, then, could Italy, after only ten months, enter the First World War on the *Entente* side? Although this decision came only after some long and troubled months of domestic debate, the outbreak of the Great War had in fact suddenly materialised all the contradictions and ambiguities at the heart of Italy's liberal foreign policy. To start with, the Anglo-German rivalry had blown up, destroying the already damaged European balance of power. Italy was now entrapped in a system of alliances that, although devised to guarantee peace, was now engaged in a mutual and unprecedented hostility. Second, with its 1911 victory in Libya, Italy had not only damaged Turkey fatally, but had indirectly contributed to strengthening the Balkan nationalist movements which were now menacing Austria-Hungary – a fact that would induce some historians to write about Italy's share of responsibility in the First World War (Bosworth 1979: 194; Croce 1929: 120).

In the face of such contradictions, and with war at its frontiers, Italian society succumbed to a period of agitation and division. On the theme of intervention, rivalling camps soon coalesced around figures such as D'Annunzio, Salvemini and Giolitti. While the nationalists and the intellectuals were eager to join the conflict, democrats were equally in favour of the intervention, but for much different reasons, namely to help the minorities in the Balkans free themselves from Austrian rule. Irredentists, on the other hand, saw the war as a good opportunity to re-claim Trieste and Trento. Finally, many favoured a policy of neutrality – this was, in fact, the majority of the country including the entire political élite, with a few notable exceptions.

In the meantime, following Austria's ultimatum, Italy had declared itself neutral on 2 August 1914. From a strictly legal perspective the defensive character of the Triple Alliance and Austria's declaration of war on Serbia made the *casus foederis* not arise. However, that decision was not really intended as definitive even by liberals (Croce 1929: 283). Rather, it was intended to buy time, until diplomats had figured out what concessions, gains and benefits Italy could reap by entering the war on the side of its allies – or, as it happened, on the side of the *Entente*.

Secret negotiations went on in parallel for about eight months, carried out by Salandra and Sonnino with the spirit of the *sacro egoismo* more than with a sense of loyalty and/or an interest in peace.[12] Austria-Hungary systematically (but rather blindly, given developments on the ground) turned down all requests for compensation from Italy. In the meantime, negotiations with the *Entente* were proceeding with fewer obstacles: in the Balkans especially Italy's support was essential to tip the balance in favour of the *Entente*, hence Britain's eagerness to further the dialogue with Italy. Thus, the Treaty of London came to be signed in secret on 26 April 1915, while negotiations with Austria were still taking place.

But by then, Italy, as mentioned, was a country fiercely divided. In Parliament, the majority was still neutralist, while newspapers and public opinion were equally divided between the two camps. The Salandra government itself entered a profound crisis, which eventually led to its resignation on 13 May 1915.

It was at this time that the political void left by Salandra's decision to resign was filled by the pro-war demonstrations of the *giornate radiose* of mid-May. In these, a vocal and well-organised minority of people portrayed war as the general will of the country, and induced the King to reconfirm Salandra and allow Italy's intervention in the First World War.[13] Within a few days, a new government was formed, and by this time the Parliament was aligned with the government. Finally, on 23 May an ultimatum was dispatched to Austria, and on 24 May Italy was at war.

The participation in the First World War would be a watershed in the history of Italy, impacting upon its domestic developments as no other event in the twentieth century: the *Grande Guerra*, with its major defeat of Caporetto (October 1917) as well as the final victorious battles of the Piave and Vittorio Veneto (June and October 1918), would enter Italy's collective memory to stay.

Despite the military victory on the ground and the total collapse of Italy's foremost enemy, Austria-Hungary, a sense of frustration at the economic and human losses caused by the war spread through the country quickly after the armistice of 4 November 1918 and the end of the war. This combined with the feeling that the expectations of war had been disappointed, and that Italy could only enjoy a half-victory, a *vittoria mutilata*.[14] As in Germany, this slowly but progressively contributed to poisoning Italy's young democracy.

As for foreign policy, the war and its aftermath proved that in the world diplomatic scenario transfigured by the war, Italy was more and more out of step. The Great War accelerated the decline of Italy's liberal regime and, with it, its foreign policy: in less than a decade, a sharp turn would characterise both domains.

Probably the clearest example of the uneasiness with which Italian foreign policy confronted world diplomacy after the First World War was to be the Paris Peace Conference of January 1919. As is well known, the Conference was formally dominated by a firm commitment to restructure European and world politics on the basis of principles of self-determination, but in fact it represented yet another attempt to secure the power of those countries, and especially France and Great Britain, that had won the First World War. The Italian delegates at the

Conference, Vittorio Emanuele Orlando and Sidney Sonnino, were resolute in their determination to claim for Italy all the territories the Treaty of London had outlined in the event of a victory of the *Entente*, together with some additions (Lowe and Marzari 1975: 160).

The insistent Italian requests for territories east of Trieste, however, soon clashed with the uncompromising stance of US President Woodrow Wilson, among others. In response, Italy's counterparts grew more and more committed to the Yugoslav cause on the grounds of the principle of self-determination. This strain quickly escalated into a full-blown diplomatic rupture between Italy and the rest of the delegates at the Conference – and especially the US – which led to the dramatic (and utterly self-defeating) withdrawal of Italy from the negotiations in Paris. Thus, the unjustified popular claim that Italy had been once again humiliated (the *vittoria mutilata*) combined with the intransigence of Wilson and the other European powers to create not only a disastrous political climate at home, but also the general sense of frustration that served as a basis for Italy's revisionist policies of the 1930s (Seton-Watson 1967: 534–5; Lowe and Marzari 1975: 171, 179–80; Scottà 2003).

The signs of an imminent crisis soon became apparent. In the few years that separated the decline of Italy's liberal regime from the rise of fascism, domestic politics and foreign policy were equally dominated by instability. To the anarchy of the *biennio rosso* of 1919–1920, foreign policy responded with a succession of five Foreign Ministers in three years. The disastrous episode of the occupation of Fiume by D'Annunzio in September 1919 once again complicated the Adriatic question and increased the hostility of all major powers towards Italy. It was only with the governments of Francesco Saverio Nitti and Giolitti (1919–1920, 1920–1921) and thanks to the mediation of the Foreign Minister Carlo Sforza (1920–1921) that a tentative 'policy of peace' was temporarily initiated in Italy's foreign relations. This new orientation was aimed at stabilising the country's position vis-à-vis the other European powers, especially regarding the issue of Dalmatia. Its major achievement came in November 1920 when a treaty to end the fifty-year long territorial dispute between Italy and Austria-Hungary was finally signed, fixing Italy's border at Fiume. It was a felicitous new course, but one which was destined to be short-lived: after only a few months a new crisis would bring down Giolitti's government, ending the liberal experiment in foreign and domestic politics, and anticipating the fascist rule to come.

Politics and paradigms of Italy's liberal foreign policy

Despite sharing a firm understanding of how critical Italy's external relations were going to be for the future of the country, as had been the case since Unification, the three major political traditions of liberal Italy – the liberal, democratic, and nationalist traditions – held different views about foreign policy and the way this descriptively and prescriptively related to the domestic politics and international relations of the time. Thus, at the turn of the twentieth century, three alternative foreign policy paradigms were vying for primacy.

The liberal position

At the turn of the century, the most notable tradition of thought by far on issues of foreign policy was that of liberalism. The liberal approach to issues of diplomacy and international relations, in fact, had almost represented the default option for an entire political class since roughly the unification of Italy to the mid-1870s and had re-emerged in the first decade of the twentieth century. Figures such as Visconti Venosta and Giolitti both belonged to this tradition, although they inevitably reflected very different stages in the evolution of liberalism in Italy (Vigezzi 1997a: 23). The main tenets of this approach can, with a degree of simplification, be summarised as follows.

First, for liberals foreign policy had to enjoy a decisive degree of autonomy from domestic politics: in particular this meant that foreign policy and diplomacy were best located 'al di sopra e al di fuori delle lotte di partito' ('over and above all party squabbles'), so that there be 'una sola politica – quella dell'Italia liberale' ('one foreign policy only – that of liberal Italy') (Ruggero Bonghi quoted in Decleva 1987: 18). Naturally, the idea that foreign policy had to be unitary had its roots in the nineteenth century and, more precisely, in the process of Unification itself – brought about by an astute diplomatic manoeuvring carried out by a handful of diplomats, among whom, of course, was Camillo Benso di Cavour.

Second, but relatedly, foreign policy was the domain of a restricted élite: in the case of Italy this included the King, the Prime Minister and the Foreign Minister. Neither public opinion nor other societal forces were allowed to influence the process of foreign policy decision-making. This principle remained central to the liberal tradition even in the first decade of the twentieth century, when the rise of a number of actors such as mass political parties, the financial-industrial complex, and the growing electorate started to present a formidable challenge. While Giolitti's reformism was aimed at enlarging the basis of consensus domestically, in foreign affairs this was not perceived as a necessarily desirable outcome.

Third, in the liberal approach foreign policy enjoyed a certain primacy vis-à-vis domestic politics. However, both the roots and aims of foreign policy were to be found, paradoxically, in domestic politics. Liberal foreign policy rested upon the 'forze materiali e morali' of the country (Visconti Venosta quoted in Vigezzi 1997a: 23). As Giolitti reiterated in his famous Turin speech of 7 October 1911, with the Libyan war underway, its ultimate goal was to provide 'una spinta a un più rapido progresso' ('a push for a greater progress') of the nation (Giolitti quoted in Vigezzi 1997a: 98).

Fourth, and last, in terms of contents and direction, liberals thought that Italian foreign policy's primary objective had to be the maintenance of the European concert of power – Italy's foreign policy ought to be a policy of peace. This state of affairs had a double advantage for Italy. On the one hand it naturally maximised Italy's strategic yet profoundly vulnerable position in the international system; on the other, it allowed the country to channel its resources into domestic politics, with a view towards strengthening the country's economic, military and societal potential. As Visconti Venosta recognised, Italy's own existence and freedom critically rested on peace:

> The persuasion that Italy's policy is essentially one of order and peace is the foundation of our good international position and of the very liberty that so far our policy has managed to maintain. [...] In Italy [...] peace is an absolute interest of ours, both for our domestic and international conditions. It is an absolute interest of ours that it be furthered as long as possible, until the time when Italy will be able to act like a great power in a European crisis, and not appear to be dominated by that sort of fatalism which is the law of the weak.
> (Visconti Venosta quoted in Vigezzi 1997a: 25, 39)

From this doctrine followed a distinctive corollary: in situations of conflict liberals had a natural preference for a policy of neutrality, which in turn reflected their view of a peaceful European society of states more generally. A cautious and moderate policy of neutrality could not only render the country 'moralmente autonoma e indipendente' ('morally autonomous and independent') (Visconti Venosta quoted in Chabod 1951: 107; see also Artom and Artom 1954), but could effectively break the 'connivenza tra gli interessi di partito e la grande politica internazionale', ('connivance between party interests and great power politics') which was deemed a great source of interference and weakness (Petrignani 1987: 91).

The democratic position

The second approach to achieve prominence around the turn of the century was that centred upon the idea of democracy in foreign policy. Drawing on Mazzini's legacy and the universalistic ideals of mass participation, this approach offered an alternative vision of foreign policy to that of the liberals. One of the best-known exponents of this approach was Gaetano Salvemini. According to Salvemini, domestic politics and especially public opinion were to be considered the real driving forces of foreign policy. The two domains, far from being separate and autonomous, derived mutual strength from their relationship. Thus, for instance, public scrutiny of foreign policy acted as an indispensable precondition for a real democratic functioning of domestic institutions as well as internal stability, as

> On the orientation of foreign policy depends military policy, and on the latter depends fiscal policy, which is the base of all domestic policies.
> (Salvemini quoted in Bracco 1998: 99)

Naturally, despite its long roots, the experience of the First World War had a decisive impact upon the coalescing of this approach. Thanks to the war, foreign policy had come out of its elitist dimension to involve the 'multitude', the 'masses' in its realisation. Democrats asserted that it was now time to institutionalise this relationship, and that this would benefit not only Italy's foreign policy, but domestic politics as well.

A democratic approach also implied a more pluralist view of foreign policy and of its actors, one more open to the idea and the possibility of peaceful change:

> When speaking of foreign policy, we are used to using collective nouns: France, England, Italy, etc. as if we were speaking of monolithic blocks which move solidly in a linear direction, as if pulled by a single force. But luckily nations are no homogeneous creations; rather, they are spiritual amalgams streaked and stressed by many different streams, which is not impossible to direct according to one's will, provided one has a clear vision as to where exactly to position oneself.
>
> (Salvemini quoted in Bracco 1998: 100)

Finally, in terms of contents and direction, the real aim of Italian foreign policy was to be peace – not a conservative peace grounded in a balance of power, but rather peace as an ideal which Italy would politically and morally promote all over Europe. In the post-war Europe, in other words, Italy had to follow

> A Mazzinian line. A policy able to transform Italy into the reformist Left of the *Entente*, while France is led by the blindness of its rulers to the position of the conservative Right; while the catapult of Lenin works as revolutionary Left; and England, by tradition, holds the balance.
>
> (Salvemini 1964: 618)

The nationalist position

Beside the democratic and the liberal approaches to foreign policy, the third and final approach vying for primacy was the nationalist approach. To start with, the nationalism which had gained strength since the turn of the twentieth century had only a tenuous connection with the liberal nationalism which had inspired so much of Italy's nineteenth century history. Indeed, it represented its ultimate degeneration: from a liberal, progressive force it had turned into a progressively conservative, imperialist movement.

According to this approach, domestic politics and foreign policy were at once separate and intimately close domains. In fact, just as the general novelty of twentieth century nationalism would be to successfully combine masses and nation, the nationalists advocated that an expansionist foreign policy be combined with popular participation and elevation of the life of the nation. What had been thus far experienced as an opposition between democracy and diplomacy, between domestic politics and international relations, was now conceptualised as a virtuous circle.

This foreign policy, far from being grounded in a conservative strategy of peace, or in the pursuit of higher ideals of democracy with a European scope, as the liberals and democrats had it, was to be based on a form of political realism. As the manifesto drafted in 1919 by the 'liberal-nationalists' Antonio Anzilotti and Giovanni Gentile urged, Italy had to adopt

> A more historically educated mentality, and one more conscious of the realistic forces that are shaping today's world order, in order to defend our most important national interests.
>
> (Anzilotti and Gentile quoted in Bracco 1998: 105)

In terms of contents and direction, the foreign policy advocated by nationalists soon became assertive, aggressive and plainly revanchist. As international politics was framed in terms of a natural antagonism between states, so must Italian foreign policy adopt the traits of a 'politica di potenza' and start claiming its national interests in the colonial world, in the Adriatic, and so on.

The competition on the international scene, in turn, was conceived of as a beneficial exercise for the young state of Italy. As Alfredo Oriani, a particularly influential irredentist nationalist, had asserted in the 1880s:

> The future of Italy lies entirely in a war which, while giving her its natural boundaries will cement internally [. . .] the unity of the national spirit.
>
> (Oriani quoted in Knox 2002: 106)

The Libyan intervention which had been lobbied for so vocally by the nationalists did much to consolidate their power, although it did not sate their appetite. But it was the Peace Conference after the First World War and the political atmosphere that followed it which ultimately crystallised their outlook. The exclusion of Italy from what was perceived as the partition of the world by the Great Powers crucially contributed to the establishment of this foreign policy approach at the forefront of the political scene.

The analysis of Italy's liberal foreign policy: the state of the art

For the sake of my argument, I will group the literature on Italy's liberal foreign policy into three broad camps. First, a great number of erudite, historical works focus on specific issues within the arc of Italy's liberal foreign policy without explicitly raising the wider question of the relation between foreign policy, Italy's domestic politics and the international relations of the time. At best these works advance an intermediate and largely indeterminate understanding of this relation, sometimes arguing that Italy's liberal foreign policy was prey to international forces, and at other times that it was geared to domestic influences (see, for instance, Pastorelli 1998). The predominance of a diplomatic history approach to issues of foreign policy and the almost disheartening absence of a strong FPA tradition can explain why these studies often merely juxtapose one another, and entirely missing from the historiography of liberal foreign policy are works resembling, for instance, Eckart Kehr's reconstruction of German Wilhelmine foreign policy – a clear reference point, not least since it deals precisely with the same time span, yet is hardly ever mentioned (Bosworth 1998: 82–105, 92–3).

A second type of approaches has clearly privileged domestic politics, focusing especially on those variables and influences upon foreign policy relating to the then emerging nation, including the importance of national ideas and ideologies (Salvemini 1970), the centrality of the national project and the Risorgimento ideals (Spadolini 1987, 1994), the relevance of public opinion in orienting and re-orienting Italy's liberal foreign policy (Vigezzi 1991), and the growing importance of economic and financial actors (Webster 1974; Mola 1980).

The most classic example of a 'domestic' reading of Italy's liberal foreign policy is Federico Chabod's *Storia della politica estera italiana.* The importance of this work in orienting the historiography on the subject is difficult to overrate and justifies quoting a few passages from the text, which Chabod introduced with a few general words on the overall style and sense of his investigation:

> It seemed indispensable to me to clarify the moral and material bases [...] the set of forces and sentiments [...] passions and feelings, ideas and ideologies, on the basis of which the diplomatic initiative [of liberal Italy] was to be pursued. [...] History does not know the abstract schemes of a foreign policy neatly separated from domestic politics, but rather sees them closely associated, dissolving one into the other [...] Of which the history of Unified Italy is a classic example.
>
> (Chabod 1951: vii–viii, x–xi)

In other words, Chabod noted that in general terms foreign policy and domestic politics, just like two 'Siamese twins', had virtually no degree of autonomy from each other. This applied especially to the case of liberal Italy. Its foreign policy, in particular, seemed to him to function as an 'offshoot' of domestic politics, with very little intervention from outside. Its history was a history of men making choices, more than a history of remote and impersonal international forces. Thence came Chabod's scrupulous attention to the 'diplomatic style' of the protagonists of the early phases of Italian foreign policy (Chabod 1951: 563–692).

The third and last category of approaches stresses the importance of 'permanent interests', usually but not always of an international kind. With his continuity thesis, for instance, Benedetto Croce intended to stress that the chequered history of domestic politics in liberal Italy did not really have an impact upon foreign policy, since this was driven by other (more permanent) forces, such as the national character of the Italian people and its 'natural' international aspirations (Croce 1929).

However, it is Santoro's *La politica estera di una media potenza* that most clearly advanced a reading of liberal foreign policy framed around international, structural factors. In his book Santoro analysed the overall trajectory of Italian foreign policy from the Unification, and with respect to the liberal period he concluded that:

> It did not appear strange to either the Germans or the Austrians, that in August 1914, when final choices were made, Italy would declare its neutrality. [...] This is rather a fundamental point in order to understand some permanent features of Italian foreign policy [...] There is indeed something *structurally* peripheral in Italy's international behaviour; something that, when push comes to shove, when other actors openly engage with one another, makes our country hesitate, give in, or even turn its back. Our thesis is that this is once again due to a profound reason of systemic and geopolitical nature, more than it is due to culture or political personnel.
>
> (Santoro 1991: 136, emphasis added)

Santoro was notoriously working from an entirely different perspective. Not an historian but a theorist, he claimed that structures – the 'divinità ascose' that Chabod ridiculed – do indeed exist. Further, he concluded that these had fundamentally decided the fate of Italian foreign policy, in August 1914 as much as at any other time.

Chabod and Santoro epitomise opposite interpretations of Italy's liberal foreign policy. The former geared foreign policy towards a set of domestic and societal elements – the 'basi materiali e morali' of the country – while the latter asserted a relative primacy for more enduring and permanent international structures such as geopolitics and the interests of the state. Naturally, the clarity of this juxtaposition – between the 'historicist' account of Chabod and the structural interpretation of Santoro – rests on a degree of caricature: both positions, in fact, do present a number of internal ambiguities and contradictions. As far as Chabod is concerned, for instance, the antagonistic character of international relations seems at times to be relatively more important than any 'diplomatic style' in driving foreign policy (Chabod 1951: 67–102). Equally, Santoro starts by asserting that it is the combination of international pressures and domestic politics that determines foreign policy, but then falls conspicuously short of analysing the complexity of such dynamics (Santoro 1991: 12).

These two accounts also represent the most common interpretative possibilities of Italy's liberal foreign policy, marking as they do two extremes in an imaginary continuum of interpretation. Is it possible to move beyond this confrontation and integrate these seemingly incommensurable readings?

Italy's liberal foreign policy: a critical realist assessment

Monocausal models

Was Italy's liberal foreign policy primarily a result of the international relations of the time? Or was it instead mainly the result of domestic and endogenous developments? The accounts offered by Chabod and Santoro tend to reproduce the causal logic of monocausal approaches as presented in Chapter 1. As such, it is necessary to probe these models once again, to assess to what extent these approaches offer persuasive reconstructions of the subject matter.

Following a form of monocausal 'primacy of foreign policy', Santoro has portrayed Italy's liberal foreign policy as the result of particular systemic, geopolitical, long-term and impersonal forces. There is no doubt that this view can account for some features of the foreign policy of liberal Italy, for instance the degree to which the international relations of the time (i.e. the European system of states) conditioned Italy's foreign policy in its freedom of action. It was not only that liberal Italy lived in 'perfect correlation with Europe' (Spadolini 1994: 7), but that in the European system of relations Italian foreign policy, to quote Giolitti's Turin speech of 7 November 1911, 'had to take into consideration events and situations which was not in its power to modify, nor sometimes even to accelerate or retard' (Giolitti quoted in Lowe and Marzari 1975: 117). This apparent declaration of impotence well epitomised the degree to which Italy had to take into account the external environment and its particular configuration of forces in order to realise its own foreign policy goals, colonial or otherwise. Further, as Santoro's work makes particularly clear, geographical factors such as Italy's very positioning between Europe and the Mediterranean offer a possible key to the diplomatic oscillation (or 'pendulum' policy) (Petrignani 1987: 37) between the Triple Alliance and the *Entente* which characterised the trajectory of much of Italy's liberal foreign policy (and beyond).

This account, however, falls short of explaining other, equally distinctive traits of Italy's liberal foreign policy. To start with, it does not leave any scope for agency. But, as we know, especially after 1910 Italian foreign policy exhibited a significant degree of assertiveness: the intervention in Libya and the handling of the war showed an unprecedented resolution (e.g. in the 'drastic' ultimatum, in Giolitti's 'brutal' approach to foreign policy). The style of Italian foreign policy, as well as its content, could not be derived from international structures. Moreover, the Libyan intervention indirectly yet powerfully started the chain of events which eventually upset the European balance of power and led to the First World War.

Second, throughout the liberal period Italian foreign policy hardly resulted simply from externally dictated developments, not even in circumstances – such as the run-up to the First World War – when international pressures and the international dynamics of security were most critical. Standard neo-realist predictions of alliance behaviour, for instance, would not be corroborated in the case of liberal Italy. Indeed, the decision to join the *Entente* and desert its previous allies came after long and convoluted negotiations and offered an example of that particular strategy of 'bandwagoning' which, according to neo-realist theory, is not only highly quixotic, but is typically induced by pressures *other than* international. Foreign Minister Di San Giuliano's own assessment in the immediate aftermath of Franz Ferdinand's assassination of 28 June 1914 contradicts rather plainly the expectations deriving from a classic neo-realist account of foreign policy:

> the real difficulty [for Italy] lay in assessing where the long-term balance of power lay since Italy, a weaker power, had to join the stronger group. In the

> long run [...] the Entente possessed the advantage, and for that reason, ultimately Italy would leave the Triple Alliance.
>
> (Di San Giuliano quoted in Lowe and Marzari 1975: 131–2)

On the other hand, the continuous diplomatic oscillation between the Triple Alliance and *Entente* could well be explained in terms of another monocausal/international account, one emphasising the geographic features of Italy's position between Europe and the Mediterranean. Yet, while intuitively attractive, an explanation framed in terms of geographical determinism would also leave the issue partly under-determined. In brief, what motivates foreign policy to change orientation in one way or the other over time given that the geography of the country is presumably not susceptible to change? What accounts, in other words, for the typical phases of pro-triplicism and pro-*Entente* policy that have succeeded one another in the years preceding the First World War? Presumably, the intervention of domestic politics. Purely international accounts are thus at a loss to explain the significant degree of change and variance in the trajectory of Italy's liberal foreign policy.

Two sets of arguments have been most frequently advanced by proponents of the 'primacy of domestic politics' thesis. Concerning the diplomatic oscillation mentioned above, the first argument asserts that the pendulum between Paris and Berlin reflected not so much presumed geopolitical necessities, but rather 'electoral cycles', i.e. the alternation of pro-French and pro-German attitudes (and ideologies) of the political élites governing Italy, and of the *Destra Storica* and *Sinistra Storica* respectively (Chabod 1951: 21–53; Petrignani 1987). A variant of this thesis highlights not just the political alignment of the élites, but also their origins: while Northern, industrial political élites would favour a continental policy, the Southern, agrarian élites would assert a stronger presence of the country in the Mediterranean.

Concerning colonial policy, the second argument states that the increasing dynamism of Italy's liberal foreign policy reflected the combined rise of a financial-industrial complex interested in opening up new markets as well as the emergence of a new wave of nationalism inside Parliament and society at large. After all, both developments acquired particular strength roughly at the time of the Libyan intervention.

On closer scrutiny, however, both sets of arguments have limits which replay those of the *Primat der Innenpolitik* from which they implicitly derive. To start with, and in reference to the claim that it was electoral cycles and the ideology of the particular élite in government which decided the direction and content of Italy's foreign policy, suffice it to consider here that it was Giolitti, a Piedmontese and natural heir of the liberal tradition of the *Destra*, who was able to successfully achieve what no other Southerners or exponents of the *Sinistra Storica* – and Francesco Crispi was both – had achieved, namely a colony in the Mediterranean named Libya. In other words, it was when the ideology of the leadership in government was *least* expected to show an interest in the Mediterranean that Italy secured its colony.

With reference to the second claim, there is no doubt that the rise of nationalist sentiments and the parallel emergence of a solid financial-industrial complex provided strong influences on the decision to intervene in Libya. Yet, they cannot explain why Italy had not intervened in Northern Africa before. By 1911 there had been roughly three decades of nationalist ferment to avenge Tunis and Adowa. Moreover, we now know that from the very beginning of his mandate Giolitti himself was (if only secretly) determined to pursue, along with his domestic priorities, 'un terzo segretissimo obiettivo' ('a third and most secret objective') – that of the Libyan war (Vigezzi 1997a: 92). Yet, for many years Italy did not act.

Neither a purely international nor an exclusively domestic account of the foreign policy of liberal Italy can entirely make sense of its overall development. Although these readings point to interesting and 'real' influences at play in the foreign policy of liberal Italy, they fall short of providing a full account. Further, there has been no agreement (indeed, there has been no debate) as to how one should go about combining the two competing accounts so that an intermediate and more fitting interpretation can be advanced.

Dualist approaches

As the previous paragraphs have shown, in the case of liberal foreign policy there are good reasons to believe that monocausal approaches are simply not corroborated by historical evidence. This leads us to consider the next set of questions, namely whether Italy's liberal foreign policy, rather than the expression of mainly international or domestic concerns, resulted from a combination of both sets of factors.

At a cursory examination, additive models seem to provide an affirmative answer to the question. After all, Italy's liberal foreign policy could indeed be accounted for by enumerating the variety of domestic and international factors that played a role in shaping the contents and direction of such foreign policy, thus positing the latter as the addition of the former. Further, Italian foreign policy-makers could be portrayed as 'brokers' between international relations and domestic politics – the double constraint under which the foreign policy process developed.

Yet, this interpretation would miss two key elements. On the one hand, it would fail to highlight how these factors not only compounded one another but more fundamentally *related* to and *interacted* with one another. Consider, once again, the Libyan intervention (to which, additive approaches would claim, international and domestic factors both contributed *equally*) and the way this impacted not only upon the international relations of the time (accelerating the collapse of the European balance of power, as mentioned above), but also upon the domestic politics of Italy (accelerating the collapse of the coalition sustaining the Giolitti's government). What was crucial in directing this foreign policy was arguably the *interaction* between international relations and domestic politics, rather than their simple addition.

Second, dualist additive approaches necessarily ignore the fact that at any given time some factors were more important than others. Consider, for instance, with what impunity Italy pursued its oscillatory diplomatic alignment between 1902 and 1912 – when the possibility of an Anglo-German conflict was even ridiculed by the foreign policy élite – and how this changed in the run-up to the First World War. Certainly, the changed international circumstances no longer allowed for a similar policy; consequently they must have impacted more heavily upon the decision-making process than they had done previously (and yet not determining any specific foreign policy).

Additive approaches to Italy's liberal foreign policy are not just implausible but, more fundamentally, they are indeterminate. They are able to provide us with a host of variables and elements which played some part in the determination of foreign policy. Yet, they provide us with very little information about the patterns of causation or inter-relation between foreign policy, domestic politics and international relations.

Could Italy's liberal foreign policy be explained by positing international relations as always relatively more important than domestic politics, as the 'nested games' approach holds? Could international relations be thought of as constantly fixing the contours of Italy's liberal foreign policy, with domestic politics deciding its details only?

If one takes the example of Italy's participation in the Paris Peace Conference, a few problems with a dualist/'nested games' explanation emerge. To start with, Italy's behaviour at the Peace Conference offered a clear example of the extent to which Italian foreign policy makers had grown out of touch with the new 'realities' of post-war international relations. This alone should make us pause and question whether the international system can really ever be said to influence foreign policy directly, if it can be so fundamentally misperceived by foreign policy actors. At a time of increasing domestic resentment, it was not surprising that Italian diplomats appeared relatively more keen to project a domestically-driven foreign policy agenda rather than one necessarily compatible with the new post-war international order. The determination of Vittorio Emanuele Orlando and Sydney Sonnino to secure a 'good deal' for Italy at the Conference was thus arguably a response to clear domestic factors, i.e. the 'vittoria mutilata' syndrome, more than international ones.

Italy's diplomatic oscillation between *Entente* and the Triple Alliance would also be difficult to decode through the lens of the 'nested games' approach. First, and in very general terms, such a contradictory foreign policy poses a challenge to any model based on a static combination of domestic and international determinants. Second, it is equally problematic to argue that this particular policy was compatible with the international system of the time. In fact, it was this contradictory policy (predicated on conditions that were rapidly evolving, in spite of Italy's interests or wishes) which in the end produced the predicament of 1914–1915.

An account grounded in the 'pendulum' framework, on the other hand, would expect foreign policy to follow the pressures of the relatively more urgent constraint – international or domestic. How does this framework score in the case of Italy's liberal foreign policy? First, as mentioned above, it was precisely at a time of high international tension such as the run-up to the First World War that Italy first reverted to a temporary neutrality designed only to buy time and, subsequently, switched its diplomatic alignment to join the *Entente.* It is therefore hard to argue that the foreign policy of liberal Italy adapted to such overwhelming international pressures by adopting a clear, externally driven foreign policy. Rather, the opposite seems to be the case.

Incidentally, this might be due, at least in part, to the fact that the decision to enter the war inevitably reflected a particular domestic climate. The *giornate radiose* and the determination of the foreign policy élite to enter the war against its former allies had in fact created a formidable tension at home. The decision to enter the war, in other words, was not generated under a relatively lax domestic constraint, but in rather intense and dramatic domestic circumstances. As is clear from Figure 1.7, however, the pendulum framework has problems making sense of precisely this type of occurrence. While this approach can explain instances where the differential of intensity of the two constraints is high (the two end points of the swing, t_1 or t_5), it cannot account for cases in which these are either both high or low. The approach to the First World War seems to constitute one of those cases in which *both* international *and* domestic pressures scored high.

Second, even considering Italy's liberal foreign policy as following the relatively more pressing constraint, nothing in the framework would account for the change in their relative importance. Thus, for instance, even granted that at the time of the Libyan intervention foreign policy followed compelling domestic circumstances – at a time when international circumstances were still relatively relaxed and undemanding – nothing in the model can explain why this combination of domestic and international forces changed as it did in the span of only a few years.

Dualist models cannot help but provide a rather static and limited account of Italy's liberal foreign policy. First, they have problems accounting for the way in which domestic and international relations not only combined, but also interrelated to generate foreign policy. Second, they cannot account for the changes in the patterns of interplay. For this reason they provide, at best, only snapshots of the subject matter, but not an account of its evolution over time.

Dialectical approaches

How do dialectical approaches score when asked to account for Italy's liberal foreign policy? If one takes the case of the Libyan intervention, for instance, it is clear that the morphogenetic approach can provide us with a clear explanatory narrative beyond the interpretative strictures of dualist and monocausal models. Neither a strictly international nor a domestic account can, in fact, make sense of the foreign policy pursued by Italy during the Libyan intervention, nor a static combination of the two.

In this case, Italy did indeed experience the constraining effect of the international system – i.e. of its system of external relations – to the degree that it was almost impossible, in the words of Giolitti, 'to make its own foreign policy'. Yet, when Italy finally acted, in 1911, it changed such patterns dramatically, restructuring parts of the context around itself. The Libyan intervention, in fact, has been explicitly related to the overall process of the collapsing of the European balance of power. By defeating Turkey in North Africa, Italy sent signals to the Slav populations of the Balkans that the Ottoman Empire was overstretched and weak. The Balkan wars resumed with more intensity, and after threatening Turkey they menaced Austria-Hungary, and with it the whole of Europe – all of which finally resulted in the events of the summer of 1914.

Just as the morphogenetic approach asserts, Italy's liberal foreign policy resulted from the interplay between a structural conditioning deriving from the international relations of the time, on the one hand, and, on the other, Italy's emergent properties, i.e. its long-cherished colonial interests. Only when given an opportunity (the Agadir crisis of 1911) was Italy in the position to assert its foreign policy and embark upon the Libyan War. This action, far from reproducing the system of relations around it (i.e. far from encouraging a morphostasis) generated feedback on the system, whose features and game-rules were consequently altered.

An interpretation of the Libyan intervention based on the morphogenetic approach is able to organise all elements into a coherent narrative, and able to explain and understand this episode in the broader context of Italian foreign policy. It also finds a natural middle way between the two extreme positions of fatalism and omnipotence which monocausal approaches would otherwise assert. Yet, it too is open to some criticism.

First of all, it does not (and indeed cannot) account for how the 'opportunity' mentioned above came about. One counterfactual consideration might help clarify this point: had Italy been more powerful, or more skilled, the window of opportunity which arguably catalysed the Libyan intervention could have come earlier, or could have been even bigger than it happened to be. This is because it is not structural conditioning per se that happens to offer or deny opportunities to actors (in this case Italy): it is the *relation* between actors and context that does so. The relational character of international politics, however, cannot be accounted for by the morphogenetic model, as mentioned in Chapter 1, because of its reliance on a (more or less stark) ontological dualism and on the assumption of the temporally distinct character of the international environment and the actor's emerging properties.

Second, in the morphogenetic model both structural conditioning and emergent properties seem to impact objectively and naturalistically on foreign policy as if they both were 'natural' and self-evident influences. The model, in other words, allows no space for the way these were perceived and made sense of in the political process. This, however, is key to the formulation of foreign policy – the one pursued and those which, instead, were not.

This brings us to the strategic-relational model. As discussed in Chapter 1, this approach tends to conceptualise foreign policy as the result of a dialectical interplay of three elements: the strategically-selective context of international relations, the foreign policy strategy elaborated through the domestic political process, and, finally, the discourses, narratives and paradigms through which these two elements are brought into a relation. Let us analyse them in turn.

In the case of Italy's liberal foreign policy, there is no doubt that the context of relations in which Italy was embedded was highly contoured: for a relatively young and weak state such as Italy, this principally meant a relatively limited autonomy and an acute awareness of its position vis-à-vis the other actors in the European system of states. At the turn of the century, in particular, the emergent confrontation between two roughly equivalent diplomatic blocs meant that Italy acquired a highly central position in the system of relations among states. Despite perhaps still being a *quantité negligeable* in absolute terms (as Lord Salisbury once famously put it), its relative position (i.e. its position *in relation to* other actors) became especially important.

In terms of strategy, this primarily involved the pursuit of a respectable status, legitimacy and rank among the other actors and translated, in turn, into the ambition for colonies and territorial gains. These sets of interests grew especially acute as the twentieth century progressed and a series of domestic developments followed: the rise of an industrial-financial complex with a vested interest in territorial expansion, the emergence of a more conservative, revanchist form of nationalism, and the progressive decline of liberal institutions.

As for the element of discourse, the way foreign affairs were discussed and the external environment perceived in the domestic political process was filtered through three alternative paradigms: liberal, democratic and nationalist. Of these, however, the liberal discourse progressively lost purchase just as the nationalist discourse grew more vocal and influential.

Can the dialectic of these three elements account for the overall development of Italy's foreign policy in the liberal period? Let us consider the Libyan intervention once again.

As already discussed, the fact that Italy had to wait for an opportunity in order to realise its colonial goals testifies to the selectivity of the international context in which liberal Italy was embedded, i.e. to the highly contoured system of relations surrounding Italy. The strategic-relational model, however, gives us a further clue as to the precise nature of the opportunity which catalysed the Libyan intervention. This was constituted not just by a change in 'structure', but more precisely by a change in the *relational* context to which Italy was oriented. With the Agadir crisis of 1911, the position of France vis-à-vis Italy's African plans changed because of its own expansion into Morocco – while Britain had already consented to Italy's intervention in 1902. It was the change in Italy's relations vis-à-vis these other actors in the system which interacted with the domestically and discursively constructed strategy to create the contingent possibility of the Libyan intervention.

It is necessary to note here that had any of these three elements not materialised, the foreign policy pursued would arguably have been different. Had the prevailing discourse (especially, but not exclusively, among the foreign policy élite) not been one of colonialism associated with a rising nationalism but, for instance, a democratic discourse of peace-promotion or a liberal discourse of balance of power, then there would have been a lesser incentive to *see* the opportunity and, more importantly, to act upon it. Had there been a different configuration of the relations among states – for instance, had there been no agreement with Britain as to the possibility of a colonial expansion in Africa – the international context would have probably selected *against* Italy's intervention. Had there finally been no colonial or strategic ambitions, the incentives to pursue a war would have been far less intense. Just as the strategic-relational model suggests, then, it is not the simple addition or linear combination of these elements that created the foreign policy in question, but rather their interaction.

Further, the Libyan intervention impacted on both the strategically selective context and Italy's own strategy (f_1 and f_2 in Figure 1.9). In this process it produced two related developments: on the one hand, given the centrality of Italy's position *in relation to* the system surrounding it, the Libyan intervention accelerated the collapse of the European balance of power; on the other, by exacerbating the nationalist component even more, it impacted heavily upon the domestic balance of forces accelerating the collapse of the liberal regime.

The strategic-relational model is able to shed light on the patterns of interaction between international politics, domestic forces and foreign policy that other models simply cannot account for. In fact, Italy's approach to the First World War can also be usefully read through this framework of analysis.

In terms of the system of relations in which Italy was embedded, this was characterised by the confrontation of two diplomatic blocs towards which Rome was equally ambivalent. As the tension between the two blocs escalated, the context became more and more impervious. It is crucial to see here that Italy's decision to switch alliances and join the *Entente* could have been different had a different strategic interest prevailed, or had a different discourse informed Italy's foreign policy makers. Nothing in the system of relations around Italy per se dictated the particular choice that was eventually taken.

In fact, even granted that Italy's only strategic interest in the run-up to the First World War was to maximise its influence, this could have been done in two different ways: either through a policy of friendship with both blocs, which at that time necessarily meant neutrality; or joining the camp which guaranteed the highest gains. While the liberals suggested the former, the conservative, nationalist movement preferred the latter. That the policy of neutrality supported by liberals no longer had a domestic constituency by the time the war broke out thus had remarkable consequences. Not only was the policy of the 'mani nette' ('clean hands') rejected even among some liberals because it was reminiscent of the humiliation suffered some thirty years before at the Congress of Berlin, but the emerging nationalist movement increasingly advocated Italy's active participation in international politics – 'marciare, non marcire' ('to go forward, not to vegetate'), in the words of nationalist and anti-neutralist Filippo Tommaso Marinetti.

A consideration of the dialectic between the strategically-selective context of the international relations of the time, the foreign policy strategy elaborated through Italy's domestic political process, and, finally, the discourses through which these two elements were brought in relation, can provide us with a convincing narrative of Italy's liberal foreign policy. Such an account avoids the pitfalls of monocausal approaches, while it also provides an answer to the puzzles that dualist or dialectical approaches leave unsolved.

Conclusions

Far from representing merely a 'low profile' policy, the foreign policy of liberal Italy has proved to be a far more complex and interesting subject of inquiry than is usually granted, yet it is often approached in light of two monocausal and largely alternative approaches. As I have argued, however, it is necessary to move beyond this stalemate and towards a more complex account of the subject matter. To this end, in this chapter I have analysed the foreign policy of liberal Italy through the lenses of the particular frameworks elaborated in Chapter 1. While monocausal approaches are to be rejected for their reductionism, dualist accounts are unsatisfactory for their view of foreign policy as the result of a simple addition or alternation of forces. Dialectical accounts, instead, are more promising as they focus on the interplay between these factors. In particular, the strategic-relational model is able to provide us with a consistent and manageable explanatory narrative.

As an application of this model suggests, Italy's liberal foreign policy resulted from the dialectical interplay between three elements: the international relations of Europe at the beginning of the century, which were a particularly selective context for Italy; Italy's domestically negotiated strategy, which primarily involved the pursuit of a respectable status, legitimacy and rank among the other actors; and, finally, the mediation of a discourse which increasingly jettisoned liberal values and ideas and acquired nationalist, conservative tones.

3 Italian foreign policy

The fascist 'ventennio' (1922–1943)

From 'arbiter mundi' to revisionist (and fallen) empire: the foreign policy of fascist Italy

That the advent of fascism to power, which followed the March on Rome of 22 October 1922, is still variously characterised either as a virtual 'coup d'État' or as a perfectly constitutional development, is perhaps the best sign of the enduring scholarly disagreement on the origins of fascism in Italy (cf. Carocci 1985: 1184; De Felice 1974: 354–80). In terms of foreign policy, however, there is wide agreement that the early years of fascist foreign policy did not stray from the pattern initiated by liberal Italy, in terms of content if not also in terms of style (Carocci 1969: 113–17; Collotti 2000: 20; Rossini 1963: xix–xx; Pastorelli 1971: 602).

Rhetorical escapades aside, when fascism rose to power Benito Mussolini had little knowledge of, but an active interest in, matters of foreign policy. Despite having emerged as a political figure thanks to his relentless denunciation of the 'politica estera rinunciataria' ('defeatist foreign policy') carried out by liberals such as Giovanni Giolitti and Carlo Sforza, when Mussolini assumed the title of Foreign Minister, together with that of 'Chief of Government' (as it were), fascism became officially represented on the international scene by a novice to foreign policy. Thus, in the early years Mussolini relied heavily upon the personnel of the Ministry of Foreign Affairs, *la Consulta*, and especially on the General Secretary, Salvatore Contarini (Cassels 1970).[1] Thus, the first few international summits (such as the Lausanne Conference in November 1922 and the Allied Conference on German reparations of the following month) saw Mussolini barely speak a word (Nicolson 1934: 290) while learning the ways of European diplomacy.

Internationally, Mussolini was favourably received by most governments and diplomats on the premise that, on the one hand, he would give Italy the stability of government it had lacked for so long and, on the other, he would protect Italy from the menace of bolshevism (Torre 1970: xi–xii; Rumi 1968: 222–23; Burgwyn 1997).[2] In this respect, British diplomats proved the most welcoming of all. In May 1923, the state visit of King George V did much to present Italian fascism to Europe and the world as a legitimate and respectable government, and

Mussolini as a 'wise and strong statesman' (King George V quoted in Seton-Watson 1967: 668–70; see also Taylor 1964: 85; Andrew 2009: 105).

France too had motives to look upon Italy with favour, especially after January 1923, when the French occupation of the Ruhr was carried out with support from Mussolini, despite Britain's opposition. As for Germany, at that stage Italy was still behaving intransigently, at least on the official diplomatic level. In fact, throughout the 1920s relations between the two countries were not developing as one would expect between 'congruent cases', as Mussolini famously characterised Germany and Italy only a decade later, in 1936 (quoted in Knox 1991: 324). Indeed, Mussolini's opinion of the emerging Nazi movement had been particularly unflattering. On the occasion of the 1923 Munich putsch, he had publicly labelled Adolf Hitler and his associates *buffoni* ('clowns'), while he constantly eschewed any official contact with his movement (while unofficially backing a number of Bavarian right-wing movements) (Cassels 1970: 166–74; Seton-Watson 1967: 674 n2, 695, 695 n2, 695 n3). Hitler, on the contrary, held Mussolini in great esteem, and considered fascism to be a model for his own movement. Such was the asymmetry in Italo-German relations of the 1920s – an asymmetry which was to be completely reversed only ten years later.

The events of the August–September 1923, however, were destined to shatter the generally positive international reception of fascism. Seizing the opportunity to strike a blow against Hellenic ambitions in the Mediterranean, as well as make a show of strength, on 27 August fascist Italy reacted to the alleged murder of its senior diplomat General Tellini by accusing Greece of having carried out the assassination in order to threaten Italy's presence in Albania and the Dodecanese. After such accusations – which were overstated, if not wholly disingenuous – Italy dispatched a drastic 24-hour ultimatum, leading to the invasion and shelling of the island of Corfù, off Rhodes.[3]

The invasion of Corfù constituted a grave episode in more than one way. The seemingly ruthless attack on the small island of Corfù outraged international public opinion and made more than one statesman wonder whether the 'strong and wise' leader of Italy might in fact represent a real threat to European peace. Mussolini, and with him Italy, had not only breached the League of Nations Covenant for the very first time since its establishment, but the invasion had been carried out in a particularly barbaric manner.

Under pressure – mainly from Britain – the League of Nations in Geneva reluctantly intervened. After a few weeks of negotiations, however, it delegated the resolution of the issue to the Conference of Ambassadors, a move which was generally seen at that time as a real 'abdication' of responsibility. The Conference eventually succeeded in forcing Mussolini to evacuate the island in September 1923, in exchange for monetary compensation from Greece, but the damage to the image of the League had been done, and Mussolini could present the episode to domestic audiences as a battle won in the name of national honour and prestige.

In the years following Corfù, Italian fascist foreign policy assumed a less assertive character. Many quickly came to forget about the episode altogether and resumed thinking of Mussolini as a nationalist, but not as an aggressive dictator. This, however, was all the more illusory. A few months after the Corfù crisis, the Matteotti assassination of June 1924 ushered Italy into a radical *fascistizzazione*, i.e. the gradual transformation of Italy into a totalitarian state (Aquaronc 1965).

Foreign policy was to reflect such a turn only in part and in time, mainly thanks to the continuity provided by the Foreign Ministry. Thus, the Locarno Conference in October 1925 featured a flawless Mussolini. At one with France, Britain and Germany in guaranteeing the post-1919 frontiers of Europe, Mussolini presented Italy as a genuine champion of the status quo – although not without ambiguities (Collotti 2000: 25–7). Locarno also marked the beginning of the phase of closest cooperation between Mussolini's Italy and Britain, which was to terminate only in 1929, with the electoral defeat of the Conservatives. Not only did the friendship between *il Duce* and Austen Chamberlain grow more intimate than ever at this stage (Seton-Watson 1967: 692, 692 n2), but Italy managed to profit from Britain's favour in at least two instances. First, in November 1926 the issue of war debts was generously settled in favour of Italy thanks to the collaborative attitude of the then Chancellor of the Exchequer and later Prime Minister, Winston Churchill; second, with the treaties of December 1925 Britain agreed to make economic and territorial concessions to Italy in parts of Libya and Ethiopia (Seton-Watson 1967: 667; Carocci 1969: 47, 270 n43; Vigezzi 1997a: 246).

Meanwhile, the progressive *fascistizzazione* of the Ministry for Foreign Affairs had introduced a turnover in personnel which was to impact distinctively upon the direction of fascist foreign policy between 1926 and 1932. The fascist *gerarca* Dino Grandi joined the government as Under Secretary for Foreign Affairs in May 1925. Salvatore Contarini, the last of the 'liberal' diplomats, resigned less than a year later, due to an inevitable (albeit well-concealed) disagreement with Grandi.

During his time as Under-secretary, and even more so in his three years as Foreign Minister (1929–1932), Grandi skilfully managed to carve out an important role for himself in the making of Italy's fascist foreign policy. With Grandi's arrival, Italy gradually turned away from a 'conservative' strategy to an open – if still moderate – revisionism in Central Europe and in the Balkans. This area, in the words of historian Giampiero Carocci, soon became Italy's 'riserva di caccia' – its hunting ground (Carocci 1969: 54). Italy's strategy was mostly aimed at challenging power relations in the area – namely, the influence of France and Jugoslavia. [4]

The other scenario which saw Grandi at the forefront of Italy's fascist foreign policy was the negotiations on disarmament, which acquired some momentum in the late 1920s before collapsing after the Conference of London in 1930 (for Grandi's own recollections of the negotiations, see Grandi 1930). However, it was Grandi's failure to enhance Italy's diplomatic profile in Europe (especially at the expense of France), coupled with his unremitting anti-German feelings, that crucially led to his dismissal as Foreign Minister in July 1932.[5]

Between 1929 and 1932 a series of developments, international and domestic, brought about a decisive turn in fascist foreign policy. Internationally, the ravaging international economic crisis was followed by the establishment of Nazism in Germany, while Japan's invasion of Manchuria signalled the beginning of a deadly crisis for the League of Nations (Watt 2001; Robertson 1971). Further, both Britain and France came to be governed by coalitions including left-wing parties, a factor which inevitably affected Italy's foreign relations vis-à-vis the two countries in negative terms. Domestically, in the same time span a new package of economic, social and financial policies gained the fascist state and Mussolini complete control of the economy and society, bringing to perfection the fascist ideal of *corporativismo* (Aquarone 1965).

Italy's foreign policy reacted to both sets of changes. The illusions of a 'decade of good behaviour' now gone, Italy's foreign relations turned their dynamism into overtly revisionist policies. On 23 October 1932 in Turin Mussolini summed up the achievements of the first ten years of fascist foreign policy and made known to Europe his vision of a 'Four-Power Pact', to be signed by Britain, France, Italy and Germany as a way to preserve peace in Europe in the face of a changing political climate. Once again, Mussolini's vision was really aimed at achieving two sets of objectives: on the one hand, the Pact would openly grant Italy the status of a 'great power', with equal standing to its partners, and with the role of 'determinant weight' (Grandi 1930: 64); on the other hand, it would create an organisation in which the kind of European revisionism in which Italy had a stake could be concerted, negotiated, and accepted.

At the core of this vision was a new and burning concern – that of Italy's relations with the new Germany of 1932, following the Nazis' electoral triumph. Mussolini's anxiety regarding the independence of Austria and, more generally, the adverse effects of German revisionism prompted the signing of the Rome Protocols between Italy, Hungary and Austria in March 1934. Italy's economic and political backing of Prime Minister Engelbert Dollfuss and of the *Heimwehr* movement of Prince Stahremberg was also reinforced as a means to discourage any further advances from Germany. Relations with Berlin cooled down again and eventually reached an unprecedented low on 25 July 1934, when Hitler organised the attempted coup in Vienna in which Dollfuss was killed.

As a reaction, fascist foreign policy underwent a full conversion away from the much-trumpeted revisionism of the early 1930s, committing itself to a status quo strategy and revamping its old *Entente* affiliation by looking not only for Britain's support, but also, more crucially, for the help of France. The Rome Accords of January 1935 (also known as the 'Laval-Mussolini Accords', from the name of the then French Prime Minister Pierre Laval) and the establishment of the so-called Stresa Front (from the Conference held in Stresa in April of the same year, which had been explicitly convened to discuss Germany's requests for revisions of the Versailles system), both resulted from such a conversion. With Italo-German relations at their lowest, Mussolini was ready to play down Italy's revisionist plans in Central Europe in return for protection against Germany's aggressive plans. In fact, Mussolini had realised that the situation in

Europe at the time would not allow any of the kind of revisionism in which Italy had a stake. At this moment, with revisionism in Europe practically beyond his reach, Italy was to turn to another 'hunting ground' – that of Africa – to pursue its vision of an Empire.

Thus, Italy's intervention in Ethiopia in October 1935 followed Mussolini's plan to avenge the national trauma of Crispi's 1896 defeat at Adowa, and was in this sense integral to his vision of foreign policy (Kallis 2000: 125).[6] After the exchange of notes between Mussolini and Chamberlain of December 1925 and the recently achieved *rapprochement* with France, in which the issue of Ethiopia had been similarly raised, Mussolini was convinced that neither Britain nor France were willing to sacrifice the unity of the Stresa front and oppose his plans for the invasion of Ethiopia (a conviction based upon a gross misunderstanding of both agreements. See Mori 1963: 165–69, esp. 167; Lowe and Marzari 1975: 258–9; Cassels, 1970: 300). Further, Mussolini noted how all breaches to the Versailles system that had operated thus far had gone completely unchallenged – including the major breach of the Anglo-German naval treaty, signed on 18 June 1935, just a few months after Stresa.

On the basis of such a miscalculation, Italy embarked upon the last colonial war of the twentieth century and declared war on Ethiopia on 3 October 1935, despite a growing wave of opposition in Britain and in international public opinion at large.[7] The League of Nations acted promptly, however, and, about a month after the invasion, economic sanctions were issued against Italy while several unsuccessful attempts were made to reach a negotiated solution to the crisis (for instance, the Hoare-Laval plan of December 1935).

However, by that stage it was already clear that Italy would accept nothing short of its Empire. Domestically, popular consensus for the fascist regime grew to an unexpected high: economic sanctions had galvanised public opinion, as had the idea that Italy was fighting its 'civilising mission' against the world alone. On the ground, the intervention quickly escalated into an atrocious war, with the Italian military making frequent use of chemical weapons against civilians, while the occupation forces were issuing what would become the first examples of fascist racial legislation, establishing a de facto regime of *apartheid* (Del Boca 1991: 232–55). The Ethiopian army outnumbered, Italy quickly secured territory after territory. Addis Ababa was seized on 5 May 1936, and on 9 May King Victor Emmanuel III was proclaimed Emperor.

The League of Nations' effort to deter Italy had been thus defeated by a number of elements: first, the success and rapidity of the intervention, which was completed in only seven months; second, by the League's own inability to agree on more effective sanctions, namely oil sanctions which had been pushed for by the United States but never approved by France (Waley 1975); and, last, by the emergence of other threats in Europe which acted as a diversion (Andreatta 2000: 137–64). In fact, in March 1936 (during the fifth month of fighting in Ethiopia), Germany had occupied the Rhineland and had unilaterally denounced the Locarno Treaty of 1925.

Thus, the state of European relations at the end of the Ethiopian crisis had worsened dramatically (Taylor 1964; Salvemini 1953: 465–8; Mori 1963: 187; Lowe and Marzari 1975: 289–90; Andreatta 2000: 137–64). The League of Nations was defeated, Italy was alienated from the Stresa front of Western democracies, and Germany was further and further down the path of aggressive revisionism. Ethiopia marked the beginning of a further re-orientation in Italy's foreign policy, this time towards Germany and away from France and Britain.

Three factors contributed to the gradual alignment of Italy with Germany, culminating in the creation, on 1 November 1936, of the 'Rome-Berlin Axis'. First, ideology and a revisionist agenda became significant elements of commonality, especially after 1935–1937. Second, and relatedly, the common involvement in the Spanish civil war did much to align Italian foreign policy with the growing transnational movement of nazi-fascism (Coverdale 1977; Cassels 1968: 88). Third, the appointment of Mussolini's son-in-law, Galeazzo Ciano, as Foreign Minister in June 1936. At the time, Ciano was a staunch supporter of the alliance with Germany and strenuously worked towards this end from the beginning of his mandate (Ciano 1980: 6 November 1937).

In order to pursue its policy of *rapprochement* with Berlin, Rome was now ready to yield to substantial concessions: between 1936 and 1937 Italy accepted that the fate of Austria was to become Germany's satellite and made no substantial opposition to the process, which culminated in the annexation of March 1938. In a speech delivered in Berlin in September 1937, Mussolini showed enthusiasm in recognising that Italy and Germany, now close partners, were marching together towards a 'common destiny' (Kallis 2000: 149; Knox 2000). Two months later Italy joined the Anti-Comintern Pact against the Soviet Union originally created by Germany and Japan, and on 11 December 1937 it pulled out of the League of Nations. A few months later, Italy also published its anti-Semitic and racial policies: in imitation of German legislation, these laws truly expressed much of fascism's own social and political agenda (Collotti 1998; Bosworth 1998).

Despite such moves, however, Mussolini was also eager to keep his options open with Britain, a policy actively supported by Ambassador Grandi in London, among others. Thus, with the British Cabinet increasingly divided – between Eden labelling Mussolini 'a complete gangster' and Prime Minister Neville Chamberlain pushing for further negotiations and concessions – in January 1937 and again in April 1938 the 'Gentlemen's Agreement' and the 'Easter Agreement' bound Italy and Britain respectively to the status quo in the Mediterranean and affirmed their cooperation in the pursuit of peace and security in Europe, the Mediterranean, and the Middle East (Collotti 1998: 329–37, 347–61; Toscano 1963a).

After Germany's *Anschluss* of Austria in March 1938, German revisionism turned towards Czechoslovakia and the issue of the *Sudeten* minority. At first Italy oscillated between a non-committal stance and a position of solidarity with the quasi-ally. The declarations of both Mussolini and Ciano, however, were most of all geared to prudence and vagueness: on the one hand, Italy was ready to reap the benefits of the German blackmailing of Western democracies, yet on the other it feared being dragged into a war over Czechoslovakia, in which it had no interests. At the apex of the crisis, in September 1938, came the British proposal of a Four-Power Conference which, in the view of Chamberlain, only Mussolini could successfully promote with Hitler.

At the Munich Conference of 28–30 September 1938, and for the last time before the war, Mussolini was once again to play the role of mediator in European affairs: the fact that both Germany and Britain entrusted him with this role, however, says more about the inherent ambiguity of fascist foreign policy in the late 1930s than about its actual indispensability. Perhaps fascist propaganda liked to portray *il Duce* as, once again, *arbiter mundi* (as at Locarno in 1925 and with the Four-Power Pact of 1933), but in fact Italy was in control of neither German revisionist agenda, nor of an effective (Western or not) strategy to counter it. As is well known, Munich succeeded only in delaying the Second World War by a year, while it signalled the definitive end of the Versailles system, the dismemberment of Czechoslovakia and the apex of the policy of appeasement. From the point of view of Italy's fascist foreign policy, Munich highlighted a few long-lasting and problematic issues in the relations with Germany (Toscano 1963b: 230).

It is worth noting that throughout all of the negotiations at Munich Germany and Italy were *aligned* as 'Axis Powers' – but not *allied* on the basis of a formal agreement. In fact, after the creation of the Axis in 1936, Mussolini had constantly avoided committing Italy to any German proposals for a formal military alliance, much to the German Foreign Minister Joachim von Ribbentrop's disappointment. When Germany started its tragically successful plan for the conquest of ever growing portions of Europe and invaded Czechoslovakia (March 1939), not only did Italy take the opportunity to present Germany with the *fait accompli* of the invasion of Albania (May 1939), but the possibility of a formal alliance grew more insistent, especially after tentative negotiations with France and Britain had come to nothing. Thus, on 22 May 1939 the 'Pact of Steel' was signed, in all haste, by Ciano and von Ribbentrop, representing Italy and Germany. The haste was such that the Pact of Steel rested on a series of grave misunderstandings. It was also inconclusive of many operational details (Toscano 1968a: 231–57; Lowe and Marzari 1975: 332–5). Thus, a few days later Mussolini issued Hitler with a memorandum (the so-called Cavallero Memorandum of 30 May 1939) which specified how Italy interpreted its obligations deriving from the Pact, as well as other strategic considerations. Among other things, in the Memorandum Mussolini made clear that:

> since an eventual war between the democracies and Italy and Germany was 'inevitable', [Italy and Germany] should therefore make preparations; but there must be a preliminary period of at least three years of peace, to allow for rearmament, and for the Rome exhibition celebrating twenty years of Fascist rule, to take place in 1942.
>
> (Lamb 1999: 251; cf. Lowe and Marzari 1975: 335–6)

Despite his initial agreement regarding the substance of the Cavallero Memorandum, Hitler requested a meeting with Mussolini to clarify a few issues. This was postponed, with vague excuses, by Hitler himself, and was finally scheduled for 11–13 August 1939, when Ciano finally met Ribbentrop only to find out that Germany was ready to invade Poland and sign a treaty with the Soviet Union irrespective of Italy's position on the matter (Toscano 1968a: 190).[8] Ciano's unremittingly pro-German policy, which dated back to the early 1930s, ended abruptly with this meeting.

Although Germany had clearly not acted in accordance with the letter of the Pact of Steel, Ciano was unable to convince Mussolini that this was enough for Italy to denounce the agreement altogether, as well as advance an alternative policy. In the late summer of 1939 Mussolini was deeply ambivalent over which strategy to adopt.

Thus, when Germany invaded Poland, on 1 September 1939, triggering the Second World War, Mussolini declared Italy a 'non-belligerent' country, while a sympathetic Hitler telegraphed Rome to express gratitude for Italy's diplomatic and political support for the war whilst excusing it for the lack of military cooperation.[9]

The showdown of fascist foreign policy had just begun, but in the autumn 1939 Europe was still expecting Mussolini to pursue a policy of peace. Yet, Italy's policy of neutrality (or 'non-belligerency', as Mussolini came to call it) was destined to last only a short time. With Germany's overwhelming success in the first phase of the Second World War, Mussolini grew more and more restless. On the side of a triumphant Germany, Mussolini thought that Italy could easily enhance its standing inside the alliance by waging its own war, a 'parallel' war, autonomously choosing its targets and tempo.

With such a miscalculation in mind, and after the defeat of France by Germany in May 1940, Mussolini declared war on Britain and France on 10 June 1940, sure that an easy victory for the Axis Power could be achieved by the end of the year at the latest (André 1963: 260). September and October 1940 thus represented the highest stage of Mussolini's hubris, months in which ambitious plans for Italy's penetration of the Balkans and occupation of North Africa were recklessly laid out in order to both expand Italy's influence and balance Germany's impressively quick conquests.

Finally, Italy attacked Greece on 27 October 1940. Though hastily decided as a response to Germany's occupation of Romania, this military operation had been planned for a long time as a way to settle the score of Corfù. The Greek campaign, however, was to end a few weeks later in a dramatic fiasco – an episode which carried enormous importance in the unfolding of the Second World War, in at least two respects. First, Greece represented the first real defeat for the Axis, and had an enormous psychological impact upon both Italy and Germany. Second, it also signified the abrupt end of any ideas of 'parallel war' for Mussolini. From the beginning of 1941, Italy lost any freedom of action and was completely subordinated to Germany – indeed, it became the first of its 'satellites' (André 1973: 125–6; Lowe and Marzari 1975: 198). Suffice it to add here that, on 5 April 1941, Hitler wrote a letter to Mussolini advising him to merely execute the orders coming from Berlin, and do nothing else of his own initiative (André 1963: 271–2). Instead of speaking up, Mussolini bowed down.

Between 1940 and 1941, Mussolini was repeatedly approached by representatives of Hungary and Romania, two countries under the formal rule of Germany that had grown deeply hostile to German occupation forces. This was to be the last chance for Mussolini to break free from its ally and form an alternative and counterbalancing bloc, and possibly a neutral bloc, as Ciano suggested (Pastorelli 1963: 278–80).[10] For fear of the German reaction, however, Mussolini let this possibility pass by and decided to follow Hitler's lead.

On 11 December 1941 Italy, together with Germany, declared war on the United States, following Japan's attack at Pearl Harbour. Mussolini rightly predicted that the opening of an Asian front would make war in Europe, and in the Mediterranean especially, easier to fight for Italo-German forces, but after a few victories in the summer, the autumn and winter of 1942 proved fatal for the Axis. With Anglo-American troops in Sicily, following their landing on 10 July 1943, and the Italian army in shambles, Mussolini once again tried to impress upon Hitler his view that it was necessary – indeed, urgent – to negotiate a separate peace; however, he failed.

Only two weeks later, Mussolini was removed from government and arrested. After less than two months of negotiations – months when anarchy and chaos swept across Italy – on 3 September 1943 the new government of General Pietro Badoglio signed an armistice with the Anglo-American forces – made public only on 8 September 1943 – and, in turn, declared war on Germany. Despite Mussolini's attempt to set up the Republic of Salò, a puppet government in the hands of Germany, and with German occupation forces meeting the increasing resistance of Italy's liberation movements, Mussolini's end was near. His capture and death in Milan followed three days after Italy's liberation on 25 April 1945.

Politics and paradigms of Italy's fascist foreign policy

The view fascism held of foreign policy derived and amplified many of the motives which were already central to the nationalist movement of the late liberal period. Indeed, as many historians have argued, the nationalist movement provided fascism with the intellectual and doctrinal apparatus that it originally lacked (Salvatorelli 1923), while there is no doubt that the symbolic heir of nationalists such as Francesco Crispi, Alfredo Oriani and Emilio Gentile was in fact Mussolini himself (Chabod 1951: 546–8; Knox 2002: 106, 138; Bosworth 1979; Bracco 1998: 105–8, 123). Fascism brought to unity many of the themes that had surfaced in the Italian political debate from the 1890s, but especially in the aftermath of the First World War.

To start with, fascism advanced a particular understanding of the nature of international politics which broke away from the liberal notion of a European concert of powers and set interests and power at the centre of the Darwinian struggle of international politics. As Mussolini stated in his first speech on foreign policy in the Chamber of Deputies on 16 February 1923:

> I see the world *as it actually is*: that is a world of unchained egoisms. If the world was a shining Arcadia, it would perhaps be nice to frisk among nymphs and shepherds; but I see nothing of that sort, and moreover when the great banners of the great principles are raised I see, behind these more or less venerable trappings, *interests* that are seeking to assert themselves in the world.[11]
>
> (Mussolini 1934: 61)

Fascism, in other words, claimed a better knowledge of the 'realistic forces' driving international politics: these were conceived in terms of 'natural laws' of eternal struggle and confrontation (for a dialogic treatment, see Wight 1952: 508–31). Rejecting any notion of 'perpetual peace' as a utopian construct, fascism considered war as the only real international institution, and foreign policy as the supreme realm of politics – 'la politica per eccellenza' (Mussolini 1932: 170–1; cf. Grispo 1963: 122). Further, international relations were not a matter to be decided upon on the basis of moral standards. Expediency provided the best guide for action.

Second, fascism managed to successfully combine nation and masses, international war and domestic revolution, into an unprecedented totalitarian synthesis. Revisionism and expansionism were necessary in order for the 'proletarian nations' to expand or – as Grandi used to put it along the lines of Hitler's idea of *Lebensraum* – simply to survive. Fascist doctrine claimed that all domestic problems such as poverty, unrest and social struggle would be solved by this kind of foreign policy: thus, the conversion of class struggle at home into an imperial struggle abroad acted as justification for adventures such as the Ethiopian invasion of 1935.

With fascism, the doctrine of the 'primacy of foreign policy' was asserted in practice and theory. 'Our preoccupation is primarily with matters of foreign policy', claimed Mussolini: it was only via foreign policy that the nation's prestige and standing on the international scene could be asserted. Hence, all interests, classes, and energies of the nation must be subordinated to foreign policy aims, following the fascist ideal of *corporativismo*:

> Italy must [...] present itself as united and compact in the arena of nations, free from all domestic troubles [...] Our formula is as follows: everything in the state, nothing outside of the state, nothing against the state. [...] Our password cannot but be: internal discipline, to present the world with a rock-solid national strength.
>
> (Mussolini 1956–80: XVII: 300, XXI: 425, XXI: 363)

On the other hand, the relations between foreign policy, war and nation also worked in the opposite direction. Foreign policy and war – both in their material and discursive/symbolic dimensions – served the function of 'educating' a nation, of forging a people.

Third, and relatedly, in the fascist doctrine foreign policy came to be endowed with qualities and attributes which were close to the very idea of life and existence. As Mussolini himself said: 'L'Italia *esiste* e reclama il diritto di esistere nel mondo' ('Italy exists and demands the right to be in the world') (Moscati 1963: 102): foreign policy was the supreme expression of a nation's life and agency. Thence, fascism's emphasis on action, which was not only thought of as a 'vehicle of implementation of ideas, but as a good in itself' (Kallis 2000: 57; Lowe and Marzari 1975: 204). This is also why, against the *politica pedestre* of Giolitti and Sforza, Mussolini announced that 'by recovering its freedom of action, Italy will take care of its interests' under fascism (Mussolini 1956–80: XIX, 20).

Last, fascism's view of foreign policy borrowed heavily from (and skilfully adapted) the geopolitical doctrines of the time so as to prove Italy's need for expansion. Hence, Mussolini's fixation with expansion in the Mediterranean: 'Si tratta di tornare ad essere la prima nazione del Mediterraneo, il che vuol dire dominare il mondo' ('We must once again be the first nation in the Mediterannean and thence we will dominate the world') (nationalist Francesco Giunta quoted in Rumi 1968: 326). Geopolitical motives were advanced to sustain Italy's activism in the Balkans from the mid-1920s to the early 1930s. Again, in 1939, in a formula reminiscent of Mackinder's more famous expression, Mussolini warned the Grand Council of Fascism that 'he who holds Bohemia, holds the Danubian basin. He who holds Albania holds the Balkans' (quoted in Lowe and Marzari 1975: 326).

To sum up, then, fascism conceptualised foreign policy as the supreme manifestation of agency in international politics, hence its espousal of an unrivalled primacy of foreign policy over domestic concerns. However, the primacy of foreign policy achieved by fascism effectively rested on the total (and totalitarian) identification/sublimation of the domestic with/into the foreign. In the case of fascism, in other words, it was the very distinction between the two realms that became blurred (Vigezzi 1997a: 24–5, 112–5). While it is certainly right to affirm that fascism embraced the primacy of foreign policy over the domestic, this is true only if one accepts that, in such a totalitarian state, the domestic ceased to exist as such and became itself part of the vision of foreign policy, forming part of its very precondition or premise.

The analysis of Italy's fascist foreign policy: the state of the art

Like fascism itself, fascist foreign policy has been at the centre of a heated and now 60-year long debate among historians and analysts of different bents and political traditions, both within and without Italy. Indeed, of all periods of Italian foreign policy, this is possibly the most widely discussed, even in contemporary research. In terms of historiography, the examination of fascist foreign policy has typically centred around three main debates (Petersen 1973; Bosworth 1998: 58–105; Azzi 1993; contrast these views with Pastorelli 1971).

First debate: the role of Mussolini

The first and probably most encompassing of all debates concerns the issue of leadership, responsibility and the role of Mussolini in shaping fascist foreign policy (Mallet 2003; Andreatta 2000: 159–62). This debate originated in the late 1930s, with the publication of one of Gaetano Salvemini's most widely read books, *Mussolini Diplomatico*. Reprinted and enlarged in the following *Prelude to the Second World War*, this contribution provided the first ever informed critique of fascist foreign policy by one of the most notable *fuoriusciti* intellectuals (Petersen 1973: 12–28; on *fuoriuscitismo*, see Serra and Duroselle 1984). In this, Salvemini famously pointed out that Mussolini

> was never the great statesman many believed him to be. [...] The man was always an irresponsible improviser, half madman, half criminal, gifted only – but to the highest degree – in the arts of propaganda.
>
> (Salvemini 1953: 10)

In its simplicity and effectiveness, the view that Mussolini was the real driving force and main determinant of fascist foreign policy rapidly gained currency and was frequently espoused by most analysts and practitioners between the 1940s and 1970s. Hence, in his *Origins of the Second World War* A.J.P. Taylor famously dismissed fascism 'as a fraud' and Mussolini as 'a vain, blundering boaster without ideas or aims'; no wonder that fascist foreign policy had been so inconsistent (Taylor 1964: 85; Kirkpatrick 1964). Winston Churchill himself, in his 23 December 1940 broadcast to the Italian people, had expressed a similar view and in a most effective way, when he had declared that 'one man alone' was responsible for Italy's misconduct in domestic and, most importantly, foreign affairs (Eade 1951: 322; Bosworth 1998: 77). Much more recently, Denis Mack Smith revamped Salvemini's thesis to show that the fundamental incoherence lying at the heart of fascist foreign policy was due to Mussolini's own incoherent leadership (Mack Smith 1976, 1981).

Many historians have contested this view, accusing Salvemini and his followers of writing a 'moralising' and highly personalised history of fascist foreign policy, while ignoring other important factors. In 1933 the Communist intellectual and later leader of the *Partito Comunista Italiano* (PCI) Palmiro Togliatti attacked Salvemini's book in the following terms:

> To consider the international relations of an important capitalist state [...] the result of the whimsicality, of the erratic behaviour, of the incompetence, of the self-celebratory fads of a single man [...] is the lowest point ever touched by democratic banality. [...] The foreign policy of fascism cannot be understood if not in constant relation with the economical situation of the country and with the material bases of Italian imperialism.
>
> (Togliatti 1964: 270)

Contributions from Marxist and left-wing authors such as Giampiero Carocci and Fulvio D'Amoja followed this lead, asserting that the 'direttrice permanente' of fascist foreign policy was its imperialist and expansionist drive. Fascist foreign policy towards the Balkans and Africa in particular exemplified such an orientation (Carocci 1969; D'Amoja 1961).

Ennio di Nolfo and Giorgio Rochat, on the other hand, downplayed the economic argument to suggest that the character and orientation of fascist foreign policy were designed mainly for domestic political purposes. Just as the spectre of a 'permanent war' was conjured up to unite the domestic front and stifle any opposition, so was the increasing militarisation, despite all fascist rhetoric, a way to cope with *internal* rather than *external* threats (Di Nolfo 1960; Rochat 1971). More often than not, in other words, foreign policy was carried out by Mussolini with an eye towards domestic rather than international politics.

From the late 1970s and throughout the 1980s, however, another set of interpretations have challenged even this last wave of scholarship. These contributions claim that rather than blaming Mussolini or the domestic nature of the fascist regime, one should give prominence to the dynamics and developments of international relations in the inter-war period.

In his massive biography of Mussolini, as well as in some of his other works, Renzo De Felice issued a number of claims regarding fascism and fascist foreign policy, some of which are deeply contentious. Substantially espousing Dino Grandi's view of Italy as the 'determinant weight' in European relations of the time, De Felice insisted that fascist foreign policy in the 1920s and '30s was nothing but a 'cautious and reasonable' strategic diplomatic action brought about by Mussolini in response to a set of objective and given international circumstances (De Felice 1973: 62).[12] In other words, fascist foreign policy was a 'normal' foreign policy (De Felice 1974: 642, 650, 706; De Felice 1998), directed at extracting benefits from the confrontation of two opposing coalitions as well as taking care of its interests in Africa and beyond (cf. Mack Smith 1975, 2000).

Rosaria Quartararo has argued even more explicitly that fascist foreign policy was 'absolutely autonomous in regard to internal policies', and only responded to international considerations (Quartararo 1980: 32; critical reviews in Bosworth 1998: 94–6; Knox 2000: 144 n121; Collotti 2000: 475). In her view, Mussolini aptly balanced Italy's German policy with his openings to Britain and France. Esmond Robertson, finally, has been less overtly revisionist in his thesis, but has equally stressed that the analysis of fascist foreign policy should not concentrate so much on Mussolini's leadership, but rather on international dynamics and the 'windows of opportunity' which opened up, especially in the 1930s.

Second debate: a foreign policy 'programme'?

The second debate relates to the question of whether Mussolini and fascism followed a 'programme' in foreign policy, or whether this was entirely erratic. Were the apparent oscillations and ambiguities in fascist foreign policy intentional, i.e. the result of a programme, or merely proof of the very lack of a foreign policy agenda? This debate originated precisely as a reaction to the progressive establishment of the 'Salveminian orthodoxy', which portrayed Mussolini as eternally in self-contradiction and fascist foreign policy as (unproblematically) expressing such constant oscillation (Petersen 1973: 15).[13]

From the 1960s, authors such as Giorgio Rumi, Ennio Di Nolfo and Giampiero Carocci all attacked this orthodoxy, albeit in different terms. According to Rumi, right from its rise to power in 1922 fascism followed a coherent foreign policy programme, its programme being fundamentally centred around the myth of the 'Third Rome' and the imperial idea in the Mediterranean (Rumi 1963: 45; 1968). Di Nolfo, on the other hand, argued that fascist foreign policy did indeed follow a programme, but this was largely determined by domestic, rather than international, objectives, i.e. the need to co-opt, appease and divert domestic public opinion through adventures abroad:

> Since the very first day, since the first words he pronounced on foreign policy issues, Mussolini had no other intention than to take care of the domestic front. If [...] Mussolini's action can appear as driven by improvisation, when it is observed from the point of view of domestic politics, it shows a clear and precocious awareness of his goals.
>
> (Di Nolfo 1960: 44)

In the last twenty years, however, this thesis has also been challenged. Many have come to suggest that while fascist foreign policy did indeed follow a programme, this was neither the result of domestic imperatives nor of imperialist drives. Blending elements of the orthodox interpretation of Salvemini with new insights, these authors argued that considering Mussolini as the key determinant of fascist foreign policy does not automatically imply the lack of a clear set of objectives and aims – in other words, a programme; quite the contrary is the case. This view has been espoused most explicitly in recent years by British historian MacGregor Knox, who has unremittingly emphasised the power of Mussolini's ideas and ideology in driving fascist foreign policy. Such was Mussolini's force, determination and clarity of thought in foreign policy that, Knox claims, already 'by 1926–27, Mussolini's programme was set in all essential details' (Knox 2000: 105).

Third debate: continuity vs. discontinuity

The third and last major debate in the historiography of fascist foreign policy concerns the issue of whether fascist foreign policy represented nothing more than a continuation of liberal foreign policy, or whether indeed the foreign policy of fascism can be dismissed as a mere 'parenthesis' – as alien to the tradition of Italian foreign policy as, in Benedetto Croce's famous metaphor, the Hyksos tribe were to the Italian population. The mainstream position here indicates that while there might have been a natural inertia in Italy's foreign policy until the mid-1920s, there can be no doubt that Mussolini's foreign policy grew qualitatively different from liberal foreign policy over time.

Many analysts and historians have tried to come up with a periodisation of fascist foreign policy able to differentiate the years of relative peacefulness and 'moderate revisionism' from those of more overt and radical expansionism – the 'decade of good behaviour' from the foreign policy of the 1930s (Halperin 1964; cf. also Cassels 394 n12, 397). Some, like Carocci, have identified the years between 1927–1928 as crucial years in this respect (Carocci 1969: 113–7); some others, such as Collotti, have deemed the turn of the decade as the decisive turn in fascist foreign policy (Collotti 2000: 20); others still have identified the years between 1932 and 1936 as providing the definitive premise for the escalation of fascist foreign policy into war (Rossini 1963: xix–xx; cf. also Pastorelli 1971: 602).

Predictably enough, these kinds of periodisation – if not the very idea of a change in fascist foreign policy – have been attacked from two distinct positions: on the one hand, by those, like Rumi and Knox, who most strongly support the view that fascist foreign policy was driven from the very beginning by a clear set of goals, i.e. by a programme, and by ideological continuity (Kallis 2000: 7), and, on the other, by those who argued (even more strongly) for a continuity of fascist foreign policy with liberal foreign policy. This latter minority view, in turn, has generated two distinct variants. There are those like De Felice who have argued that:

> Mussolini's foreign policy from 1922 to 1924, and even later – roughly to Locarno – was a policy of prestige, but largely in the manner, in the tradition of the Italian foreign office.
>
> (De Felice quoted in Azzi 1993: 196)

and have substantially defended the claim, already illustrated above, that fascist foreign policy was a 'normal' foreign policy. Carlo Maria Santoro similarly claimed that 'il ventennio fascista non sconvolse radicalmente le basi di politica estera italiana' ('The fascist *ventennio* did not revolutionise the foundations of Italian foreign policy in any radical way'), and while the style was perhaps different, the substance was not (Santoro 1991: 159).

The other variant of the continuity thesis has been advanced by R. J. B. Bosworth over the last two decades. In brief, Bosworth argued for a more 'structural' interpretation of fascist foreign policy, by highlighting the enduring constraints under which both liberalism and fascism in Italy carried out their foreign policy. Nationalism, expansionism and the myth of the 'Third Rome' were not exclusive to fascism – indeed, they were already apparent in the foreign policy of liberalism, constituting the real driving force of interventions such as the one in Libya in 1911. Thus, rather than being the result of Mussolini's leadership, fascist foreign policy was nothing less than 'the natural result of Italian history' (Bosworth 1983b: 79) and national identity, as 'the major difference [between liberal and] fascist Italy lay in the method rather than in the contents of foreign policy' (Bosworth 1979: vii).

Italy's fascist foreign policy: a critical realist assessment

Differently from the foreign policy of liberal Italy, fascist foreign policy has attracted a substantial amount of scholarly attention and sparked fierce and long-lasting debates. Studies have been pitched at different levels of analysis and have emphasised different narratives and explanations along the domestic/international continuum. How do the models elaborated in Chapter 1 fare when measured against Italy's fascist policy?

Monocausal approaches

The claim that fascist foreign policy was an exclusive function of the international relations of the time has been advanced by some historians (De Felice and Quartararo, for instance) to explain Italy's external behaviour – and, by the same token, to advance a fundamentally exculpatory reading of Mussolini's role in shaping it.

De Felice's and Quartararo's readings have evident overlaps with those monocausal models of foreign policy stressing the 'primacy of foreign policy'. Particularly in its 'offensive' version, neo-realism conceives of states as fundamentally interested in maximising their gains, hence fascist Italy should constitute an easy case to account for. After all, Mussolini's own understanding of foreign policy was framed around the primary concern of enhancing Italy's power and freedom of action in international politics. The invasion of Corfù of August 1923, i.e. only ten months after Mussolini's rise to power, then, could be thought of as providing a most evident corroboration of neo-realist hypotheses: states naturally expand in pursuit of power, and so did fascist Italy.

Yet, the overall trajectory of fascist foreign policy presents other episodes that are just as convincing as Corfù in challenging this thesis. Most of all, neo-realism would be at pains to explain Italy's behaviour from the mid-1930s and especially in the run-up to the Second World War. When confronted with a clear and compelling threat – that of Nazi Germany – Italy decided to side with it, rather than against it. In March 1938 Mussolini summarised the peculiar strategic calculations behind this choice saying 'it may be observed that when an event is fated to take place, it's better if it takes place with you rather than despite of, or worse still against you' (Mussolini quoted in Lowe and Marzari 1975: 291; cf. also Ciano 1980: 16 March 1940). That fascist Italy decided to bandwagon instead of balancing against Germany already presents a problem for a pure, neo-realist theory of foreign policy that excludes any account of domestic politics from its explanatory framework and would expect states to 'naturally' balance.

The second monocausal international perspective, geopolitics, also has its problems when understood in purely objectivist, naturalistic terms. In so far as, for instance, Santoro asserts that geopolitics played a major role in directing Italy's foreign policy and, in particular, its alliance strategy (Santoro 1991: 157ff.), this claim is once again difficult to measure and sustain against the empirical record. A succession of orientations and re-orientations brought Italy first on the side of the Western democracies (formerly the *Entente* powers; then to the position of leading the revisionist powers of Central Europe; later into a position which Grandi would characterise as 'splendid' isolation; then to re-align with the Western democracies; and finally to the side of a radically revisionist and strengthened Germany. If this oscillatory policy is simply ascribed to Italy's ambiguous geographical location between 'continental' Europe and the Mediterranean, as Santoro suggests, then it becomes deeply problematic to explain exactly why Italy's policy changed in one or the other direction at each particular stage, given that presumably its geography was not susceptible to change. Naturally, it is the intervention of 'politics' (necessarily entailing a domestic component) that needs to be accounted for in these cases. Yet, monocausal interpretations framed around geopolitics – such as Santoro's – seem to be ill-equipped to provide such an account.

The third international perspective used by historians of fascist foreign policy has focused on the dynamic of the international economy. In particular, the international economic cycle of the late 1920s has been related to Italy's imperialist policy of the mid-1930s, and the Ethiopian intervention of 1935 has been interpreted as a response to the 1929 economic depression (Baer 1967; Catalano 1969). Despite its merits, this thesis also leaves a few aspects unexplained. First, it cannot account for the timing of the war, since by 1935 the economic depression had in fact already exhausted its worst effects. Second, this thesis underrates the extent to which the Ethiopian intervention responded to a long-standing programme of ideological revisionism on the one hand, and, on the other, could not have been waged in any international scenario but rather had to wait for the particular international conjuncture of the mid-1930s.

If international monocausal approaches to foreign policy have troubles in adequately accounting for foreign policy, domestic monocausal perspectives are equally lacking, although in different respects. Consider, for instance, the explanations focused on fascism as a particularly and naturally aggressive regime, a line of argument which today resonates in the democratic peace theory. There can be very little doubt that fascism, as a political doctrine imbued with virulent nationalism, attributed a paramount importance to war. As seen at the outset of Section 2 ('Politics and paradigms of Italy's fascist foreign policy'), war was not only thought of as the supreme proof of the nation's virility, but was also a privileged instrument for achieving perfect domestic unity in a fragmented state such as Italy. Thence, for instance, Mussolini's emphasis on the ambiguous concept of 'permanent war' (Kallis 2000).

However, it is undeniable that if one considers the relation between fascist Italy and war the first puzzle with which one is presented is the wide gap between intentions and actual actions. After Corfù, no major military operations were launched until the mid-1930s. Both the strict intentionalist (Mussolini-centred) and the 'primacy of the domestic' readings of fascist foreign policy cannot be stretched to explain why, despite all the revisionism and aggressively military rhetoric of fascism, despite its 'programme' of war, despite the ideology and the authoritarian nature of the regime, the actual propensity for war remained relatively low for most of the fascist *ventennio*. To put it bluntly and rather provocatively, if fascism meant war, why was there so little of it?

Let us once again take the example of the Ethiopian war. As we know, the war which eventually broke out in 1935 had been planned through the 1920s and early 1930s in great detail. Thus, over the years many historians have wondered why Mussolini waited throughout the 1920s and early 1930s to fulfil the vision of an Empire, which he had inherited from Crispian nationalism, and which, already in the 1920s, he considered 'imperative' for fascism. A. J. P. Taylor was among them:

> Revenge for Adowa was implicit in Fascist boasting; but no more urgent in 1935 than at any time since Mussolini came to power in 1932. [...] For reasons which are still difficult to grasp, Mussolini decided in 1934 to conquer Abyssinia.
>
> (Taylor 1964: 118–9)

What is implicit in Taylor's remarks is the consideration that a reading purely grounded in ideology, the role of Mussolini, or domestic politics cannot explain why a war that was so integral to fascism was not waged until 1935. The predictions of a purely cognitive, idiosyncratic approach, as well as those of the democratic peace theory, are hardly met by the foreign policy of fascist Italy.

Further, domestic politics or ideology are also relatively powerless in explaining another important feature of fascist foreign policy, i.e. the pace and trajectory of Italy's policy of alignment with Germany. Briefly stated, if ideology was really the driving force of fascist foreign policy, why did Italy avoid aligning (even informally) with Nazi Germany until 1936, i.e. three long years from the spectacular rise to power of Nazism in Germany? Why did the years between 1932 and 1935 mark the highest stage of rapprochement between *il Duce* and Western democracies in the 1930s, climaxing in the Stresa Conference and not in an alignment with Germany? Finally, why did Italy wait until 22 May 1939 – i.e. eight months after the Munich Conference and three years after the 'Rome-Berlin Axis' – to finally sign its first and only formal alliance with Germany, the Pact of Steel, if the ideological bond between the two regimes had been so decisive for its foreign policy? Thus, if ideology or the nature of the regime were the only forces at play, the diplomatic wavering of fascist Italy between 1932 and 1939 would be simply unintelligible.

It is striking that monocausal models based on the primacy of foreign policy or of domestic politics both fail to perform in a case, such as fascist Italy, which could be methodologically considered 'easy'. On the one hand, monocausal international approaches fail to make sense of Italy's behaviour precisely when international relations were in a particularly tense state and the international constraint particularly stringent, e.g. in the run-up to the Second World War. On the other, domestic approaches are insufficient to explain Italy's foreign policy despite the obvious importance of ideology and nationalism throughout the fascist *ventennio*.

Dualist approaches

Among the dualist approaches, the additive model starts from the assumption that foreign policy can always be understood as the combination or addition of international influences and domestic factors. These approaches could be thought of as providing a simple, commonsensical account of Italy's fascist foreign policy. Consider, for example, Italy's progressive alignment with Germany.

Following the logic of additive approaches, one could argue that Italy's siding with the Nazis resulted from the addition of two distinct influences. On the one hand, the rise of German power on the continent presented Italy with the possibility of entering into association with the future hegemon of Europe, and thus benefiting from its protection for its own revisionist programme. On the other, the ideological affinity binding the two regimes acted to reinforce rather than mitigate this tendency.

In terms of the balance between domestic and international elements, therefore, one could argue that fascist foreign policy resulted from the combination of both the domestic/ideological motive and the strategic/international preference. Pressures at the international level added up to those at the domestic level so as to bring about the observed outcome. Yet, this explanation skims over a few rather important issues.

First, it fails to account for any variations in the relative importance of international vs. domestic factors. Second, it cannot accommodate their dynamic interplay, in spite of the fact that this was historically crucial in the development of Italy's alliance with Germany. Had the strategic/international and the ideological/domestic motives always been equally paramount in impacting upon Italy's foreign policy, then one could not explain why, as already mentioned, a preliminary agreement with an ideologically similar and strong power such as Germany was pursued only three years after the rise of Nazism (Rome-Berlin Axis, November 1936) and why a formal alliance had to wait a further three years to materialise (Pact of Steel, May 1939).

Similarly, in the case of the Ethiopian intervention of 1935–1936, additive accounts cannot explain the changes within international relations and domestic politics which were brought about by the Ethiopian intervention itself. However, in unveiling Britain's hostility to Mussolini's radically revisionist plans and reinforcing the ideological and transnational component of fascist foreign policy, the intervention in Ethiopia arguably did much to bring about Italy's progressive siding with Germany. Hence, it was not just that the relative importance of international vs. domestic factors changed over time, but that these factors interacted in a way which escapes the simply additive logic of the approaches in question. Though sound in descriptive terms, dualist/additive accounts have trouble accommodating complexity.

Does it perhaps makes more sense to posit fascist foreign policy as the result of a dual constraint in which international relations provided the *grandes lignes* while domestic politics determined the details of fascist foreign policy? How do 'nested games' approaches fare in this case?

As discussed in Chapter 1, some approaches belonging to this category have been elaborated precisely to deal with the case of 'revisionist states', of which fascist Italy is a clear example. For their particular domestic characteristics, it has been argued, these states divert the natural international stimuli into 'unnatural' behaviour – thus, for instance, Italy's bandwagoning in the run-up to the First World War, which has been explained in terms of its high degree of ideological revisionism.

However, if such an argument is accepted, then it becomes unclear why systemic variables should be accorded a relative primacy at all. Indeed, if one accepts that the revisionist regimes by definition aim at changing the international relations of the time, then it becomes especially hard to argue that the latter, rather than the former, determine its foreign policy, at least in its *grandes lignes*. With Corfù, but especially with Ethiopia, fascist Italy aimed precisely at revolutionising the international order born out of the First World War, and institutions such as the League of Nations. It would have been impossible to do this in ways 'compatible' with the international relations of the time, because the whole point for the fascist regime was to change those relations. In fact, what Corfù and Ethiopia contributed to was the decline of the order negotiated at Versailles and the creation of a new one, something which would hardly have come about in the absence of such revisionist regimes.

Thus, not only does the implicit hierarchy of the 'nested games' approaches seem dubious and unable to account for important features of fascist foreign policy; more generally, these approaches (as all other dualist models) have problems accommodating agency-initiated change. This, however, was as integral an aim as anything else to the foreign policy of fascist Italy.

According to the pendulum model, foreign policy responds to those pressures, international or domestic, that are relatively more intense. Can fascist foreign policy be usefully read through the lenses of this approach?

As already mentioned, in the case of the highest international tension – the run-up to the Second World War – fascist Italy's foreign policy did not adapt to international factors only. Even the most recalcitrant neo-realist analysts have conceded that domestic politics did play a role in the choice of how to cope with the German threat by eventually joining the bandwagon of Nazi Germany. Thus, in so far as the first end-point of the pendulum trajectory is concerned (t_1 in Figure 1.7) there does not seem to be much evidence in favour of the pendulum approach.

In terms of domestic politics, pressures from this arena were arguably high throughout the two decades of fascist rule, and especially after the mid-1920s, when the *fascistizzazione* of the Foreign Ministry (and society at large) ensured that no domestic influences other than fascism could shape Italy's external behaviour. However, even at this level of intensity, domestic politics was clearly not the only influence bearing upon Italy's foreign policy. As mentioned above, the alliance strategy that Italy pursued, especially vis-à-vis Germany, is hardly accountable in terms of domestic politics only, but needs to be complemented by an assessment of the particular international situation of the mid-1930s. Hence, not even at this end of the pendulum (t_5 in Figure 1.7) does there seem to be much evidence in support of the pendulum approach.

On closer inspection, the failure of the pendulum model can be hypothesised to derive from the fact that both sets of pressures remained high at least from the mid-1930s onwards, which is difficult to account for in the model.

Dialectical approaches

Can the morphogenetic model provide a more fitting account of the evolution of Italy's fascist foreign policy over the years? Can it make sense of the interplay of international and domestic developments and of the way these impacted upon foreign policy?

Consider, for example, the Corfù crisis of 1923 as a sequential combination of international and domestic factors. Up until the crisis, fascist Italy, in international terms, enjoyed relative autonomy to plan and carry out the operation. Thus, the 'strategic conditioning' on Italy's foreign policy was rather weak: international relations among states were in a rather permissive and de-polarised state. No great powers, and least of all the League itself, were expecting the crisis to take place, and they were insufficiently prepared to cope with it. Further, when the crisis finally took place, France was determined not to oppose Italy's action completely, lest the League discuss its own occupation of the Ruhr, only recently carried out. Britain was the only power that supported strong measures against Italy (the possibility of a British naval attack was, at some point, seriously contemplated). The crisis itself, however, produced a decisive tightening of the international constraint: military pressure from Britain stepped up, which in turn prompted the intervention of the League of Nations and finally led to the evacuation of the island.

The morphogenetic model would claim that it was thanks to the working of the actor's emerging properties (in this case, fascism and the establishment of Mussolini's leadership on foreign policy), that foreign policy could impact upon the pre-constituted and structured environment around the actor (the international relations of the early 1920s), changing its features. Corfù started off as an expression of the aggressive foreign policy programme of fascism to produce a partial restructuring of the system surrounding it.

This interpretation of the crisis has the merit of reconciling and integrating the causal role of international and domestic factors into a coherent account, able to overcome the strictures of the monocausal accounts and emphasise their dynamic interaction. However, it too presents some problems.

First, it tends to assume that international relations and domestic politics are separate, their interaction unproblematic and their causal power objectively measurable. The mediation of political discourse is absent from the model, although this arguably constituted the locus of such interplay. At its most simplistic level, it is hard to argue that the rhetoric of fascism played no role in crises such as Corfù and Ethiopia.

Second, the notion of 'structural conditioning' cannot effectively convey the idea of a particular system of relations in which fascist Italy was acting and towards which it was orientated. Any changes in this system produced a more or less favourable environment for Italy to pursue its foreign policy goals and hence were crucial in prompting Italy's fascist foreign policies. It was not structure per se that conditioned foreign policy, but rather the specific context of relations of which Italy was part.

Can a strategic-relational model be more successfully applied to Italy's fascist foreign policy? Is the dialectic between strategically-selective context, strategic action and political discourse, in which the model is grounded, able to capture the nature and evolution of Italy's fascist foreign policy?

To start with the first element of the dialectic, one should consider the 'uneven terrain' of international relations which fascist Italy faced and how this evolved over the decades. Despite Italy's much-trumpeted revisionism, in fact, there is no doubt that the international relations of the 1920s did impose a constraint on Italy's fascist foreign policy. After all, with the exception of Corfù, no overtly revisionist operations or military campaign were launched until the mid-1930s. Had Italy been more powerful in relation to the other actors in the system – i.e. had the environment been less constraining – it would have been easier to pursue that radically revisionist foreign policy which formed the core of the fascist foreign policy programme from its very rise to power. Instead, during the first decade after the march on Rome of October 1922, the relative position of Italy was such that it could easily perform and profit from the role of pivot between the democratic and revisionist camps. Arguably, this tendency climaxed in the proposal of the Four-Power Pact (March 1933), but re-emerged in the late 1930s. With the rise of Nazi Germany, however, the horizon of Italy's external relations changed, and thus did its relative position. In particular, the rise of an ideologically contiguous and powerful actor such as Germany increased the likelihood and appeal of a bandwagoning strategy.

In terms of strategy, there is no doubt that, on the one hand, fascist ideology aimed at enhancing Italy's profile and, on the other, it intended to change the environment surrounding it. The progressive loss of influence of the foreign policy professionals of *la Consulta* also meant that Mussolini's role in deciding over foreign policy grew stronger as the years went by. Just as with the process of *fascistizzazione* of Italy's entire society, the foreign policy process became less plural, more hierarchical, and unified at the top.

This also enabled the establishment of one prevalent political discourse. On the one hand, the way international relations were perceived was strongly influenced by a combination of Darwinism and *Machtpolitik* which made international competition for power the standard feature of relations among states. On the other hand, Italy's role in the world was associated with imperialist myths such as that of the 'Third Rome' and of the alleged superiority of the Italian race.

How did the dialectical interaction between the strategically selective international relations of the time, the strategy initiated by fascist Italy, and the establishment of a particular discourse around foreign policy shape Italy's fascist foreign policy? Consider, for instance, the Ethiopian intervention of October 1935–May 1936.

Up until the mid-1930s, the relations between the states of Europe provided an uneven and selective terrain for fascist foreign policy; the situation deterred any military intervention in Europe or colonial adventures abroad until 1935 because the likelihood of a response by the front of Western democracies was arguably high. In April 1935 Mussolini finally secured the agreement with France which, together with the one signed with Britain ten years before, 'settled' the issue of Ethiopia in Italy's favour – or at least, this was Mussolini's interpretation of the agreements. On the other hand, the growth of German power on the continent constituted an important and favourable change of the international context. Thus, with Petersen,

> The attack on Ethiopia was to be scheduled, it seems, for the precise moment in which national-socialist Germany would be strong enough to resist interventionist pressure [...] and, on the other hand, the level of Germany's armament would not allow threatening initiatives against Italian hegemony in South-East and Central Europe.
>
> (Petersen 1973: 54–5)

In other words, Italy profited from the opportunity given by the rise of Germany, under the illusion that the democracies of the Stresa front would never risk the future of the coalition (and Italy's participation in it) for the sake of Abyssinia. Thus, the 'programme' of ideological revisionism had to wait until the changing conditions of the international situation and, most notably, the rising threat from Germany, provided the window of opportunity necessary to carry it out.

Further, the Ethiopian intervention generated a powerful feedback on both the system of relations of which Italy was a part and Italy's own domestic politics. As for the former, by directly challenging the institutions upon which the post-war international order had been built, the Ethiopian intervention hastened the collapse of peace in Europe. As for domestic politics, the Ethiopian intervention further reinforced the strategy of aggressive revisionism of fascist Italy.

Neither a purely international nor an exclusively domestic account would be able to capture the combination of influences that generated Italy's fascist foreign policy. Moreover, had any of the three elements in the dialectic been different, a different outcome would probably have followed. Had the prevailing discourse not been colonised so forcefully by the aggressive imperialism of fascism, the incentive to embark upon the last of the colonial wars would have been far less intense. Had the system of relations surrounding Italy been different – had Nazism not yet risen in Germany, for instance – the intervention would have been less likely, while the attempt to negotiate the annexation of Ethiopia would have remained probable. Had Italy's strategy not been linked to a long-held revisionist foreign policy programme, the opportunity to gain Ethiopia would not have been considered vital. A dialectical account which takes into consideration how the context, strategy and discourse of Italian foreign policy evolved over time is able to offer a complex and persuasive reconstruction of a key episode in Italy's foreign policy behaviour under fascism as well as of its overall development.

Conclusions

In this chapter I have analysed Italian foreign policy under fascism from the point of view of its domestic and international orientation. As I have argued, the discussion around this issue has been often framed around the confrontation between domestic accounts and international explanations. These contributions have typically failed to engage with one another due to the excessively empiricist ethos and fragmentation of the historiographical scholarship. Further, this lack of engagement has further led to ignorance of the wider theoretical and normative implications that such debate has proved to have.

By drawing on the conceptualisations sketched out in Chapter 1, I have suggested more complex and theoretically-informed accounts of the subject matter and have assessed their limits and virtues. All models point to interesting elements and processes at play in Italy's fascist foreign policy, although only dualist and dialectical accounts advance ways to integrate them in a coherent narrative. Among dialectical accounts in particular, the strategic-relational model offers an exhaustive account of the subject matter centred on the dynamic interplay of context, strategy, and discourse.

4 Italian foreign policy

The 'First Republic' (1943–1992)

From fallen to 'normal' power: the reinvention of Italian foreign policy

With the fascist regime in ruins and the Second World War in its last phases, the dramatic events of autumn 1943 laid the first foundation for the democratic reconstruction of Italy. After Mussolini's fall on 25 July and the signing of the armistice on 8 September, the first foreign policy act of the Badoglio government came with the declaration of war against Germany on 13 October. Although the position of Italy was to change formally from that of enemy to that of 'co-belligerent', from then on the country was to experience possibly the most difficult and ambiguous phase of the conflict. On the one hand, it suffered the advance of Nazi Germany and the occupation of the country's entire Northern territory; on the other, the South was transformed into a military base from where the Allied forces, together with the Resistance movement, launched the long campaign for the liberation of the country (Aga Rossi 1985).

In itself, this turbulent military situation created much of the scope for the ambiguity which characterised the Allied Powers' political relations with the 'new' Italy (Poggiolini 1990; Ellwood 1977, 1985; Harper 1987). On the one hand, Britain was in favour of a 'punitive' solution to the Italian problem and was supportive of the monarchy as the institution that could hold in check the dangerous revolutionary ferments which were sweeping through the country; on the other, the US ('the nation least offended and damaged by fascist policies in peace and war' – Tarchiani 1955: 80) was pushing for a more lenient treatment of the ex-fascist state, for greater cooperation with the Vatican, and for the establishment of a truly democratic form of government (Stuart Hughes 1953; Quartararo 1986; Rostagni 1990; Di Nolfo 1978).

The ambiguities of policy combined with the economic and social unrest to create a period of formidable tension and uncertainty, which in turn fed back into Italy's nascent foreign policy. Between 1943 and 1945 the country was torn between the desire to quickly re-legitimise itself internationally and the fear that the peace treaty – despite widespread talk of a 'just peace' for Italy – could bring about an even greater humiliation (Di Nolfo 1986; Cialdea 1967; Poggiolini 1990). A step forward in the direction hoped for by the Badoglio government – and especially by the Secretary General to the Foreign Ministry, Renato Prunas – came on 4 March 1944 with the USSR's diplomatic recognition, the very first since the armistice (Arcidiacono 1990; Di Nolfo 1985). Besides the obvious surprise and irritation expressed by the United States and Britain, neither of which had been informed of the move by the Soviet ally, this development accelerated important domestic political dynamics in Italy. The return of Palmiro Togliatti from Moscow and the so-called 'svolta di Salerno' – the announcement that the PCI was ready to join all the other democratic political forces to create the first truly democratic government, to be led eventually by the anti-fascist Ivanoe Bonomi – marked the beginning of that period of 'national unity' which was to end three years later, in March 1947.

Amidst revolutionary outbursts and signs of economic collapse, the second Bonomi government – featuring the Christian Democrat Alcide De Gasperi as Foreign Minister, after the British had vetoed the more experienced (but anti-monarchist) Carlo Sforza – announced Italy's liberation on 25 April 1945, two weeks before the general European armistice. The political life of the 'new' Italy was to be tentatively reorganised around the rejection of the monarchy and the establishment of the Republic (2 June 1946), and the drafting of a new Constitution by the *Assemblea Costituente* (which would come into effect in January 1948).

Just as these developments unfolded in Italy, the unity of the international coalition against nazi-fascism came under increasing pressure, a process which was to slowly escalate into the Cold War. As the region around Greece and Turkey came to be progressively identified as the theatre of the confrontation between the two superpowers, so too did interest in the country of Italy – in its fate and positioning – suddenly increase, especially in Washington and Moscow (on US strategic interests and the 1945 Cleveland Memoradum, see Aga Rossi 1985: 38). De Gasperi, who had been brusquely refused an invitation to visit Washington in March 1945, was now granted one in January 1947, thanks to the mediation of Vatican officials and the keen involvement of the Italian Ambassador in Washington, Alberto Tarchiani. As is well known, this visit had important (if not historic) repercussions not only on the international profile and positioning of Italy, but also on its domestic politics – although probably, at that time, neither of these had been entirely intended by Rome and Washington (Del Pero 2001; Collotti 1977; Scoppola 1977: 295–318; Galante 1980).

After the eruption of a new crisis of government, De Gasperi formed his fourth government in May 1947, calling Carlo Sforza to the Foreign Ministry. This time, however, the government excluded the forces from the Left (PCI and the *Partito Socialista Italiano*, PSI). It was the end of the period of 'national unity' started in 1944, the beginning of that *conventio ad excludendum* which would keep the PCI out of power for the greatest part of the post-war years, and the final establishment of the *Democrazia Cristiana* (DC) as the ruling party until the end of the 'First Republic'.

A few days later, on 5 June 1947, George Marshall announced at Harvard the launch of a massive plan of economic aid to Europe, which Italy had long invoked. By then, US President Truman had already set out his vision for the adoption of the doctrine of containment (12 March 1947) and, just a few months later, he went so far as to guarantee – under direct recommendations from the Central Intelligence Agency (CIA) – that the US would support democracy in Italy in the event of revolution (Del Pero 2003; Newell 2011: 50).

In the nascent bipolar confrontation, then, Italy was taking its first steps towards joining the Western camp. This process, however, was far from inevitable or straightforward. In 1948 De Gasperi frustrated American and European expectations by refusing to join the initiative launched by Ernest Bevin on 22 January – which was to lead to the signing of the Brussels Pact (in March 1948) and the creation of the Western European Union (WEU) in 1954 – arguing that Italy could not enter such negotiations on a par with other countries, given the inferior status to which it had been relegated by the peace treaty. Washington naturally condemned Italy's behaviour and, more generally, its continuous oscillation between East and West (Pastorelli 1987: 123–56; Sterpellone 1967: 212–3). The atmosphere of profound uncertainty thus reached a climax in the run-up to the first democratic elections (April 1948), and started to wane only when it became clear that the DC had secured an overwhelming success (on the role of the CIA in the 1948 elections, see Galante 1978: 142–7).

Italy was to approach the negotiations for the Atlantic Treaty with a broad majority in government, but having to fight ill-disguised hostility from most European powers (with the exception of France; Serra and Duroselle 1984) and the US. In the end President Truman's reluctant invitation to take part in the decisive stages of the negotiating of the Atlantic Treaty gave way to a fierce parliamentary debate in Italy, with the PCI and PSI opposing the treaty, and the DC, the *Partito Socialdemocratico Italiano* (PSDI), and the *Partito Liberale Italiano* (PLI) in favour of it (Varsori 1990). De Gasperi's solid rule of his party and majority – which many party members stigmatised as somewhat absolutist – proved crucial in obtaining the vote the government needed to make Italy sign the Treaty on 4 April 1949 (Vezzosi 1990: 215).

A similar uncertainty surrounded Italy's participation in the first phases of the European integration process (Pastorelli 1987: 145–208; Sforza 1952). Italy joined the negotiations for the European Coal and Steel Community (ECSC) from their inception, but again the Italian parliament was the last to ratify the treaty, in yet another sign of reluctance and uncertainty. The same dynamics would resurface in the case of the negotiations for a European Defence Community (EDC). On the one hand, De Gasperi and Sforza resolutely took the lead – suffice it to mention here De Gasperi's campaign for 'article 38' of the EDC treaty, the one designed to establish a political community.[1] On the other hand, the complications on the domestic front multiplied (on Trieste, see Novak 1970; Favaretto and Greco 1997). Eventually, the eighth and last De Gasperi government – formed after the turbulent electoral campaign of spring 1953 – fell before the treaty had been ratified; this, together with the rejection of the French *Assemblée Nationale*, was enough to make the EDC project collapse.

Despite the end of the De Gasperi era, with its broad and stable parliamentary majorities, a certain line of Europeanism in Italian foreign policy carried on through the 1950s. Heading the Foreign Ministry from September 1954 to May 1957, Gaetano Martino took the initiative to convene the Messina Conference of June 1955 which was to re-launch the integration process after the EDC crisis. When the negotiations were successfully completed and the treaties ready to be signed, he also took pride in suggesting Rome as a suitable venue for the signing ceremony, which took place on 25 March 1957 (Battaglia 2000). Italy ratified the treaties establishing the European Economic Community (EEC) and the European Atomic Energy Community (EURATOM) only after a difficult parliamentary debate, which featured the vocal opposition of the PCI, the quasi-abstention of the PSI, and the disillusionment of the federalists like Altiero Spinelli, who resented the lack of a political dimension to the newly born economic community (Spinelli 2000).

By the mid-1950s, however, the general political scenario of Italian foreign policy had changed substantially. In particular, the election of the former NATO-opponent and staunch neutralist Giovanni Gronchi as President of the Republic in April 1955 came to symbolically mark the end of the first phase of post-war foreign policy – that of reconstruction through the choices for Europe and the Atlantic Pact. Only 10 years after the momentous events of 1945, Italy was ready to embark upon a markedly different course of foreign policy – active to the point of revisionism (Magrini 1992: 58–73). Capturing a sentiment particularly widespread in Italy at the time, the foreign policy manifesto which the President enthusiastically presented in his swearing-in speech featured the intention to strengthen Italy's relations with the USSR and with the People's Republic of China (whose entry into the United Nations Gronchi came to sponsor), but also the need to reform the pillar of the Western political bloc, NATO. Not surprisingly, this turn was met with apprehension and alarmism in Washington – and in Rome by the fiercely anti-Communist US Ambassador Claire Booth Luce – where many feared that Italy 'was going Communist' (Nuti 1999; Ortona 1986: 52–7, 128–31; Wollemborg 1983: 34). When Gronchi visited the US in February 1956, however, many realised that Italy's loyalty to NATO was not at stake. In an inspired speech to the American Congress, Gronchi talked with unexpected eloquence of the need to reform NATO, and in particular article 2 of the treaty, in order to strengthen political consultation and solidarity among the allies.[2]

More generally Gronchi – and, with him, Amintore Fanfani, Foreign Minister and later Head of Government (July 1958–February 1959, July 1960–June 1963 respectively) – sponsored a host of initiatives (usually inconsequential and unwelcome, see Andreotti 1988: 35–43) aimed at promoting détente and placing Italy as a bridge and mediator between the West and the East, the North and the South (Vigezzi 1992; Coralluzzo 1991). Gronchi's eccentric and somewhat nationalist approach naturally converged with some of the claims expressed by the then emerging non-aligned movement, although the political and cultural closeness to this movement was never allowed to put Italy's role in NATO seriously at stake (La Pira 1971; Fanfani 1978). Further, this approach combined with the larger trends of progressive decentralisation, pluralisation and fragmentation characteristic of Italian foreign policy in the late 1950s. It was at roughly this time that economic foreign policy started to run parallel to (and at times collude with) the official foreign policy of Italy, with the effect of multiplying the country's diplomatic channels, especially towards the East and South (On Enrico Mattei, see Frankel 1960; Perrone 1989).

As gradually became apparent, Gronchi and Fanfani were merely preparing the ground for a change which had long been expected in Italian domestic politics, i.e. the first turn towards the Left. For the first time since the period of post-war national unity, between 1962 and 1963 Italy came to be governed by majorities which – aside from the hegemonic DC – included (or benefited from the external support of) the PSI. While the latter had progressed in its acceptance of NATO as a 'purely defensive' yet indispensable pillar of a stable international order through the 1950s (especially after the repression in Hungary of 1956), since the end of the De Gasperi era the DC had seen the emergence of a powerful internal faction led by Fanfani himself (the so-called *base* – 'grass-roots') which lobbied intensely in favour of an opening to the Left. The rise of the leadership of Aldo Moro in the 1962 DC party congress of Naples acted as a catalyst for the first government of the centre-left.

The inevitable concerns and apprehensions voiced in Washington felt much less urgent this time. As a matter of fact, when the first centre-left government was finally formed in February 1962 it had already received the *ex-ante* blessing of the newly appointed President of the United States, John Fitzgerald Kennedy, as well as that of the Vatican.[3] Indeed, the changing political scenario in Italy seemed to tie in extraordinarily well with Pope John XXIII's reformist zeal and pacifist orientation, as well as JFK's enlightened leadership.

Despite the novelty brought about by the new political arrangement, the foreign policy of centre-left governments did not stray much from the one pursued by DC's *monocolore* (single-party governments) of the 1950s. In Europe, Italy showed determination in working for that vision of a 'new Euro-atlantic community' which President Kennedy had laid out in his Philadelphia speech of 4 July 1962. Most notably, this implied a firm support of EEC enlargement to Britain and a harsh confrontation with De Gaulle's France, which grew particularly intense after France's exit from NATO's integrated command in March 1966 (Pistone 1989: 181).

The year 1968 proved crucial in the development of centre-left governments and, more generally, in the politics of Italy, ushering the country into one of its most difficult decades since the Second Word War. First, the economic miracle of the late 1950s and early 1960s – and the social stability associated with it – started to give way to a creeping economic recession and a phase of social unrest, already sweeping through Europe and America, which was to escalate further in Italy during the 1970s (Santoro 1977: 185–202). Second, at the international level the tragic repression of the Czech insurrection by Soviet forces in August 1968 provided the catalyst for the further distancing of the Italian PCI from the Cominform and, in turn, paved the ground for the gradual affirmation of the so-called Euro-communism (Rizzo 1977; Bonanate 1978). Third, the war in Vietnam highlighted once again the divisions between Italy's public opinion and official foreign policy – especially vis-à-vis the US – torn between the traditional Atlantic loyalty and the search for a greater role as mediators between the two blocs (Sica 1991).

The elections of spring 1968 saw the heavy defeat of the party that had just been admitted to share in government responsibilities – the PSI – while the DC and especially the PCI gained substantially. In electoral terms, then, the centre-left experiment had revealed itself to be a failure. The political situation had deteriorated into an open polarisation between the DC and the PCI, and a strengthening of the neo-fascist movement. After the experiment of the centre-left and the brief 'adventure' of the centre-right Tambroni government, the only viable alternative appeared to be a coalition government including the PCI – a political formula which came to be known as the *compromesso storico* ('historic compromise') and which would characterise the government of the emerging DC leader Giulio Andreotti (July 1976–March 1978) (Romeo 2000).

No doubt such a move had been made possible by the PCI's gradual acceptance of the Western pillars of Italian foreign policy – NATO and the EEC – which the party leader Enrico Berlinguer ultimately made known in a famous interview with *il Corriere della Sera* on 15 June 1976. The formation of the first government of national solidarity, however, was seen in Washington as posing a grave menace to the stability of Italy and Europe. The apprehensions were such that the American Ambassador in Rome, John Volpe, and later the US President Jimmy Carter himself, publicly opposed such a development, the main reason why relations between the two countries remained tense until the end of the decade (Olivi 1978; Wollemborg 1983: 441, 447, 559).

The government of 'national solidarity' born out of the 'historic compromise' pursued a 'consensual' and low-profile foreign policy, without the substantial involvement of domestic public opinion and political parties (Mombelli 1967). In Europe, Italy resuscitated the idea of a 'conference on East-West security', especially through the Foreign Ministers Nenni and Moro, in the belief that, differently from the 1950s, détente was now inevitable. When Moro signed the final Act of the Conference on Security and Cooperation in Europe (CSCE) in August 1975, as both President of the EEC and Head of Government, Italy symbolically attained one of the foreign policy objectives most dearly cherished over the previous twenty years – namely the completion of a process of détente in which it could claim the role of protagonist (Gaja 1995: 201–9). In matters of foreign policy Italy also came to enthusiastically support the establishment of those mechanisms and institutions which gave birth, in the early 1970s, to European Political Cooperation (EPC) (Bonvicini 1983).

Thanks to skilful diplomatic manoeuvring, and despite the opposition of some countries such as Germany, Italy also managed to join the 'Group of 7' from its initial meeting in Rambouillet, in November 1975. Further, throughout the 1970s all of the major parties (DC, PSI, and PCI) converged around the need to strengthen Italy's pro-Arab policy in the Middle East and the Mediterranean. In this area, as in so many others, Italy used the EPC as a 'cover' and a 'multiplier' to give more credibility to its international initiatives, which included strengthening diplomatic and economic relations with states such as Libya and Algeria – especially in the wake of the 1973 oil crisis, as a means to differentiate energy supply – as well as promoting the cause of the Palestinian Liberation Organization (PLO) as the legitimate representative of the Palestinian people. Finally, in 1972 Italy launched the plan for a Conference on Security in the Mediterranean, to parallel the process of détente and dialogue which had been initiated between the two blocs in Europe.

The experiment of the 'historic compromise' – and with it its 'consensual' foreign policy – ultimately ended in tragedy when, in March 1978, the *Brigate Rosse* kidnapped and later killed the DC leader (and catalyst of the turn to the left) Aldo Moro. This tragic (and still obscure) episode marked the apex of the domestic crisis of the 1970s but, at the same time, it also marked the beginning of its end. One year later, in a significantly changed international context, the DC leadership of Francesco Cossiga, and especially the rise of the new PSI leader Bettino Craxi, ushered Italy into a new political phase.

NATO's decision of December 1979 to 'modernise' its nuclear weapons in Europe (the so-called 'Euromissiles') provided one key test, demanding that countries such as West Germany, Belgium and Italy open new sites. Against the background of growing opposition from public opinion and the extreme Left, the Cossiga government managed to gain a comfortable majority of votes in the Parliament thanks to the support of the PSI, whose new leader Bettino Craxi was increasingly eager to prove his Atlanticist credentials (Cremasco 1984; Lagorio 1998).[4]

Domestically, the end of the economic crisis and of the acute phase of terrorism of the late 1970s gave way to the progressive consolidation of two parties in particular: the DC and the PSI. It was the latter – with the cooperation of the leftist factions of the former – that revamped Italian foreign policy to make the country a dynamic (if not always unambiguous) player in several international arenas (Aliboni 1985).[5]

In Europe, Italy's attempt to re-launch the process of European integration which had stalled in the 1970s produced the two notable initiatives: arch-federalist and PCI member Altiero Spinelli's ambitious project for a full political union, which came to be examined and approved by the European Parliament in July 1982, and the 'Genscher-Colombo plan' of 1981 (from the names of Italian and German Foreign Ministers Emilio Colombo and Hans-Dietrich Genscher), for cooperation in the fields of foreign and security policy justice and culture, which produced the 'Solemn Declaration on the European Union' of Stuttgart in 1983 – but little else.

During the country's EEC Presidency semester, and once again on the strength of the European 'cover', Italy skilfully managed to enhance its role in the Mediterranean and the Middle East, supporting that process of Euro-Arab dialogue which led to the Declaration of Venice (June 1980) and sponsoring the request that Arafat's movement be associated with the on-going negotiations on the Arab-Israeli peace process. More generally, Italy's pro-PLO policy ran almost uncontested through the 1980s – supported mainly by the PCI, the leftist factions of the DC (led by Andreotti himself), the Vatican and the PSI, and opposed only by lay parties such as the PLI and Spadolini's *Partito Rebuppli-cano Italiano* (PRI).[6]

But it was in 1985 that Italy was to gain much profile and exposure in European affairs. Welcoming Jacques Delors' attempts to speed up the completion of the common market, and amid the euphoric anticipation for the headline goal of '1992', Italy concluded its Presidency semester at the December Milan European Council by pushing through the decision to open the Intergovernmental Conference (IGC) which would produce the Single European Act two years later. Controversy was caused by the decision of the European Council's President Craxi not to accept vetoes and to put the decision to a majority vote, triggering a furious reaction from Britain, and opposition from Denmark and Greece (Varsori 1998: 234ff.; Olivi 1993: 278ff.). Greeted with triumphalism and satisfaction in Italy, Craxi's show of resolve was in fact short-lived and soon tempered by the more tactical and defensive approach favoured by Foreign Minister Giulio Andreotti (August 1983–July 1989).

Rather inevitably, however, Italy's Mediterranean policy was to clash with the Middle Eastern policy of the United States following the revolution in Iran. The Sigonella crisis of October 1985 came to epitomise this tension (Cassese 1987; Silj 1998; Martini 1999). After the hijacking of the cruise-boat *Achille Lauro* by a group of Palestinian extremists, Italy actively collaborated with Arafat, his emissaries, and Mubarak in Egypt to obtain the release of the hostages, possibly with a view towards legitimising the two leaders as interlocutors of the West. Their release was followed by US intervention against the hijackers, who were forced to land at the Sicilian base of Sigonella. Here, however, the US forces intending to capture the terrorists met with armed resistance from the *Carabinieri*, in a dramatic stand-off. The tension only waned following personal negotiations between US President Reagan and Craxi. Sigonella came to epitomise the dilemma of Italian foreign policy in the Middle East – caught between its pro-Arab leanings and the country's loyalty to the Atlantic Alliance and, at its heart, the US.[7]

From the mid-1980s, however, the most important scenario for Italian foreign policy was that of East–West relations in Europe. After the tensions which had followed the December 1981 coup in Poland and the attempted murder of Pope John Paul II in May of the same year, Italy resumed political contact with the countries of the Eastern bloc at a time of change in the leadership in the USSR. The advent of Mikahil Gorbachev was greeted with particular enthusiasm in Rome (Gaja 1995: 239; Chiesa and Medvedev 1989: 190; Romano 2002: 234–7). Gorbachev's vision of a stronger Europe as a political interlocutor of the USSR and, most notably, of a 'common European home' – the former announced to Craxi during Italy's 1985 Presidency of the EEC and the latter to Head of Government Ciriaco De Mita during a visit to Moscow in 1988 respectively – gained immediate and widespread popularity among the political élite as well as public opinion at large. When the prospect of substantial reductions in conventional and strategic arms in the context of the Strategic Arms Reduction Treaty (START) negotiations were further improved by the Reykjavik summit of October 1986 between US President Ronald Reagan and Gorbachev and the Washington Treaty on the Intermediate-range Nuclear Force (INF) of December 1987, the jubilation of Italian foreign policy-makers was almost uncontained. Many saw Italy's traditional approach of engagement and cooperation with the USSR being vindicated. Gorbachev's visit to Rome in November 1989, just a few days after the historic fall of the Berlin Wall, predictably marked the highest point of Italy's relations with the USSR in the late 1980s.

However, the consequences of the events of November 1989, and especially the appearance of the issue of German re-unification on the European agenda, found Italy unprepared and, if anything, irritated by Kohl's activism on the one hand, and by the exclusion from the negotiations which were to lead to the '2+4' Treaty of July 1990, on the other. The uncertainty with which Italy approached the events of 1989–1990 also affected Italy's presidency of the EEC in July–December 1990, which followed a few months after the momentous decision to convene the IGC on Economic and Monetary Union (De Michelis 1996, 2003).

Such uncertainty, however, did not dissuade Foreign Minister Gianni De Michelis (July 1989–June 1992) from pursuing his pet project of a closer partnership between Italy and Central and Eastern European countries – now free from the Soviet orbit, but not yet in Germany's (IAI 1991; Mastny 1995). The *Pentagonale*, however, soon evolved into a loose framework for economic and cultural cooperation – and was transformed into the 'Central European Initiative' in July 1992 – with its political value greatly impoverished by its increasing geographical extension and, above all, by the rapid dissolution of one of its founding members, Yugoslavia.

The break-up of Yugoslavia and the simultaneous war in the Gulf provided the first real tests of foreign policy after the end of the Cold War. In the first case, Italy was surprised by the declaration of independence from Slovenia and Croatia in June 1991, and frustrated by Germany's unilateral initiative to grant such recognition (December 1991), which came after De Michelis' repeated efforts to push for a concerted European solution (Brioni Accords, July 1991) and after Germany's initial agreement to a collective European decision. Following the veto from Croatia and Slovenia over a possible Italian role in the peacekeeping mission, Italy's participation in the conflict was to be limited to a supporting function, at least in the first years of the conflict: mainly, the use of the NATO bases on its Eastern coast and the WEU-NATO sponsored monitoring of the embargo against Serbia-Montenegro in the Adriatic Sea.

The conflict in the Persian Gulf of January 1991, on the other hand, provoked a much larger debate in the Italian political élite and public opinion at large (IAI 1992; Guazzone 1992; Coralluzzo 2000: 308–38; Davidson 2011: 59–63). After the failure of all attempts at mediation – including, among others, one led by Gorbachev himself, which Italy had expectantly supported – the Andreotti government decided to contribute three frigates and eight *Tornados* to the US-led but UN-sponsored *Desert Storm* operation – a contribution which at the time could not but be defined 'symbolic' – and the use of the NATO bases in Sicily. The growing protest within public opinion and the outright opposition to the war from the Vatican posed severe problems for the government, but in the end these were overcome by the rapid conclusion of the operation. What was less easy to take in was Italy's exclusion from the series of talks held between the US, Great Britain, France and Germany at the end of the Gulf war.

It was during these crises that the Italian political system underwent the most dramatic changes of its entire Republican history. In the span of two years (1992–1994) the three political parties which had dominated the political scene for the previous five decades disappeared from the horizon. The PSI and DC were shattered under the pressure of the anti-corruption judicial operation called *Mani Pulite* ('clean hands'): their establishment on trial, many of the political figures who had occupied positions of government in the last fifty years disappeared or were jailed. At the January 1991 Congress the PCI split into two distinct parties – the *Partito dei Democratici di Sinistra* (PDS) and *Partito della Rifondazione Comunista* (PRC) – after a long and troubled process of reflection on the party's new role after the end of Communism. The wave of popular referenda held between 1992 and 1993 – especially the electoral law, which was to favour the creation of a bipolar system – summed up the country's long-held desire of political change: the year 1992, symbolic in so many other ways, marked the end of the 'First Republic'.

Politics and paradigms of Italy's foreign policy in the 'First Republic'

The military occupation which followed the armistice of 8 September 1943 represented, for a few years, the most tangible and inescapable manifestation of how international relations could penetrate a country to impose their own logic on possibly every aspect of political life, including foreign policy (Catalano 1967: 419–54). The progressive institutionalisation of the Cold War further sharpened the awareness of Italy's foreign policy makers, as well as its leading political figures, that the domestic politics, foreign policy and international relations of their country were to be inter-linked for many decades to come.

After the brief period of national unity between 1943 and 1947, which reflected the then reigning climate of international solidarity, the issue of what foreign policy to adopt – if to adopt one at all – and, most importantly, how to connect it to the domestic politics and international relations of the new and democratic Italy, gained great prominence in the political debate. On the one hand, inevitable ideological differences started to emerge; on the other, the post-war conditions which had made the international anti-fascist coalition possible were rapidly giving way to an overt confrontation between the two blocs. It was in this context that the main political parties and protagonists of the new Italian democracy started to articulate their different visions of foreign policy.

The years between 1943 and 1953 thus marked a 'creative phase' in the political debate with regards to foreign policy – indeed, possibly the most creative in the history of post-war Italy. As Spinelli notes, these debates were 'forse gli unici dibattiti di politica estera condotti nel nostro paese col senso dell'importanza della posta in gioco' ('perhaps the only foreign policy debate carried out in the country with full awareness of the issues at stake') (Spinelli 1967: 51).

In fact, from around 1953, a progressive convergence brought all major parties of the political spectrum to agree on a set of international and foreign policy priorities. As Pastorelli notes, from 1953

> The consensus around the government's decision started to expand, slowly but steadily. It reached its apex when, on 1 December 1977, the Communist party signed a motion defining the Atlantic Treaty as a 'key reference' for Italian foreign policy.
>
> (Pastorelli 1987: 233)

It was the birth of the experiment of 'national solidarity' of the late 1970s, of the 'historic compromise' and its bipartisan, consensual (if not 'unanimous') foreign policy (Tamburrano 1973). In what follows I briefly review the three main discourses of foreign policy articulated by the three main political parties – DC, PCI and PSI – between 1943 and 1977.

The Democrazia Cristiana: primacy of the international?

The traditional historiographical reading of the role which the DC, and especially its post-war leader De Gasperi, played in Italian foreign policy is both simple and powerful. Thanks to De Gasperi's Atlantic and European choices, thanks to his vision of a foreign policy firmly tied to the Western camp – as the interpretation usually goes – Italy could not only resume its proper place on the international stage in a remarkably short time, but could also enjoy the benefits of American and European assistance in economic and security matters.

Admittedly, the logic of the argument captures the fundamental correspondence between international alignments and domestic equilibria on which the DC constructed its foreign policy: Italy's international participation in NATO and the EEC, that is, meant stability and prosperity at home. Though a member of the PRI, Sforza's views were representative of this position:

> Italy is much more exposed than other countries, actually it is doubly more exposed: since it is disarmed, it can be attacked in two different ways [internal and external] [...] Only one point was not negotiable: there should be *no gaps* between our international commitments on one side, and support and guarantees for our rearmament on the other.
>
> (Sforza quoted in Vigezzi 1990: 32, emphasis added)

Yet, this narrative does not do justice to the ambiguities and uncertainties which accompanied its slow and difficult articulation. To start with, how can it accommodate the fact that it was De Gasperi himself who, in early 1948, turned down the first offer to join the Western camp (in the forming Brussels Pact) and secure a place for Italy among the nations of Europe?

Even more importantly, this interpretation plays down the vast neutralist sentiments which were present in the party, especially on the left. In 1948, for example, soon-to-be President of the Republic Giovanni Gronchi was among the most vocal opponents of the decision to join the Atlantic Alliance, together with Giuseppe Dossetti. Although with different ambitions and results, they supported a policy of neutrality or equidistance between the forming blocs. As one of their followers put it,

> To us America is not the bearer of the absolute good. [...] Neutrality is and will be for many Italians [...] the ideal aim not only of today but of the future as well. Today the policy of 'clean hands' should be the great policy of Christian Italy.
>
> (Marinelli quoted in Vezzosi 1990: 212)

In this position, two issues combined: on the one hand, the wish to de-link Italian domestic politics from international relations, i.e. not to compromise the social and political development of the country in the name of international structures of power; on the other, a doctrinal and fervent anti-Americanism.

The latter motive was especially influential not just on the Left, but also among many Catholics (and liberals such as Manlio Brosio; see De Leonardis 1990). Indeed, sectors of the Vatican visibly embraced anti-Americanism during the post-war years (Rostagni 1990). The faction led by one of its most influential figures of the time, mons. Tardini, for instance, as well as several Catholic publications such as *Civiltà Cattolica*, were overtly supportive of a strategy of neutrality (and for the affirmation of a federal European 'third force' between the two blocs) on the grounds that Italy's social and moral fabric had to be preserved from corruption from America, not to mention the USSR (Rostagni 1990: 186–7).

It was mainly due to De Gasperi's extraordinary grip on the party and the realisation that Italy, weak as it was, had more to gain from Europe and NATO than from a possible neutrality that the 'pragmatic' policy of Atlanticism and Europeanism were adopted. These allowed De Gasperi's DC – in contrast to Togliatti's PCI – to exchange the international 'impotence' of a foreign policy subserviently tied to the Western wagon for the consolidation of power and autonomy inside the country (Galante 1990: 356).

Through the 1960s and 1970s these principles were to be confirmed and strengthened by Italy's periodical re-affirmations of its Atlantic orientation. Still, some of the ambiguities that had characterised the early phases of elaboration of such a vision resurfaced intermittently to complicate the neat correspondence between inside and outside. Not by chance, from 1955 Gronchi again represented the main inspirer of such an adaptation. The turn to the left of 1963 paralleled a return to some of the concerns voiced in the late 1940s – and again, equidistance became a desirable foreign policy priority (Vasile 1967: 1012–20).

The 1970s confirmed such trends, and the rise of the leadership of Andreotti was crucial in shaping Italy's foreign policy, both in terms of style and content, towards an ambiguous 'pacifist Atlanticism' (Hassner 1975). While Italy's participation in NATO was never seriously put into question, the pacifist and ecumenical character of the country's foreign policy combined with Andreotti's tactical and subtly nationalist diplomatic style to produce a distinctive course: this featured a further opening to the Soviet bloc, an intensification of all those measures designed to facilitate détente as well as an overt support of the Palestinian cause in the Middle East (Romeo 2000). As I shall illustrate below, around this uneasy combination of policies wide sectors of the other two major parties (PCI and PSI) converged.

The Partito Socialista Italiano: primacy of the domestic?

Although the PSI was only intermittently in government between 1943 and 1977, the party elaborated a clear vision of not only foreign policy, but also of the relation between foreign policy, domestic politics and international relations from the very beginning of the debates of 1947–1948 (Benzoni *et al.* 1993). After all, Nenni was to serve as Foreign Minister for a brief period of time in 1946 and then again in 1968, the only non-Christian Democrat, apart from Giuseppe Saragat, ever to hold this position.

At the heart of the Socialists' understanding of foreign policy was the consideration that, to use Nenni's words, Italy could only have 'the domestic politics of its foreign policy':

> We would have had the domestic politics of our foreign policy. This is what happened with the Triple Alliance, and with the Rome-Berlin axis. In both cases, domestic politics had been strongly constrained by military alliances.
> (Nenni quoted in Canavero 1990: 225)

By this Nenni meant that the domestic political development of Italy – which was the real area of concern of the party – was to be decided by the foreign policy choices made by Italy. Just as the Christian Democrats, the Socialists too understood that there existed a perfect correspondence between the international relations and the domestic politics of Italy. They differed from the DC in that they feared the very solution which De Gasperi's party was advancing. This was Nenni's motivation in serving as Foreign Minister before the collapse of the government of 'national unity' in 1947: to avoid Italy being entangled in an alliance with 'conservative' powers.

Precisely because the party's real interest lay in domestic politics, and aware of the close relationship between this and foreign policy, the Italian Socialists looked at the international relations of the time with special concern. The reformist character of the PSI, and the so-called 'principle of unity' with the Communist party – progressively to be abandoned by Nenni's party – meant that in the late 1940s the Socialists could not accept that the joining of the Western camp could halt the process of those domestic social reforms on which the moral greatness of the country depended. Thus, Italy's entry in the Atlantic Pact was, according to Nenni, 'un delitto storico' ('a historic murder'), and indeed paralleled the break-up of the domestic national front: they were 'due aspetti dello stesso fenomeno' ('two aspects of the same question') (Nenni quoted in Benzoni 1967: 928, 936).

From this it followed that the foreign policy favoured by the PSI from the late 1940s to the mid-1950s was one inspired by pacifism and international solidarity, equidistance and neutrality between the two blocs. Indeed, the function of Italy was to advance and preserve the dialogue between the West and the East, entertaining political but also economic relations with both – Italy's role was to embody a synthesis between Orient and Occident (Nenni quoted in Benzoni 1967: 935).

The foreign policy position of the PSI, however, was to evolve quite visibly in the following decades. As early as the mid-1950s, and especially after the events in Hungary of 1956, the PSI was the first to welcome the signals of the first phase of détente as a positive development for international affairs. Indeed, as they expected, détente was to have beneficial domestic effects, which materialised in the creation of the first centre-left government: this included the PSI in 1963.

Progressively, the PSI moved further away from its original position of anti-Atlanticism to identify international peace with international stability. This finally led to its acceptance of NATO as a 'purely defensive' organisation and as a pillar of the international order, as Nenni defined it in a parliamentary debate of January 1962. The Atlantic and Europeanist motives combined with a special emphasis on the role of the UN, the institution most fit to deal with threats to international security and peace, and an interest in the Third World. This movement towards the positions of the DC was the first sign of that convergence which would lead, together with the contribution from the PCI, to the formula of the 'historic compromise'.

The Partito Comunista Italiano: between internationalism and a 'national way'

Because of its position as avant-garde of the Communist front in Italy, or 'fifth column' as it would later be called, from its very inception the vision of foreign policy of the PCI had to combine a national and an international dimension. The climate of international solidarity which accompanied the PCI's 'svolta di Salerno' and its inclusion in the government was the precondition for the adoption of a foreign policy of 'amicizia con tutti, specialmente con l'Unione Sovietica' ('friendship with everyone, especially the Soviet Union') (Galante 1990: 289).

The motive of internationalism which the PCI advocated for Italy and its foreign policy, however, was bound to clash with an increasing international polarisation which, for the PCI, primarily meant the danger of co-optation from the USSR. Precisely to *avoid* this nexus between international and domestic politics – which for the PCI was even more strict than for any other party in Italy – Togliatti's party started to claim that Italy had its own 'national and democratic way' to socialism. A way, in other words, that would enable the party to have that basic level of autonomy from Moscow, which in turn formed the precondition for any participation in the political life of Italy. In the words of the successor of Togliatti, Luigi Longo, as early as 1945:

> We are infinitely grateful to the USSR, England and United States of America who endured the most severe trials to free Europe and the world from nazi fascism [...]. But [...] we will be infinitely more grateful to them as soon as they will allow us to govern our own matters.
>
> (Longo quoted in Galante 1990: 297–8)

Naturally, this process, as well as developments in the Soviet bloc, was also at the basis of that strategy of *policentrismo* which Togliatti promoted from 1947 to 1956 in an attempt to loosen up the Cominform's grip on European Communist parties (Galli 1967: 950–2). As with the Socialists, the PCI's primary concern was domestic politics, and this translated primarily into a determination to avoid a conservative turn in social and political affairs (Galli 1977: 96).

Both of these concerns (primacy of domestic politics and rejection of any undue pressures from Moscow) led the PCI to consider foreign policy beyond its scope of action and, therefore, to adopt a balanced approach in this area. In concrete terms, this meant a strong opposition to Italy's participation with NATO (and, in the early years, Europe), but an equally strong condemnation for the Soviet's actions in Hungary 1956 and in Czechoslovakia in 1968.

The progressive convergence of the PCI towards the acceptance of NATO – which started off in 1968 and culminated in 1976 – was the logical conclusion of a process which privileged the domestic political consequences of the party's actions (the 'historic compromise') rather than international affairs per se. In the titanic confrontation between domestic politics, with its own equilibria, and international politics, with its own logic, the PCI deliberately made foreign policy a casualty, sacrificing it on the altar of participation in government (Sassoon 1976, 1981).

1977–1992: patterns of convergence

As mentioned above, the 1970s marked the convergence of the three major Italian political parties not only around a common domestic political platform (Moro's famous 'parallel convergences'), but also around a set of foreign policy objectives. As Giulio Andreotti noted in 1976,

> Not only are the Atlanticist and European issues not contested, but also the policy of détente and the North-South policies (that is, the relations with the developing countries) [...] are included in this vast area of consensus.
>
> (Andreotti quoted in Sassoon 1978: 98)

Now that the conflictual stage of the 1940s and 1950s was gone, foreign policy became consensual or – to use the words of Luigi Vittorio Ferraris – 'unanimous'. By the same token, because of the nature of the political debate of the 1970s–1980s (mainly inward-looking and concerned with the domestic political situation of Italy) foreign policy was also pushed to the margins of the political debate, increasingly neglected, neutralised, and ultimately stalled (Putnam 1977).

Naturally, differences among the three main parties persisted, but in the field of foreign affairs these were no more significant than the internal factions which each party had to accommodate. Thus, within the DC Atlanticist leanings coexisted with universalist tendencies, and 'minimalist' understandings of foreign policy were side by side with 'maximalist' visions of Italy's role in the world (Vannicelli 1974).

Throughout the 1980s and early 1990s, when the international developments leading to the end of the Cold War suddenly materialised, most of the traditional and bipartisan party foreign policy priorities, such as détente and East–West dialogue, variations in the ideas of foreign policy of the DC, PSI and PCI were minimal. Even the Socialist experiment of the 1980s to revamp Italy's foreign policy more or less followed the traditional course of moderate Atlanticism and opening to the East, complemented by a stronger resolve to make Italy's voice heard in the realm of European and transatlantic affairs.

Only the domestic political crisis of 1992–1994 substantially restructured the debate around foreign policy. In time, this led to the articulation of new and competing visions of foreign policy in its relations with the domestic politics and international relations of Italy.

The analysis of Italy's foreign policy in the 'First Republic': the state of the art

The study of Italian foreign policy between 1943 and 1992 is marked by a wealth of works and publications devoted mostly to two temporal segments: the 'creative period' between 1943 and 1960, and that of the end of the Cold War. The great majority of these works are historical and descriptive in nature, but more analytical contributions are also well-represented. Theory, however, is almost wholly absent.

Doubtless this is due, at least in part, to the scarce purchase which theory enjoys in international studies in Italy – a phenomenon affecting not just foreign policy, but from which foreign policy suffers with particular intensity. However, part of the reason also stems from the paradoxical landscape of the extant works, which seem to be locked in a long-standing confrontation between two opposing camps: on the one hand are the works which see Italy's foreign policy as having been ineluctably determined by the iron logic of the Cold War; on the other, there are those who argue that in fact Italian foreign policy was for its most part the expression of domestic dynamics. Both strands of analysis recognise that foreign policy, domestic politics and international relations have interacted in a complex fashion. What they radically differ on is the issue of causation from one domain to the other, and from both towards foreign policy.

International explanations

A first group of analyses has stressed international determinants such as the Cold War and bipolarism, Italy's participation in the Western alliance and especially NATO, or the hegemonic influence of the US on Italian foreign policy. This is possibly the most frequent and popular interpretation of Italian foreign policy during the 'First Republic', an outlook exemplified by Paul Ginsborg's description of Italy as simply the 'Bulgaria of NATO' (Ginsborg 1994: 260). Along these lines, Carlo Maria Santoro suggested that,

> During the republican period, the dynamics of the global context was indeed the key independent variable in deciding Italian foreign policy, much more so than in the two preceding periods (liberal and fascist age).
>
> (Santoro 1991: 198)

By 'global context' Santoro meant not only the bipolar character of the international system and Italy's participation in a hegemonic and asymmetric subsystem such as NATO, but also Italy's geopolitical position, on the border between East and West. In stressing Italy's particular geopolitical position, Carlo Jean (1995: 225ff.) advances a similar interpretation, as does Sergio Romano:

> Facts proved that the biggest international asset of defeated Italy was constituted by two items: its geopolitical position and the disputes among the winners. That was the starting point for Italian foreign policy at the end of the war.
>
> (Romano 2002: 34–5)

Interestingly, together with the geopolitical motive Romano adds another determinant of Italian foreign policy, equally international in nature, i.e. the particular systemic position of Italy between the two blocs, which enabled the country to pursue a policy of 'determinant weight' or exert a form of 'blackmailing power'. The issue of the autonomy (or lack thereof) which Italy enjoyed in its foreign policy is, thus, another typical concern of these analyses (see, most recently, Ratti 2012). Given the rigid and neat bipolar geometry of the international system, these contributions deem the margins of autonomy left to Italian foreign policy since the Atlantic choice of 1949 rather narrow.

Similarly, both Santoro and Romano tend to put forward the view that structural factors such as Italy's geopolitical position determined cross-historical continuities in the foreign policy (and foreign policy style) of Italy, such as the so-called 'presentism', its declaratory nature and micro-nationalism. Far from being the result of particular domestic political arrangements or of personalities, these were in fact caused by external, environmental factors.

In addition, these interpretations usually extend their reach to consider not only foreign policy, but domestic politics as well in its connection to international politics. For instance, political developments such as the turn to the centre-left in the early 1960s, or the 'historic compromise' of the mid-1970s, are interpreted as the result of a change in the international context rather than in Italy's domestic political climate. Again, Romano suggests that,

> Berlinguer's analysis on the question of the PCI's participation in government [...] proved the importance of the international situation in the political life of Italy. Foreign policy [...] 'made' Italian domestic politics. That had happened at the beginning of the Sixties, when the formation of the centre-left government had been eased considerably by the beginning of détente. It happened again [...] in the second half of the Seventies.
>
> (Romano 2002: 190–1)

This view, then, maintains that the international system of the early Cold War years penetrated Italy's fragile domestic environment to reproduce its defining conflict on a national scale (Pasquino 1974). Thus, just as bipolarism was opposing the US to the USSR, so was ideological polarisation responsible for the latent political struggle between the two major parties, the DC and PCI. Just as détente came to interrupt this confrontation, so did the turn to the left open a period of collaboration among the major parties.

Last, just as this interpretation was thought to be particularly apt in accounting for the formative years of Italian foreign policy, not coincidentally it resurfaced powerfully in the academic debate at the end of the Cold War. When the domestic political system of Italy started to crumble at the beginning of the 1990s, it became commonplace to blame the end of the Cold War and the upsetting of its stable equilibrium (for instance, Coralluzzo 2000).

Domestic explanations

At the opposite end of the interpretative continuum, the second group of perspectives tends to privilege internal and domestic factors, rather than international dynamics. These contributions recognise that the ideological confrontation between the DC and PCI mirrored the international bipolar divide since the late 1940s – with this correspondence being especially close in the formative years of the Republic – yet they assign greater explanatory force to the former, rather than the latter. Thus, for instance, Daniel Sassoon argues that

> The Italian system exhibits a high degree of linkage between internal and external developments. [...] Italy must be considered as an extreme case of the subordination of foreign policy to domestic politics once the major choices of 1947–50 were made.
>
> (Sassoon 1978: 198)

Similarly, in presenting Primo Vannicelli's study of Italy's accession to the EEC and NATO, Stanley Hoffmann affirms that

> The foreign policy choices of Italy were above all geared to, and shaped by the domestic scene. [...] The two basic choices of Italian foreign policy [Italy's entry into NATO and the EEC] started as a means of establishing within Italy a certain kind of political majority. [...] Later, they became a means of keeping the Centre in power. [...] By making the test of the 'aptitude to govern' a foreign policy test, the Italian political system cleverly defused domestic tensions, since it shifted the vocabulary of politics from explosive internal issues to rather Byzantine external ones.
>
> (Hoffmann 1974a: ix–x; see also 1974b)

Last, Angelo Panebianco advances a similar thesis by explicitly relating the phase of 'low profile' which occurred in 1970s to the characteristics and dynamics of the party system of the time:

> In the Italian case, it is possible to argue that the foreign policy system was characterised, after the initial settling phase of the Christian democrats' regime, by an incompatibility between domestic goals (protection of the political equilibria) and external goals (enhancement of the national status). [...] The domestic aim [...] required [...] a constant 'minimisation' of all the tensions coming from foreign policy [...] Hence [...] the neutralisation, the 'de-politicisation' [...] of Italy's international action.
>
> (Panebianco 1977: 863)[8]

Although aware of the powerful impact of the international context on Italy's foreign policy, these interpretations advance the view that foreign policy has not been so much determined by its bipolar logic, but rather by the peculiar characteristics of Italy's domestic system. It is no coincidence that these three contributions were written around the years in which the 'historic compromise' loomed at the horizon of Italian domestic politics. The consensual (and necessarily minimalistic) foreign policy pursued by Italy did indeed parallel the consensual phase of the political debate; these authors perceive this parallel as being more than merely coincidental – indeed, as a causation effect from the domestic level to that of foreign policy.

This 'bottom-up' interpretation of foreign policy has also influenced those who have carried out research of a more critical bent. For instance, scholars have argued that during the 'First Republic' the military arm found its actual rationale in the controlling of domestic tensions and revolutionary ferments, and not so much in foreign policy (Bova and Rochat 1974).

At the end of the Cold War, this view was re-articulated through the debate over whether the Italian domestic political system had indeed been revolutionised by the end of bipolarism or by endogenous dynamics. Although strictly centred on *domestic* developments, rather than developments in foreign policy, the analysis of Stefano Guzzini once again suggested that the causes of the dramatic end of the 'First Republic' (and presumably of its foreign policy as well) are to be found inside, rather than outside, the country – although at times of globalisation, Guzzini argues, it is this very distinction that collapses:

> Although not lacking in insight, [the top-down, end-of-the-Cold-War thesis] fails to give a coherent and complete account of what is happening in Italy. [...] Changes in Italy *could have happened in any international context* short of heightened East-West conflict or war. It is the implosion of a clientelistic-consociational system.
>
> (Guzzini 1994: 11, emphasis added)

Italy's foreign policy in the 'First Republic': a critical realist assessment

Was Italy's foreign policy primarily a result of the international relations of the time, as the 'international' explanations discussed above suggest? Was it instead mainly the result of domestic and endogenous developments? It is time to probe these explanations further and examine Italy's foreign policy in the 'First Republic' with a view towards measuring the validity of the frameworks elaborated in Chapter 1 against the empirical record.

Monocausal approaches

As discussed above, the thesis that Italian foreign policy has been an exclusive function of some particular features of the international relations of the time has been advanced by a good number of scholars. What are the limits and strengths of these positions?

To start with, geopolitics and neo-realism would be at one in advancing an explanation of Italian foreign policy from 1943 to 1989 as, most of all, a response to that particular international context which was the Cold War. After all, the iron curtain separating East and West placed Italy close to the forefront of the bipolar confrontation in Europe. Given the high level of proximity to the Soviet threat, neo-realism would infer, Italy had a strong incentive to follow the systemic imperative of bipolarism and align its foreign policy to the dictates of primarily NATO and West European integration.

This explanation would not, however, account for some of the very defining features of Italy's external behaviour in the period at hand. To start with, an exclusively international reading framed around the geopolitical and security dynamics of the international relations of the time could not account for the numerous instances in which Italy pursued a policy of *rapprochement* and cooperation with the Soviet bloc: from the recognition of China (which Italy came to sponsor, against Washington's approval, from the mid-1950s) to the exceptionally close economic cooperation with the USSR in the late 1950s and 1960s, or the attempted mediations at the height of the Berlin crisis of 1961.

Second, relations with the Arab world were often driven by considerations other than those deriving from the country's international commitments within NATO. The Sigonella affair in 1985 and relations with Libya more generally, for instance, showed the degree to which Italy was willing to challenge or at least complement its 'official', Western-oriented foreign policy with a course of action inspired by a logic *other than* that following from an exclusively neo-realist or geopolitical reading of the bipolar confrontation.

Italy, in other words, constantly diverged from a purely 'rational', externally driven foreign policy and instead pursued parallel and often contradictory policies at the same time. Even at those times when the bipolar confrontation grew especially intense, Italy followed the imperatives of the alliance of which it was a part, but not without ambiguities. Hence, for instance, at the time of the second Cold War and NATO's dual track decision, Italy did follow the imperatives deriving from its participation in the alliance but not without voicing other concerns as well. The so-called zero clause – with which the decision to install NATO's missiles was explicitly linked to the possibility of negotiations with the Soviet bloc – responded to the desire, especially felt by the then opposition, to keep a 'soft line' with Moscow, even at a time of dramatic confrontation such as that which followed the USSR's invasion of Afghanistan.

On the other hand, an explanation exclusively emphasising the binding logic of international institutions such as NATO and the then EEC would be able to account only for parts of the trajectory of Italian foreign policy during the 'First Republic'. In so far as NATO is concerned, Italy's moderate exceptionalism and pacifist Atlanticism has been illustrated in the example discussed above. As for the EEC, here the constraint of European integration grew stronger as the decades progressed. Certainly, by the end of the 1970s a socialisation effect had driven Italian foreign policy makers to develop their policies within the EPC framework. Yet, exceptions to this rule were not infrequent: suffice it to mention here the case of Libya, towards which Italy maintained a rather soft line even at the time of most intense crisis, and in spite of the rather critical stance taken from most EEC members.

While international explanations might provide a parsimonious account of the foreign policy of Italy during the 'First Republic', when measured against the empirical record they also tend to offer ultimately unsatisfactory readings of the subject matter. This is not surprising, given the characteristics of these theories. Yet, it is an important result for the exercise that follows.

The thesis that Italy's foreign policy during the 'First Republic' followed domestic rather than international pressures has, on the other hand, found an equally numerous group of supporters among historians and analysts. Of the various monocausal theories belonging to this category, the ones stressing the nature of the regime and its institutional features have been especially popular.

Domestic accounts of Italy's foreign policy in the period in question certainly provide an illuminating view of many aspects of the country's diplomatic activity, and of its style. They capture, for instance, the degree to which strong political parties (and weak governments) distinctly influenced the pursuit of foreign policy – for example, the degree to which Italy's relations with certain regions were shaped relatively more by party-political, factionalist or even clientelistic interests, rather than those of the entire political system. Suffice it to mention here Italy's relations with Somalia in the 1980s, upon which political parties such as the PSI came to have a remarkable influence. Or, again, the overall influence that some key figures of the DC had in the context of Italy's relations with the Arab world, especially but not exclusively with the PLO.

More generally, interpretations framed around the 'primacy of the domestic' capture the degree to which Italy's foreign policy during the 'First Republic' was pursued with an eye towards the domestic political debate and was mostly influenced by party/political dynamics. Although interesting, however, these accounts are not entirely effective in explaining some of the defining traits of Italy's foreign policy during the 'First Republic'.

If one takes into account the formative period of 1943–1947, for example, it is difficult to see how an exclusively domestic-based account of Italy's foreign policy could be stretched to explain Italy's eventual siding with the West. Indeed, as Aldo Garosci points out in relation to domestic politics,

> At the moment of the Liberation Italy was evenly divided between ideals of conservation and ideals of renewal. *If, by an absurd hypothesis, these ideals had existed outside* [...] *of any international equilibria*, it is most likely that, at least for a period, the forces of renewal would have prevailed.
>
> (Garosci 1967: 546, emphasis added)

Italy's domestic situation alone would not have produced the foreign policy it eventually did in *any* international environment – as would be the case if domestic causes were really sufficient. Suppose, in fact, that the spirit of the international alliance against Nazi-fascism had continued, instead of breaking up around 1946–1947: most likely, the neutralist sentiments that were in fact prevalent in the country would have prevailed in directing foreign policy away from the path that it eventually took.

More generally, the Cold War provided a constraint that came to direct Italy's foreign policy in very fundamental ways. Consider, for instance, an episode such as the settlement over the city of Trieste in the 1950s, on which powerful domestic political dynamics were at play, and endogenous interests (apart from ideology) were clearly at stake. As the then Italian Ambassador to London Nicolò Carandini was forced to admit, in that circumstance (as well as in so many others during the Cold War), 'la questione non è fra noi e la Jugoslavia, ma fra la Russia e gli Anglo-Americani' ('the issue is not between ourselves and

Yugoslavia, but rather between Russia and the Anglo-Americans') (quoted in Poggiolini 1990: 79).

The autonomy that Italy enjoyed to pursue an exclusively domestic-driven foreign policy was therefore limited. The international relations of the time provided a constraint to even the most 'heartfelt' initiatives of Italy's foreign policy makers, some of which could not therefore be pursued. As in the case of monocausal/international approaches, this result might appear trivial, yet it is an indispensable and logical step for moving on to examine more complex accounts of the subject matter.

Dualist approaches

Dualist/additive models can provide a more effective answer to the puzzle of explaining Italy's foreign policy from 1943 to 1992. After all, as these models suggest, one could argue that Italy's foreign policy simply responded to both sets of influences – international and domestic – at the same time, with foreign policy makers acting as mediators and brokers between these two domains, and foreign policy resulting from the combination and mediation between these two opposite forces. Thus, for instance, the 1979 decision to accept NATO's missiles on Italy's soil, including its 'zero clause', could be thought of as the result of the *addition* of international pressures (the need to comply with NATO's decision, the rising Soviet threat) and domestic needs (pressures from the PCI and left-wing factions of the DC to keep options open with the USSR).

This straightforward account, however, would miss several aspects of the decision in question and, more generally, of the way in which international and domestic influences were brought to bear on Italy's foreign policy during the 'First Republic'. First, it would not be able to account for the varying degrees in which international circumstances or domestic politics affected foreign policy during the 'First Republic'. Both degrees, however, are likely to have changed over the decades, presumably according to the state of both domestic and international politics of the time – contrast the way in which Italy was constrained by the international relations of the post-war years, between 1943–1947, with the extent to which détente influenced Italian foreign policy three decades later.

Second, the particular mechanism which additive explanations adopt to account for foreign policy, i.e. a simple addition of international and domestic forces, cannot make sense of any form of dynamic interplay between variables. However, this was crucial, for instance, in the Euromissiles episode of 1979 just as, more generally, in the foreign policy of Italy during the 'First Republic'. In fact, consider the way the decision to accept the missiles fed back into Italy's domestic politics to strengthen the pro-Atlanticist position and thus marked the beginning of a decade, the 1980s, in which Atlanticism remained a key point of reference for governments.

Thus, while providing a simple and descriptively sound account of the subject matter, additive accounts cannot account for variance and change in the patterns of interplay between international relations, domestic politics and foreign policy.

Could one perhaps advance an argument along the lines of the 'nested games' approach to suggest that international relations have been always relatively more important than domestic politics in deciding Italy's foreign policy between 1943 and 1992?

In so far as the 'nested games' approach represents a weaker version of the 'primacy of the international' thesis – as illustrated in Chapter 1 – this view has obvious overlaps with what has been discussed above in relation to monocausal/international explanations, except that this position accepts that domestic politics has some limited influence on foreign policy (i.e. only on its details). Thus, in the case of Italy's foreign policy during the 'First Republic' an application of this model would lead us to argue that while international relations determined Italy's belonging to the Western camp, domestic politics decided the style of this participation. This, in turn, generated a foreign policy solidly grounded in Atlanticism and Europeanism and yet eccentric and contradictory – hence Hassner's formula of 'pacifist Atlanticism'. Domestic politics, in other words, functioned as an 'imperfect' transmission belt and diverted clear systemic pressures into unclear foreign policies.

However encompassing and intuitively fitting it may be, this account raises a few puzzles. Consider, for instance, the period around 1975 to 1978, i.e. the highest point of East–West détente. What kind of foreign policy should have responded to such international circumstances according to the 'nested games' approach? If international relations are considered to decide over the *grandes lignes* of foreign policy, then one would have expected Italy's foreign policy to follow the spirit of détente and multiply its initiatives towards the Soviet bloc, while confirming its Atlanticist leanings. However, except for the signing of the final act of the CSCE, this period marked the phase of *lowest* profile for Italian foreign policy, which became neutralised and almost non-existent. It is difficult to argue that the domestic political situation of the 'historic compromise', with its broad convergence and consensus, only influenced the 'details' of Italian foreign policy, rather than its very essence.

The last dualist model to offer a way to solve the problem of how to reconcile international and domestic determinants of foreign policy is the 'pendulum approach'. If we apply this approach to the question at hand, we could argue that Italian foreign policy has oscillated between the two poles of domestic and international politics between 1943 and 1992. Over this period it has stopped at different points of the pendulum's trajectory, according to the uneven combination of international and domestic pressures (see Figure 4.1).

Thus, after a brief phase (t_1: 1943–1946) in which domestic politics influenced the foreign policy initiatives of the nascent state of Italy towards a vague yet at the time functional neutrality or equidistance (e.g. the March 1944 diplomatic recognition from the Soviet Union, which was prompted by Prunas and Badoglio), the coming and progressive consolidation of the Cold War (t_2: 1947–1954) brusquely inverted this tendency and tied Italian foreign policy to primarily international imperatives. That these were relatively more pressing than domestic ones is apparent in more than a few instances: in the early 1950s the Italian

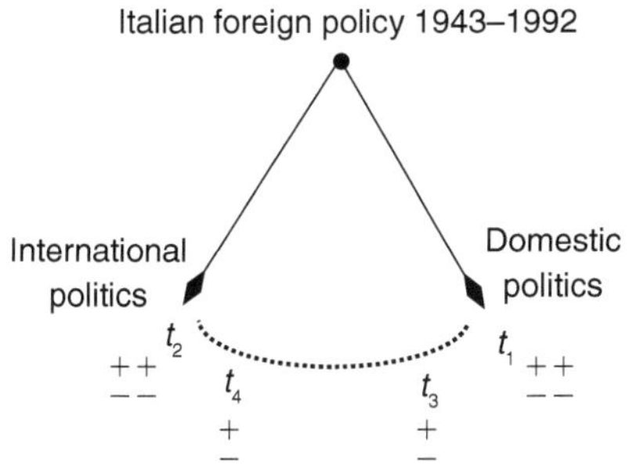

Figure 4.1 A 'pendulum' approach to Italian foreign policy 1943–1992. The application of the 'pendulum model' to Italian foreign policy, with t_1–t_4 being the following four temporal segments: t_1: 1943–1947; t_2: 1947–1954; t_3: 1954–1979; t_4: 1979–1992.

Ambassador to Moscow, Pietro Quaroni, somewhat brutally informed the Ministry in Rome that

> Nobody cares about Italy. We are nothing but a pawn, and not even one of the most important ones, in this struggle between giants. [...] Today Italy's troubles, compared to the big questions in front of us, are just secondary issues: we are the state of Temeswar of this new Versailles ... *If Talleyrand had been foreign minister of Italy today, he could not have done any more than has already been done.*
>
> (Quaroni quoted in Arcidiacono 1990: 120–1, emphasis added)

Apart from noticing the dramatic narrowing down of Italy's autonomy in foreign policy, Quaroni implicitly denied that domestic politics could really make a difference for Italy's foreign policy at a time when it was the international fact of the Cold War which counted most – not even Talleyrand, let alone Italy's foreign policy makers, would have been able to change this state of affairs.

From the end of the De Gasperi era (t_3: 1954–1979), however, Italy seemed to 'lose its clear international compass' (Spinelli 1967: 68) and started pursuing a foreign policy more tied to domestic concerns. The opening to the left accompanied Italy's opening to the East as well as the beginning of a more autonomous foreign policy during the 1960s. In the 1970s, instead, the profound domestic crisis impacted heavily upon foreign policy, mainly as an inhibiting factor, with the result that foreign policy was neutralised and sacrificed on the altar of domestic stability. Naturally, despite the relative primacy of domestic factors, international pressures did not disappear. Indeed, the fact that it was the easing of the international constraint and the first glimpse of détente in the mid-1950s which allowed this re-balancing of forces is compatible with the pendulum model – in fact, it makes sense of the oscillation.

Last, the phase of t_4 (1979–1992) marked the reappearance and decline of the more stringent international constraint of the 'second Cold War', which impacted upon Italy's foreign policy quite dramatically, directing it first towards a greater alignment with the West and finally to embrace (though not unequivocally) the end of the bipolar confrontation between the USSR and the US. Naturally, as in the previous phase, despite the relative prominence of international factors, domestic politics (for instance, the rise of the PSI and of its leader Craxi) did not disappear from the equation – rather, it had only a minor impact upon foreign policy.

Such a 'pendulum' model has numerous limits and ambiguities, but in this case also some merits. In particular, it raises the question of the different functions that foreign policy performs in international and domestic affairs: on the one hand, international functions such as the maximisation of security; on the other, the domestic function of consensus-building and the legitimisation of leadership. What an application of the pendulum model to the case in question suggests is that between 1943 and 1992 the foreign policy of Italy responded relatively more to a domestic or international rationality at different times.

However, how does one account for the movements of the pendulum? How does one explain, in other words, the changes in the combination of international and domestic influences over time? As with all other dualist models, change cannot be explained endogenously. Further, how does one account for the phases where both constraints were equally acute? The idea that foreign policy responds to *either* domestic *or* international pressures has, as seen above in the case of monocausal models, inevitable limits when measured against the empirical record. Last, the pendulum model also seems ill-equipped to deal with the problem which constituted the very starting point of this analysis, i.e. the interpenetration and interplay of the three domains: foreign policy, domestic politics and international relations.

Dialectical approaches

The morphogenetic approach conceives of foreign policy as the result of a dynamic and sequential interplay between international relations and domestic politics. Can such an approach make sense of the foreign policy of Italy during the 'First Republic'?

To start with, while it is certainly possible to indicate phases of powerful 'structural conditioning', such as the one which occupied the formative years of 1947–1954 of the 'First Republic', it is less frequent to find examples of a foreign policy able to impact upon such a structure to create an instance of 'morphogenesis', i.e. an alteration of the international relations surrounding Italy. As mentioned in Section 1 ('From fallen to "normal" power: the reinvention of Italian foreign policy'), from the mid-1950s to roughly the coming of the second Cold War in 1979 Italy did pursue a foreign policy aimed at détente. However, it would be far-fetched to assert that this has contributed to the eventual materialising of phases of détente between East and West.

Further, if we take out the possibility of *morphogenesis* from the model, then what is left of the approach is a sequence of structural conditioning from international relations and periodical interventions from domestic politics, the dynamic combination of which would constitute foreign policy. This position, however, would closely resemble that of the 'nested games' approach, in which international relations always has a relative (and temporal) primacy over domestic politics in defining foreign policy, and in which domestic politics intervenes only marginally. This would run into the series of problems illustrated in the examination of the 'nested games' approach and would put us primarily back into a 'dualist' framework of analysis, with all its limits.

Last, the morphogenetic model cannot account for the way international relations not only conditioned but created opportunities for Italy from 1943 to 1992. More importantly, it cannot explain how these came about or how these related to the particular actor in question, namely Italy. Once again, the undifferentiated view of structure of the morphogenetic model makes it difficult to clarify the process of interplay between foreign policy, domestic politics and international relations because it tends to represent this as sequential and fundamentally additive.

The strategic-relational model, on the other hand, rejects both monocausal and dualist logic to conceptualise foreign policy as the result of a dialectical interplay between three elements: a strategically-selective context, a strategic actor, and, finally, the discourses through which the two elements are brought into relation. How can one apply this model to the case of Italy's foreign policy between 1943 and 1992?

To start with, one should consider the context of relations in which Italy was embedded, and how this changed over the period in question. Consider, for instance, the 'formative years' – 1943–1946 and 1947–1954. As illustrated earlier in the chapter, the institutionalisation of the Cold War changed the horizon of Italian foreign policy as it altered the relative position of Italy vis-à-vis the other main actors, such as the two superpowers and the other European states. It was because of the institutionalisation of the confrontation between these two blocs that the position of Italy became significant in relative terms, i.e. in *relation* to its context. Hence, for instance, the intensification of contacts between Italy and the US starting from the end of 1946, i.e. only when it became clear that there was no chance of collaboration with the Soviet Union.

While constraining, it was precisely the system of relations associated with the Cold War that progressively offered opportunities for Italy to pursue its own foreign policy. Had Italy not been placed close to the border between East and West, or had the cooperation between the US and the Soviet Union continued, Italy's relative position would have been different and, with it, the opportunities and constraints to its foreign policy.

In terms of strategy, the re-legitimisation of an entire nation and the enhancement of Italy's international status acted as the driving concerns for foreign policy-makers of post-war Italy. With the tragic end of the fascist experiment, nationalism had ceased to be a legitimate source of inspiration for foreign policy, just as the military option had become a virtually impossible instrument of foreign policy. Thus, the political and symbolic objectives of foreign policy became especially important, much as the participation in the main diplomatic fora on a par with other actors.

Finally, concerning discourse, there were at least three alternative paradigms of Italy's relation with the 'international' which, from the late 1950s, progressively blurred into one another, as mentioned in Section 2 ('Politics and paradigms of Italy's foreign policy in the "First Republic"'): an idea of foreign policy solidly grounded in the values and institutions of the West, a vision of foreign policy which privileged external neutrality (or equidistance between the two blocs) and domestic reformism, and, finally, a conception in which foreign policy had been in itself neutralised in favour of a full participation in the government of the country. While these last two discourses were popular, it was the first which prevailed, at least in the first, post-war phase of Italian foreign policy.

The interrelated elements of context, strategy and discourse interacted dialectically between 1943 and 1954 to produce Italy's post-war foreign policy. More interestingly, had any of these elements been different, another foreign policy would have been likely. First, had the context not crystallised around the confrontation between the two superpowers, the incentive to join either side would have been less intense. Second, had the strategy been not one of international re-legitimisation at all costs, and willingness to participate actively in world affairs, the option of neutrality would have been perhaps more viable. Finally, had the prevailing discourse not been one of solidarity with the West, the attempt to establish 'equidistance' would have probably been successful.

Consider now the period immediately following the formative years of 1943–1954. The first détente of 1955–1956 partially changed the system of relations in which Italy was embedded by providing a greater opportunity to further Italy's foreign policy of cooperation with the West and with the East. Italy's foreign policy strategy and discourse also changed in part. With the rise of the leadership of Gronchi and Fanfani, Italian foreign policy started projecting itself further afield in international politics. The main instrument of this 'new course' in foreign policy was the political and economic dialogue initiated by Italy, especially vis-à-vis the Eastern bloc and the Arab world.

Thus, to those measures aimed at confirming Italy's presence in the Western bloc (e.g. the acceptance of the Jupiter missiles, 1959) Italy added those aimed at intensifying its relations with the Eastern bloc (e.g. Fanfani's visit to Moscow and attempted mediation over the status of Germany, 1960). Besides the consolidation of Italy's position in the Western bloc (e.g. acceptance of the Euromissiles, 1979) Italy pursued a parallel and contrasting foreign policy with the Arab world (e.g. the Sigonella crisis, 1985).

Context, strategy and discourse interacted dialectically to produce the foreign policy pursued by Italy in the mid-1950s. Once again, had any of these three elements been different, Italy would have likely pursued a different diplomatic course. First, had the discourse been still inspired by De Gasperi's intransigent line, such that 'non possiamo oscillare. [Non possiamo assumere] una funzione di ponte, nel senso che l'Italia possa presumere di stare come a cavallo dei due mondi' ('we cannot waver. [We cannot behave as a] bridge, with the presumption that Italy can straddle two worlds') (De Gasperi quoted in Sterpellone 1967: 334), Italy would have had less of an incentive to intensify its relations with the Soviet bloc. Second, had the context of relations of which Italy was a part still been informed by an open confrontation between the two blocs, Italy's foreign policy would have probably been frustrated or would have risked a rupture in Italy's Atlanticism. Finally, had Italy's strategy not featured an increasing (and moderately revisionist) determination to raise the country's profile in international affairs, the opportunity offered by the 'first détente' would not have been seized upon.

Third, and last, consider the example of the end of the Cold War. Here too a consideration of the context, strategy and discourses through which Italian foreign policy was framed might explain a few important aspects of how Italian foreign policy reacted to that historic change. To start with, the collapse of bipolarism significantly altered Italy's relative position and altered the system of opportunities and constraints in which the country had been embedded over the previous five decades, making its position possibly less central. Further, Italy's strategy progressively featured the desire to enlarge the country's margins of influence and pursue a more dynamic foreign policy, especially in the Mediterranean and in Central Europe. Finally, thanks to the activism of the Foreign Minister De Michelis in particular, the discourse which prevailed was that of affirming Italy's continued participation in world affairs, combined with a renewed attention for the geopolitical 'opportunities' brought about by the end of the Cold War.

The interaction of all three elements led to the foreign policy of the late 1980s and early 1990s. Had the system remained that of the Cold War, initiatives such as the *Pentagonale* would not (and most likely could not) have been pursued. Had Italy's strategy and discourse still been framed by the architecture of the Cold War, status quo and détente would have been preferable to the measure of revisionism which Italian foreign policy came to acquire in the post-Wall era.

Conclusions

As this chapter has attempted to make clear, the foreign policy of Italy between 1943 and 1992 is a complex subject in need of complex explanations. In particular, there is a certain urgency to move beyond the stalemate which currently characterises the explanations available in the academic debate, as illustrated in the chapter.

Drawing upon the models elaborated in Chapter 1 I have thus advanced alternative ways to conceptualise the complex interaction between the domestic politics, foreign policy and international relations of Italy between 1943 and 1992. While monocausal models have been rejected, dualist and dialectical frameworks have been considered more helpful, and their strengths and weaknesses have been compared and contrasted. Two models have proven particularly useful in this examination: the 'pendulum' model and the strategic-relational model. While an application of the former is able to capture the idea that Italian foreign policy has responded to different functions – international and domestic – at different periods during the Cold War, the strategic-relational model offers a more generally valid account of the subject matter, centred around the idea of a dialectic between context, strategy and discourse. Most of all, by promoting a better engagement between opposite interpretative traditions, this chapter aimed at liberating some space for more creative ways to address the subject, beyond the current theoretical, normative and epistemological straitjacket.

5 Italian foreign policy

The 'Second Republic' (1992–2011)

Losing a status and finding a role? Italy in search of a foreign policy

The years immediately following the fall of the Berlin Wall saw Italian foreign policy seized by a fit of remarkable dynamism. Initiatives such as the *Pentagonale*/Central European Initiative (May 1990), the Conference on Security and Cooperation in the Mediterranean (CSCM, September 1990), and the proposal for a European seat at the UN Security Council (September 1990) were launched in the span of three years. Finally, Italy was involved – although more in diplomatic than military terms – in the Gulf War as well as in the early phases of the conflict in the former Yugoslavia (Brioni Accords, October 1991). Just as this dynamic trend in foreign policy was consolidating, however, Italy's domestic politics was entering that deep state of crisis which would result in the end of the 'First Republic' (Hine 1992; Leonardi and Anderlini 1992; Hellman and Pasquino 1992). The 'gap between the external dynamism' of Italy's foreign policy and the 'internal ineffectiveness' of the political system left Italy stranded in a 'dual crisis' – of its Cold War international and domestic anchorage (IAI: 1993).

In the domestic political arena, after the historic evolution and split of the PCI into the PDS and the PRC (January 1991), between 1992 and 1994 Italy's two other major parties – the DC and the PSI – suffered a total electoral collapse and, eventually, extinction. As for the former, pushed well below 30 per cent of preferences for the first time in its post-war history in the elections of April 1992, the DC initiated a process of long-suppressed internal reform which ultimately proved fatal: the party ceased to exist in January 1994 and was replaced by the *Partito Popolare Italiano* (PPI, centre-left) and the *Centro Cristiano Democratico* (CCD, centre-right). At the same time, leading figures of the DC establishment such as Arnaldo Forlani, Severino Citaristi, Cirino Pomicino and, most notably, Giulio Andreotti, came under judicial inquiry for fraud, corruption and – in the case of the latter – association with the *Mafia* (Scoppola 1997; Follini 1994; Andreotti 1995).

But it was the PSI that was to suffer most dramatically from the notorious judicial campaign of *Mani Pulite* (operation 'clean hands') initiated by a team of judges in Milan in the early 1990s. With the arrest of Milanese businessman

Mario Chiesa on 17 January 1992 a series of judicial inquiries began uncovering vast networks of systematic collusion between the political, institutional and business worlds – starting from the PSI-controlled region of Lombardy. In the span of a few months, the entire party establishment – including Gianni De Michelis, Claudio Martelli, Giuliano Amato and Bettino Craxi – found itself in the eye of the storm. The collapse of the party followed in November 1994.

With the end of the party system which had 'governed' Italy from 1945 (the so-called *partitocrazia*, 'rule of the parties'), a climate of growing institutional instability spread across the country, climaxing in the assassination of Giovanni Falcone and Paolo Borsellino (May 1992), in the devaluation and exit of the Italian *lira* from the European Exchange Rate Mechanism (ERM, September 1992), and in the ominous bomb attacks in Rome, Florence and Milan (1993). By the same token, new actors erupted onto the political scene: above all, the *Leghe*, of which the *Lega Lombarda* led by Umberto Bossi was the most prominent, but also political/civil society movements such as the *Patto per l'Italia*, led by reformist Mario Segni, who rose to special notoriety for promoting a series of referenda designed to set the reform of Italy's shaky political institutions in motion. Thus, on 18 April 1993 an overwhelming majority of voters resolved to replace the proportional representation electoral law with one designed to encourage bipolarism and a healthy alternation in power. This vote, more than anything else, was hailed in the press as the sign that a new political system – the so-called Second Republic – was in the making, while the 'First Republic' had finally imploded in on itself (Pasquino and McCarthy 1993; Mershon and Pasquino 1995; Katz and Ignazi 1996).

It was in this context of extreme uncertainty that Italy was called to express a foreign policy vis-à-vis the international political crises of the day, and especially the Balkans and Somalia. With the dissolution of Yugoslavia – an outcome which between 1990 and 1991 Italian foreign policy makers, *pace* the Vatican, had done so much to avoid – Italy came to border the new Republic of Slovenia. The issue of the Treaty of Osimo, signed with Yugoslavia in 1975 concerning precisely that border, came to the fore from September 1992 when Italy acquiesced in Slovenia's determination to take over the obligations deriving from the treaty from the old Yugoslavia. This move, in fact, foreclosed any possibility for the renegotiation of the treaty. The political row which erupted – with the right-wing movement of the *Movimento Sociale Italiano* (MSI) as well as the PLI and PRI accusing the government and Foreign Minister Emilio Colombo of betraying Italy's national interests, and with the issue of property rights of the minorities high on the agenda – signalled the start of a three-year long *querelle* between Rome and Ljubljana (Favaretto and Greco 1997).

In the meantime, the crisis in Bosnia escalated. Despite the government's reiterated willingness to participate in the humanitarian mission promoted by the UN (United Nations Protection Force, UNPROFOR), in September 1992 the country was excluded from peacekeeping operations on the basis of its status as a border country. NATO's airbases on the Adriatic coast of Italy, however, played an important role in the logistical organisation of the humanitarian mission and, from March 1993, provided a veritable 'launching pad' for NATO's subsequent military intervention *Deny Flight*. Considering also Italy's pivotal contribution to the NATO/WEU-sponsored operation *Sharp Guard* (the monitoring of the arms embargo against Serbia-Montenegro), there was enough for Italy to protest at the lack of political involvement in the management of the crisis. In fact, as early as May 1993 Italy found itself excluded from the nascent 'Contact Group' formed by the USA, Russia, France, Great Britain and, later, Germany (Greco 1994; Bellucci 1997).

The other arena of activity for Italian diplomacy between 1992 and 1994 was that of Somalia, where the fall of Siad Barre's regime (which Italy, and the PSI especially, had done so much to support throughout the 1980s) had given way to a ruthless civil war. Italy's dubious colonial legacy in Somalia and constant involvement in its post-independence internal affairs provided reasons for caution (Tripodi 1999). However, the desire to enhance Italy's international and regional profile in the Horn of Africa, as well as strengthen its international credibility in the midst of a devastating domestic political crisis, prevailed. In December 1992 the Parliament approved the mission IBIS, consisting of around 2,500 peace-keepers to join the United Nations Operation in Somalia I (UNOSOM), later United Nations Operation in Somalia II (UNOSOM II) (Sica 1994; Del Boca 1993; Ercolessi 1994; Croci 1995).

On the strength of its contribution on the ground – and more or less as it had happened in Bosnia – in the spring of 1993 Italy presented the request to be associated in the management of the operation. Again, just as in Bosnia, the request was immediately turned down by the US and dismissed as inappropriate by the UN. This was the beginning of a phase of protracted hostility which characterised Italy's relations with the US and the UN throughout the remainder of the mission.

After a number of severe setbacks and ambushes in Mogadishu, all of which inevitably exposed the weaknesses of the UN strategy in Somalia, accusations of having turned a humanitarian mission into a war were publicly voiced by General Bruno Loi, commander of the Italian troops in Somalia (Loi 2004). The response from the UN – namely Vice-Secretary General Kofi Annan's order to remove General Loi from its position – was received in Rome (and especially in the Defence Ministry) with defiance and the withdrawal of Italy's peace-keepers from the capital Mogadishu (August 1993). This only managed to further heighten the tension, and in the end accelerated the operational *impasse* in which UNOSOM II found itself. A few months later, the rising death toll – especially among American peace-keepers – as well as the pressure exerted on American public opinion by the televised coverage of the crisis convinced both Washington and the UN that the operation 'Restore Hope' had ended, in a disaster. Their analyses of its failure did indeed seem to vindicate some of the criticisms voiced in Rome.

As the crises in Somalia and Bosnia unfolded, Italy's domestic situation evolved further. The continuing political instability and growing fragmentation which marked the political landscape of the 'new' Republic were suddenly contrasted by the spectacular affirmation of a new party, *Forza Italia* (FI), led by Milanese media-tycoon Silvio Berlusconi. Appealing especially to those voters of the centre who could no longer vote DC or PSI, and putting forward a bold programme of institutional, economic and social reforms, FI acquired extraordinary popularity soon after Berlusconi's decision to 'enter the political field' in November 1993 (McCarthy 1996). No-one, however, could have anticipated the electoral triumph leading to the formation of Berlusconi's first government in May 1994, whose supporting coalition included Gianfranco Fini's right-wing *Alleanza Nazionale* (AN, formerly MSI), Bossi's *Lega Nord per l'Indipendenza della Padania* (LN) and the DC-splinter party CCD.

Because of Berlusconi's dubious judicial record and glaring conflict of interest, but also given the inclusion of the ex-fascist party of AN in his government coalition, the international reaction to the coming to power of Berlusconi's government was little short of hostile. After all, just one month before the elections, Fini had famously declared that he considered Mussolini to be the greatest Italian statesman of the century (*La Stampa* 1994; *The Economist* 1994; Neal 1996).

In terms of foreign policy, the change of government coincided with a change in the style, if not always in the substance, of Italy's role on the international stage: a greater assertiveness and frequent talk of 'national interests' characterised the action of the government and of its Foreign Minister, Antonio Martino (May 1994–January 1995). In Europe, Martino favoured a position of qualified integrationism and was critical of the logic underlying the then nascent European Monetary Union, all of which already stood in sharp contrast to Italy's traditionally integrationist and rather a-critical attitude (Bonvicini 1996; Neal 1996).

In the case of Bosnia, Italy continued to support the intervention and demand to join the Contact Group. The request was met with a degree of embarrassment given that in the electoral campaign preceding the elections of May 1994, AN had overtly called for a redrawing of Italy's Eastern border and a renegotiation of the Treaty of Osimo. When the government went so far as to publicly veto the negotiation of the Association Treaty between Slovenia and the EU, the reaction from Italy's international partners was one of unanimous condemnation – so much so that Italy soon found itself isolated in Europe (cf., however, Romano 1995).

The attempt by the Berlusconi government to re-nationalise foreign policy was, however, short-lived. After only six months, the coalition supporting the government collapsed due to the defection of the LN. Despite the change in government, some of the assertiveness expressed by the centre-right government did not disappear; in fact, a nationalist vein subtly permeated the technocratic government of Lamberto Dini (January 1995–May 1996).

In the case of the Bosnian conflict, Italy was finally invited to join the negotiating table after it agreed to a greater involvement in the operation, in particular contributing eight *Tornados* and six *AMX* to the operation *Deliberate Force.* When it turned out, however, that the invitation to the club had been extended on a consultative basis only – due especially to German and French pressure – the reaction from Rome was immediate and harsh: in September 1995 the US Stealth bombers directed to Bosnia were denied access to the NATO bases in Italy (Romano 1996; Donatucci and Lucarelli 1998). Symbolic and extreme as this measure was, it ironically reaped only meagre results, partly because by then the bombings had already weakened the Serbian resistance – making the *Stealth* bombers less and less necessary – and partly because from then on the decisional mechanisms of the Contact Group were gradually replaced by those of NATO proper.

In Europe the Dini government maintained a more traditional integrationist line and was to initiate many of the strategies that Italy would follow in the next five years under the centre-left governments of Romano Prodi (May 1996–October 1998), Massimo D'Alema (October 1998–December 1999, December 1999–April 2000), and Giuliano Amato (April 2000–June 2001). Such continuity in foreign policy was made possible not only by the ideological contiguity of the governments, but also by Dini's uninterrupted presence at the *Farnesina* for the entire legislature (Dini 2001).

Thus, in the context of European integration the Dini government – called upon to open in Turin the IGC leading to the Amsterdam Treaty in March 1995 and to hold the EU Presidency Semester between January and May 1996 – reaffirmed Italy's commitment to integrationism, particularly in view of the launching of the European Monetary Union (EMU) and the threatened exclusion of Italy from its 'core' (Daniels 1997).[1] Italy also lent its full support to the 'Barcelona Process' started in November 1995, as a way to counterbalance the impending opening of NATO to countries in Eastern Europe (Aliboni 1999; Attinà 1998). It also pushed for measures such as the gradual inclusion of the WEU into the EU, a greater recourse to qualified majority voting (QMV), and a stronger role for the European Commission (Daniels 1997; Missiroli 1997).

As it turned out, the Dini government paved the way for the electoral success of the centre-left coalition led by Romano Prodi in the elections of May 1996. The coalition – comprising, among others, the PDS, the PPI and the Greens, with the PRC externally supporting the government – reaped a historic victory by allowing ex-Communist parties to fully participate in the government of the country after the *compromesso storico* of almost two decades earlier.

Arguably, Europe represented the paramount scenario of Italian foreign (and domestic) policy between 1996 and 1998, as frequent talk of the imperative to 'stay in Europe' or 'join Europe' made clear. Indeed, the objective of meeting the convergence criteria set at Maastricht and thus entering the EMU from its very beginning absorbed the greater part of the government's activity until May 1998, when the aim was finally attained (Letta 1997; *Limes* 1997; *Il Mulino* 1998). In this process the government overcame international scepticism (especially from France and Germany) by adopting a number of fiscal and financial measures stringent enough to substantially cut Italy's debt (Sbragia 2001; Hay and Rosamond 2002).

The determination of the Prodi government to qualify for the first round of the EMU reflected the more general objective of enhancing Italy's role in multilateral frameworks by adopting a strategy of 'active multilateralism' (Andreatta and Hill 2000: 252–8). Prodi's government was determined to prove that Italy was no longer a free rider in NATO and the EU but rather a 'security provider' (Dassù and Menotti 1997; Zannoni 1997). In the UN the Prodi government also re-launched the proposal for the reform of the Security Council which successfully blocked the prospect of an enlargement of the Council's permanent membership limited to Germany and Japan (Andreatta 1993b; Dini 2001: 30; Fulci 1997, 1999: 13–14).

But it was the case of Albania that provided the real test for Italy's foreign policy under the Prodi government. After the failure of the pyramid savings scheme and the ensuing financial crisis of February 1997, Albania fell into political and social chaos. First and foremost, the crisis constituted an immigration emergency, but also a further factor of instability in the nearby Balkans. While France and Greece shared this assessment, Germany and Britain were more cautious, and in the end vetoed a possible EU/WEU sponsoring of a humanitarian mission to Albania (Ferraris 1997).

It was in this context that Italy took the lead of the 6,500-men Multinational Protection Force (MPF) code-named *Alba* which came to operate under UN Resolution 1101 from March 1997 (Sciortino 1998; Tripodi 2002; Perlmutter 1998). Operation *Alba* proved unique in many ways. First, contrary to an established UN practice, it was led by a border country (and one with long historical ties with the target country). Second, its command structure included a multinational political steering committee with a permanent Secretariat at the Foreign Ministry in Rome, which proved to be not only effective and reliable, but also avoided situations of competing command chains *à la* Somalia. After one major setback in March 1997, when a collision with an Italian ship caused the sinking and death of about eighty Albanians, the intervention largely succeeded in meeting its objectives, and by August 1997 the conflict had been de-escalated.

Despite the success on the ground and in terms of enhanced international credibility, however, domestically the management of the Albanian crisis dealt a fatal blow to the centre-left coalition led by Prodi. Forsaken by the increasingly vocal PRC, the government relied on the votes of the opposition to pass the financing of the mission *Alba*. By then, however, the crisis in the government had erupted and internal wrangling in the coalition continued until October 1998, when the Prodi government resigned due to the lack of a majority in Parliament. Its fall produced another centre-left coalition government, this time led by Massimo D'Alema, the first ex-Communist to lead a government in Italy.

As analysts soon pointed out – and D'Alema himself later admitted (D'Alema 1999a: 3–4) – foreign policy was to provide a real benchmark, if not the ultimate test, for his government, whose majority included (aside from the DS, the PPI and the Greens) the *Partito dei Comunisti Italiani* (PDCI), a splinter party of the PRC. In foreign policy the D'Alema government sought to find a pragmatic way out of a number of impasses created by the tension between the ideological drive of his centre-left coalition and the necessity to prove Italy's continued credibility abroad, especially in Washington.

First, the 'Öcalan affair' opened a crisis not only between Italy and Turkey – regarding the extradition to Turkey of the leader of the Kurdistan Workers' Party (*Partiya Karkerên Kurdistan*, PKK) Abdullah Öcalan, arrested in Rome – but also in the newly formed government, which included sympathisers of the PKK and of its leader's request for political asylum. The crisis was averted only by treading a cautious line, which in the end facilitated Öcalan's 'voluntary' exit from the country on 16 January 1999 (Aliboni and Pioppi 2000; cf. Dini 2001: 55–61). The Öcalan affair also contributed to a bad start in Italy's relations with the US, already strained after the 'Cermis accident' of February 1998 – when a US aircraft flying below its authorised altitude in a Trentino valley provoked the death of twenty people (*La Repubblica* 1999; D'Alema 1999b) – and Italy's condemnation of the US bombings on Iraq.

The escalating conflict in Kosovo thus provided a real test case for Italo-American relations (Greco 2000; Croci 2000; Cremasco 2000; D'Alema 1999a: 3). Italy approached the Rambouillet negotiations preceding the war with the intention to avoid an armed conflict at all costs and favour an agreement between the Kosovar and Serbian delegation (Dini 2001: 62–3; Fubini 1999). What was perceived in Rome as American intransigence, however, made operation *Allied Force* inevitable.[2] Further, the fact that no UN Resolution was passed to legitimise the intervention was deeply problematic for Italy, especially for a centre-left government such as D'Alema's, as was Russia's continued opposition.

Yet, from the inception of the operation, the Prime Minister made known that Italy would 'do its share' to stop the ethnic cleansing in Kosovo but also to allow Italy to take its part in the stabilisation of the Balkans (*International Herald Tribune* 1999). Apart from its participation in the military mission – officially limited to NATO's system of 'integrated defence' and the usual, crucial logistic assistance – Italy soon took the lead in terms of humanitarian assistance of the Albanian refugees, launching operation *Arcobaleno* and thus astutely justifying the intervention on mainly humanitarian grounds.

Throughout operations, the government maintained a strategy of critical involvement. It expressed scepticism towards NATO's strategy of air-bombings, as in the occasion of D'Alema's first visit to Washington on 5 March 1999, with Foreign Minister Dini especially vocal in lamenting NATO's bombing of non-military targets, such as the Serbian TV headquarters and the Chinese Embassy (Croci 2000: 43–4; cf. D'Alema 1999b: 34–9). Equally, Italy sponsored several attempts to favour a 'political' solution to the crisis – including the one led by Armando Cossutta of the PDCI who, in the middle of the war, visited Belgrade. Interestingly, Italy was also the only Western country to keep its Embassy open in Belgrade during the war (Balfour *et al.* 1999: 75). It was with relief, then, that Italy welcomed Russia's involvement in the G-8 sponsored peace plan which ended NATO's bombings in June 1999 and paved the way for the intervention of a UN stabilisation force.

In Kosovo, just as elsewhere, the D'Alema government made its proneness to 'dialogue' a principle of foreign policy, especially vis-à-vis problem countries such as North Korea, Libya and Iran (Dini 2001: 123). With the former, Italy was the first Western country of the G-8 to open full diplomatic relations in March 2000, after a controversial visit from Foreign Minister Dini which included an homage to the statue of Kim Il Sung. In the case of Iran as well, both the Prodi and the D'Alema governments made every effort to legitimise the moderate turn in its domestic politics. Finally, but perhaps most importantly, under the second D'Alema government Rome inaugurated a new phase in its relations with Libya and brought to fruition the diplomatic efforts initiated by the Dini and Prodi government in 1996, with a number of economic joint-ventures marking a high point in the strategy of engagement with Libya (Guazzone 2000: 433–44; Pioppi 2002: 50–6).

After yet another implosion of the centre-left governing coalition (and much personal wrangling between D'Alema and Prodi), the Amato government succeeded D'Alema in April 2000. In foreign policy as in many other areas, however, the 'new course' initiated by the centre-left in 1996 seemed to have exhausted its momentum, with Italy failing to land the membership of the UN Security Council for 2001–2002 as well the post of United Nations High Commissioner for Refugees (UNHCR), despite its aspirations to both.

The *Casa delle Libertà* (CdL) led by Berlusconi capitalised on the growing dissatisfactions of the electorate with the centre-left so as to reap the electoral triumph of May 2001, initating a five-year rule (May 2001–April 2006). The coalition formed by FI, AN, the CCD (later *Unione Democratica Cristiana*, UDC) and the LN gained an overwhelming majority in Parliament – the largest in the history of the 'First' and 'Second' Republics.

The events of 11 September 2001, only a few months after Berlusconi's victory, provided a compelling incentive for a re-articulation of Italian foreign policy (Andreatta and Brighi 2003; Ignazi 2004; Aliboni 2004). The centre-right government proved zealous in endorsing the US' 'Global War on Terror', including its framing of 9/11 as an attack upon a 'superior', Western civilisation (*Il Corriere della Sera* 2001). Berlusconi also shared the talk of 'old' versus 'new' Europe coming from Washington, enthusiastically signing the 'United We Stand' initiative by the leaders of the self-proclaimed 'new' Europe (*The Wall Street Journal* 2003) and showing little patience for European predicaments regarding the military campaigns in the Middle East (Brighi 2011).

Italy's contributions to the actual operations on the ground in Iraq (3200 men in the operation code-named *Antica Babilonia*) and Afghanistan (2800 men integrated in NATO's International Security Assistance Force [ISAF] mission) were constrained by the constitutional imperative to avoid being engaged in war, with Italy adopting a most ambiguous position of 'benevolent neutrality' at the start of the war. Yet, during the years of the centre-right, the missions managed to garner both a substantive majority in Parliament as well as commendation from Washington (Davidson 2011; Coticchia and Giacomello 2011).

In Europe, despite an unwavering commitment to ESDP and contributing to virtually every military mission launched under its umbrella, excluding the French-led operation *Artemis* in Congo, on issues such as the European arrest warrant, the EMU and the Constitutional Treaty, and after the early departure of

Foreign Minister Renato Ruggiero, Italy often ended up being stigmatised for its eccentric positions, aside from being associated with the infelicitous rhetorical escapades of its Prime Minister (Rossi 2002; Missiroli 2007; Carbone 2008; Carbone and Quaglia 2011).

Berlusconi's appetite for bilateral 'special relationships' able to bolster his image at home was in part to blame. Thus, quite aside from the frequent trips to the US, including one to Washington in 2006 where he solemnly addressed a joint session of Congress, the centre-right government invested in maintaining close relations with Russia and Israel – at the cost of defending the former's human rights abuses in Chechnya while Berlusconi was serving as EU President in November 2003 and backing the latter's counter-terrorist policies such as the controversial 'Separation Wall' (Del Sarto and Tocci 2008). To testify to the deliberate selectivity of its foreign policy commitments, as well as its eccentricity in Europe, the Berlusconi government also deliberately passed on the opportunity to join the 'Big Three' in the EU mission to Tehran over the nuclear dossier (*La Repubblica* 2005) – only to then lament the country's exclusion from this *directoire* for the rest of the centre-right government's mandate.

At the elections of April 2006 the centre-right was narrowly defeated by a broad centre-left coalition formed by nine parties, led by the *Democratici di Sinistra* (DS, formerly PDS) and headed once again by Romano Prodi (May 2006–April 2008). Despite the desire to categorically distance itself from the centre-right record on foreign policy, the centre-left pursued a pragmatic trajectory which led to continuity on a number of fronts (Walston 2007; Brighi 2007a, 2011). In Europe Prodi's government clearly prioritised institutional reform and backed the Lisbon process, though not without occasional obstructionism. In terms of relations with the US, despite moving quickly to withdraw its troops from Iraq – a move which Berlusconi himself had hastily announced in the run-up to the elections and in the aftermath of the Calipari affair (Brighi 2007b) – Italy reaffirmed its commitment to the transatlantic alliance by not only continuing to support the ISAF mission in Afghanistan but by not reneging on the agreement to host a controversial new US military base in Vicenza. On both issues the governing coalition was deeply divided, and indeed on one occasion, in February 2007, the Prodi government temporarily collapsed due to a vanished majority in Parliament (Croci 2008: 295–6).

The Prodi government was, however, especially keen to prove that Italy remained a responsible and ethical foreign policy actor on the international scene, in the tradition of the centre-left governments of the 1990s (Walston 2008). In the summer of 2006 it did so by working relentlessly on a mediation to cease the hostilities between Israel and Hezbollah. When that failed, it took the lead of a substantial peacekeeping mission to Lebanon (United Nations Interim Force in Lebanon, UNIFIL II) which was not only endorsed by the UN and the EU, and to which Italy contributed 2,500 troops, but which met with the approval of the US, reassured that Italy was not disengaging from its commitments in the Middle East (Menotti 2007: 439–40).

The delicately balanced foreign policy approach adopted by the Prodi government, however, could not survive the tears within the centre-left coalition, with its shifting majority in Parliament. New elections were called for April 2008, and this time the centre-right coalition organised under Berlusconi's *Popolo delle Libertà* (PDL, formerly CdL) was given yet another comfortable majority in both houses.

The foreign policy record of the fourth and last Berlusconi government was a mixed bag of volatility and reassertion. On the one hand, Italy showed a predictable return to the Atlanticist tropes of earlier centre-right governments, although now vis-à-vis the less ideologically congruent US Administration of Barack Obama. After the rather undiplomatic 'open letter' from NATO ambassadors in February 2007 (Silvestri 2007) and persistent requests from Washington to do more in Afghanistan, Berlusconi agreed to contribute substantively to 'the surge', bringing the Italian ISAF contingent to over 4000 troops, whilst also proving keen to accelerate Italy's disengagement, no doubt with an eye towards the budget and public opinion (Ratti 2011).

The centre-right government kept cultivating the special bilateral ties with Russia and Libya that the centre-left government of Romano Prodi had also substantially invested in, in both cases following strong energy interests. However, in 2008 Berlusconi went as far as defending Russia's military campaign in Georgia, again breaking the European front and attracting the telling epithet of 'Europe's Trojan horse' (Carbone 2008). In the case of Libya, the 'Treaty of Friendship' signed in August 2008 was presented as historic by Berlusconi and celebrated rather lavishly over the four official visits of Muhammar Ghaddafi in less than a year, the last one in August 2010. When the UN-sponsored and French-led multinational coalition initiated its bombardments over Libya to stop Ghaddafi's attacks against civilians only nine months later, in March 2011, Berlusconi's response was one of embarrassed indifference, after obstructing a European initiative for sanctions and lamenting France's unilateralist attitude. Faced with the prospect of intervention, the centre-right coalition started to show its cracks. Italy's participation was only ratified after the reassurance, which turned out to be empty, that its *AMX* fighter planes would not fully engage in war. Soon, however, Rome recognised the National Transitional Council as the new and legitimate government of Libya, which paved the way for a new memorandum on energy signed in August 2011 (Lombardi 2011).

But it was Europe that proved to be the most difficult and ultimately losing game for Berlusconi's last government. While the early part of its mandate (July 2008) featured an enthusiastic ratification of the Lisbon treaty, Italy managed to alienate the support of its European partners on a number of issues, including its immigration policies towards the Roma, the continued support of Israel's military operations in Gaza but, especially, its debt crisis and slow growth, as well as the personal scandals and lawsuits involving Berlusconi himself. In November 2011 the pressure from European markets combined with unrest within his own coalition to mark the end of Berlusconi's centre-right government and, for some, of an era.

Politics and paradigms of Italy's foreign policy in the 'Second Republic'

In the two decades since 1992, the political and party system has exhibited three main tendencies. First, it has restructured itself around a loose bipolar dynamic. Second, it has shown a high party fragmentation at the extreme wings of the political spectrum. Third, its stability has been increasingly compromised by parliamentary practices such as crossing the floor and defecting reminiscent of the era of *trasformismo* (Sabbatucci 1990). Broadly speaking, electoral competition has revolved around the confrontation between two main coalitions of parties along the right–left axis. However, while the core of the coalitions has remained relatively unchanged over the last ten years, differences in their composition have been frequent and noticeable (Ceccarini Diamanti and Lazar 2013).[3]

In terms of the foreign policy paradigm, the end of the Cold War and the beginning of the 'Second Republic' catalysed a restructuring of the imagery and discourse around foreign policy. Thus, between 1992 and 2005 the two coalitions expressed two largely alternative views, not only of domestic politics, but of Italian foreign policy as well. These visions were predicated on significantly different ideas of the relationship between foreign policy, domestic politics and international relations in the case of Italy. Since the disengagement from Iraq announced in 2005, however, a process of 'parallel convergence' has toned down most substantive differences, narrowing the gap between these alternative foreign policy visions. On the fringes of the political spectrum, however, foreign policy discourse continues to differ radically, and indeed increasingly so (Andreatta 2008a; cf. Andreatta 2008b; Coticchia and Giacomello 2011).

The centre-right: a national foreign policy?

The centre-right led by Silvio Berlusconi developed its vision of foreign policy around the idea that in the post-bipolar world Italy enjoys greater freedom to assert its national interests (Frattini and Panella 2004; Berlusconi 2002):

> The fall of the bipolar system makes the international situation bear much less on our foreign policy. Our potential sphere of action is now enlarged. [...] We are no longer simply a subject belonging to one of the two poles; once again, we are now capable of an autonomous foreign policy. [...] A coherent foreign policy, one which is not tempted by any kind of utopian universalism, is the most modern and productive investment that a State can make in the world to defend national interests, increase its own welfare, and at the same time foster the world's development and international cooperation under the rule of law.
>
> (IAI 1994a: 221)

As Roberto Aliboni, Ettore Greco and Gianni Bonvicini have noted, the advent of the centre-right in power heralded the coming of a moderately nationalist vision of foreign policy, centred around the idea of a greater assertiveness in pursuing foreign policy goals and a greater autonomy in engaging with the international environment (Aliboni and Greco 1996; Bonvicini 1996).

The centre-right translated these principles into a set of policy guidelines.[4] First, the attempt to enhance Italy's profile in international politics by privileging a strategy of active bilateralism and by embracing the principle of 'effective multilateralism', i.e. privileging multilateral context only in so far as they meet interests and deliver results, rather than correspond to values or ideals (Frattini 2004). Second, a less deferential attitude towards the process of European integration and a more spare, if not overtly mercantilist, engagement with its institutions. Third, centre-right governments have strengthened the economic aspect of diplomacy by promoting the penetrative function of foreign policy, especially towards developing markets, in a strategy to raise the economic and diplomatic profile of the country (Forza Italia 2004: 20).

These guidelines point to an understanding of foreign policy that is first and foremost domestically/nationally based: the emphasis on national culture, the projection of the national economy and the use of bilateralism rather than multilateralism all point in this direction (Fisichella 1997: 192–5).

This vision has also exhibited significant ambiguities and limits over the last decade. First, it is not clear whether the 'national' basis of foreign policy is in fact taken to justify the definition of interests on a purely private/personal basis – i.e. mainly but not exclusively relating to Berlusconi's own business/political empire. For instance, the kind of bilateralism pursued by the government has been personalised and, at times, privatised to a degree unprecedented in the post-war history of Italian foreign policy. More generally, however, this criticism points to the notorious ambiguities of the very concept of 'national interest' – hardly a general interest, more often the encounter of specific and particular interests – around which the centre-right has failed to promote a genuine debate.

Second, it is striking to note that despite all the emphasis on its national vocation, the foreign policy of the two Berlusconi governments has in fact often been reactive rather than strategic. Especially since 11 September 2001, Italy has adapted to the increased tension in the international system not so much by emphasising its own indigenous interests, but rather by giving in to an externally driven foreign policy, mainly tied to the redefinition of interests promoted by the USA and a revival of Atlanticism.

If one compares this strategy with the original foreign policy agenda of the centre-right, therefore, one cannot miss the fundamental contradiction between its own alleged 'national' basis and its actual 'international' driver. The idea that foreign policy is essentially a continuation of domestic/national politics (if not the result of a personal 'primacy') is simplistic in so far as it fails to take into proper account how the international system comes into play. Surely an exaggerated reaction to the end of the Cold War, the centre-right vision of Italy's foreign policy has tended to overestimate Italy's autonomy in the current international system as well as under-rate the constraints under which Italian foreign policy is actually articulated.

The centre-left: an international foreign policy?

The foreign policy vision of the centre-left is based on a series of assumptions – about both the new nature of the international system after the Cold War and the consequences for Italian foreign policy – which are not entirely dissimilar to those held by the centre-right. However, the policy conclusions drawn from these assumptions are radically different:

> To Italy the end of the bipolar era offers the opportunity of pursuing a foreign policy less conditioned by the international constraints of the past. [...] [However] our country should not really conceive of unilateral foreign policies; on the contrary, it should operate more actively and consistently [...] in the main multilateral contexts. This is the only choice in line with the international interests of Italy.
>
> (IAI 1994b: 241)

This principle has been translated into a firm internationalism.[5] Even the category of 'national interest' has been redefined to take into account the international framework in which Italy's foreign policy is necessarily to be articulated (hence, the 'international', rather than national, interests in the quote) (L'Ulivo 2004). Thence, the centre-left's emphasis on the centrality of European integration, and the fundamental value of Italy's participation in it:

> We entered the XXI century in a deeply changed world. [...] The transformations of our world enter [...] our homes, but it is not from there that we can guide them. It is Europe that allows us to do so. It is Europe which can and must operate efficiently to correct the wrong paths of globalisation, to foster peace, democracy and equality.
>
> (L' Ulivo 2004)

The same principle of reliance upon international frameworks for the articulation of Italy's foreign policy interests is the basis for the strategy of 'active multilateralism' which has been the tenet of the centre-left strategy when in government. Inspired by the lucid reassessment of Italy's role in the post-bipolar international politics by the former Foreign and Defence Minister Beniamino Andreatta (1993a, 1993b), the strategy of 'active multilateralism' promoted by the centre-left translated into two main imperatives. On the one hand, the need to enhance Italy's role in all multilateral frameworks by raising its political profile within them as well as increasing its level of contribution to their activities; on the other, the acknowledgement that integration is a value in itself, and that its promotion is fundamental to the attainment of Italy's true national interests.

In terms of the balance between domestic and international drivers of foreign policy, then, the foreign policy vision put forward by the centre-left privileges, at least in theory, the international dimension of foreign policy. After all, the Euro episode clearly demonstrated that a set of decisions taken on an integrated (if not international) level was able to influence foreign policy for a significant period of time and with considerable repercussions for domestic politics. By the same token, it is fair to say that the national dimension of foreign policy has remained under-conceptualised in the centre-left discussion of foreign policy, for well-known historical and political reasons.

Yet, despite all the emphasis on the 'international', it has often been the case that when in government the centre-left ended up pursuing distinctly national, if not subtly nationalist, foreign policies. Dini's permanence at the Foreign Ministry certainly contributed to this result – with his determination to raise the stakes with NATO over Bosnia, for instance, or the eccentric policy pursued vis-à-vis 'problem states' like North Korea and Libya – *despite* the opposition of European partners, the UN and the US at the time, i.e. those very multilateral frameworks of which Italy is part. This seems to feed into a larger trend, however, one that goes well beyond the role of particular personalities. By anchoring Italy's foreign policy solidly to a number of international frameworks, Italy is able to pursue limited, yet distinctly national policies, with the added advantage of an international cover. This is the continuation of a particular strategy which Italy and many other small European states pursued throughout its post-war participation in the process of European integration. Thus, to some extent the centre-left foreign policy outlook shows a degree of continuity with the Cold War, despite the dramatic changes which have taken place in the international system post-1989.

2005–2011: new (and old) patterns of convergence

If the first decade of the 'Second Republic' presented strikingly and substantively different foreign policy narratives between the two dominant coalitions, in the second decade the trend has been somewhat inverted. On the one hand, the centre-right has toned down some of its more 'nationalist' and 'revanchist' themes, emphasising the principle of responsibility as well as that of autonomy in foreign policy. Thus, the kind of systematic Euro-sceptic rhetoric which permeated much centre-right discourse of the first Berlusconi government has been abandoned by all but the LN. The discourse surrounding the ratification of Lisbon treaty is a case in point, and no doubt the actual experience of government has helped in shaping the narrative in this direction (Carbone and Quaglia 2011: 172). On the other hand, the centre-left has undergone an often divisive but necessary process of soul-searching regarding important aspects of foreign policy, such as the use of force in humanitarian interventions and the role of the US in the management of global security. In the debates over the military campaigns in Kosovo, then Afghanistan and Iraq and, more recently, over Libya, the discourse of pacifism and radical internationalism has been definitively appropriated by the extreme left. The centre-left coalition, on the other hand, has coped with or actively supported interventions even when the normative umbrella of the UN was missing (e.g. Kosovo). Equally, it has exceeded all expectations in its profession of Atlanticism, as the episode of the US military base in Vicenza has recently confirmed, leaving the more critical or overtly anti-American outlooks to the radical left (Andreatta 2008b).

In terms of foreign policy then, despite the high level of litigiousness in the everyday political competition, the differences in foreign policy paradigms between the coalitions are not only less marked and substantive than they were at the start of the 'Second Republic', but are also less marked and significant than are the differences *within* each coalition. While this could have translated into a bipartisan consensus on foreign policy, the outcome has rather been one of neutralisation and de-politicisation of foreign policy. Thus, since around 2005 and the 'consensual' decision to withdraw Italian troops from Iraq, foreign policy has virtually disappeared from the political platforms presented at the 2006 and 2008 elections by the two main coalitions, and has remerged only when explicitly tied to domestic political considerations.

The analysis of Italy's foreign policy in the 'Second Republic': the state of the art

The 1990s: nation, identity, geopolitics

In the intellectual and academic debate of the early 1990s, interest in international politics, and the role of Italy within it, peaked unexpectedly. This was due, at least in part, to the end of the Cold War and the opening up of many scenarios in which Italy could play a role. In terms of foreign policy, the debate has developed along a number of avenues.

The first avenue of exploration developed in relation to the extraordinary resurgence of interest in the concept of 'national interest'. Given the transformations of both the international and domestic political system, many contributions called for a re-evaluation not just of Italy's foreign policy strategy, but of the very concept of nation, a word which had remained taboo throughout the post-war history, because of its association with fascism. Authors such as Ernesto Galli della Loggia and Gian Enrico Rusconi were amongst the most vocal in denouncing Italy's lack of a clear national identity as the single most important cause of the country's troubled domestic development and, consequently, of its fragile international performance since 1943 (Galli della Loggia 1996; Spadolini 1994; Rusconi 1993, Santoro 2001).

It was, in other words, time to rediscover Italy's national vocation in domestic politics, which also meant initiating a thorough reassessment of Italy's strategic priorities in international affairs:

> Today we can do it, because the end of bipolarism allows everyone to be oneself. It brings Italy back to its autonomous responsibility, since the

> international system which kept the country on its feet has fallen. Now we have to decide who we want to be.
>
> (Galli della Loggia 1993: 103)

Relatedly, Sergio Romano proposed a domestic view of Italian foreign policy polemically centred upon the idea of its 'death' in the aftermath of the dual crisis of 1989/92. Since the *blocco storico* ('historic establishment') which formed the basis of Italian foreign policy between 1943 and 1992 – mainly, the collusive party system and the business élite which supported it – had been swept away by domestic and international turbulence, Romano argued, Italian foreign policy was facing an inevitable death. In particular, as long as the country's energies were absorbed by the on-going economic, political and financial crisis, Italy was destined not to have a foreign policy – whether national or European in nature (Romano 1992, 1995).

A veritable anxiety to rediscover Italy's *interesse nazionale* together with the country's *identità nazionale* permeated the intellectual and academic debate on Italian foreign policy from the early to mid-1990s. This led to a wealth of publications devoted to launching and sustaining a debate on Italy's role in contemporary international relations, as well as Italy's capacity to project its interests abroad in a unitary and coherent fashion (CeMiss 1997; Corsico 1998). Needless to say, this debate inevitably came to reinforce the emergence of a moderate yet distinctively nationalist political discourse, which roughly corresponded to the rise to power of the centre-right coalition (Merlini 1993, 1994).

The rediscovery of the theme of 'national interest' tied in well with the other intellectual fashion of the early 1990s, namely the resurrecting of geopolitical thought. As with the 'national interest', the resurgence in interest in geopolitics was spurred mainly by the end of bipolarism, but also by the perceived need to provide Italian foreign policy makers of the 'Second Republic' with a system of analytical and conceptual tools with which to examine contemporary world politics and Italy's place within it. Thus, the birth of *Limes: rivista italiana di geopolitica* – certainly the most remarkable editorial success story in the Italian field of international relations/foreign policy in many decades – but also the proliferation of geopolitical thought in journals, reviews and newspapers (Brighi and Petito 2012; Lucarelli and Radaelli 2004).

Both tendencies displayed a characteristic propensity to jettison the foreign policy of Italy between 1943 and 1992 as wholly inconsistent and ambiguous, and called for a more assertive and confident course. However, each of these strands of thought had its own ambiguities and contradictions: in the end, the most visible one was the lack of realism – not the theoretical school, which they both praised, but the more down-to-earth capacity to acknowledge the reality of Italy's domestic and foreign policy and avoid replacing it with abstract and idealised notions (Bonanate 1997; Ferraris 1993; Santoro 1996):

> Italy has interests because it is an important actor in the international arena, and not the other way around. Otherwise we would run the risk of creating

> artificial and ephemeral interests, as if made in a laboratory, which would not be in tune with the country and thus would not be perceived as such.
> (Andreatta 1997: 137)

In the end, it was this lack of political realism which condemned both strands of thought to a progressive loss of influence, which materialised at the end of the 1990s.

The 2000s: continuity vs. discontinuity and levels of analysis

The debate on how to explain Italy's foreign policy was revived in 2001, mainly due to another dual change. On the domestic level, the victory of the centre-right and, more visibly, the affirmation of the leadership of Berlusconi attracted a vast body of commentary. On the international level the 'big bang' events of 11 September 2001 prompted an analysis of the ongoing restructuring of the international system and its effect upon countries such as Italy. This dual change soon triggered a sustained debate about the relative importance of variables such as leadership, domestic politics and international relations in Italian foreign policy.

Thus, there have been those who have interpreted Italian foreign policy through the lens of leadership and personality, arguing that Italian foreign policy needs to be understood in terms of the idiosyncrasies and eccentricities of Italy's dominant political figure and four-time Prime Minister, Berlusconi (Ignazi 2004; Rossi 2002; Romano 2006). Other contributions have challenged this view, responding that a focus on personality not only misses the big picture, but also 'engenders a misleading trivilization' of foreign policy, failing to acknowledge how Berlusconi's foreign policy course reflects more deeply seated concerns and interests (Brighi 2006: 3).

This debate has fed into the larger question of the impact of domestic politics upon foreign policy. In particular, analysts have discussed the impact of changes in government, i.e. the alternation of centre-right and centre-left coalitions in government, on the foreign policy of Italy. A group of scholars have argued that this alternation has brought a significant degree of discontinuity (Andreatta 2008b, 2008c; Carbone 2007; Carbone and Quaglia 2011). Others have been more cautious in advancing the argument that while this alternation has certainly changed the rhetoric, it has not changed foreign policy outcomes besides a few nuances (Davidson 2011; Nuti 2005; Walston 2007). A third group of scholars have denied that the change in governing coalitions has significantly impacted upon foreign policy, as this is determined relatively more by international variables such as alliances or geopolitics which, incidentally, have not changed much since the Cold War (Bellucci 1997; Croci 2005, 2008). Finally, some analysts have drawn on versions of neo-realism (neoclassical realism and structural realism, respectively) to more strongly and formally argue for the relative primacy of international variables over domestic variables in explaining Italy's foreign policy after the end of the Cold War (Cladi and Webber 2011) or, indeed, across time

(Ratti 2012). Interestingly, little has been advanced in terms of relating these explanations and their variables together in the attempt to come up with a genuinely integrative framework of analysis (but see Menotti 2007; Brighi 2007c).

Italy's foreign policy in the 'Second Republic': a critical realist assessment

Drawing on the conceptualisations developed in Chapter 1, is it possible to arrive at a fuller and more critical understanding of Italy's foreign policy during the 'Second Republic'? How do these conceptualisations fare when measured against the empirical record and how do they move us beyond the current analyses of the subject matter?

Monocausal approaches

To start with the primacy of the international accounts, there is no doubt that the changed international environment impacted upon Italy's foreign policy to some degree. The fall of the Berlin Wall and the end of bipolarism arguably brought about a greater autonomy and freedom of action in orienting and re-orienting the foreign policy of all countries, including Italy. As many commentators have noted, and as mentioned in Section 3 ('The analysis of Italy's foreign policy in the "Second Republic": the state of the art'), for Italy in particular, the disappearance of the Soviet threat signalled the end of the 'privileged' status inside the Atlantic Alliance derived from Italy's positioning along the East–West frontier.

From a neo-realist perspective, the 'distribution of power' in the international political system has changed considerably since 1989, and so to has the geopolitical landscape. In particular, instead of the East–West axis of bipolarism, in the early to mid-1990s the most important geopolitical scenario ostensibly moved from the centre of Europe to that of the 'arc of instability' stretching from the Balkans to North Africa.

How did Italy's foreign policy respond to these interrelated changes in the international environment surrounding it? To some extent, its foreign policy has validated some of the expectations generated by monocausal international perspectives. First, the disappearance of the bipolar structure has certainly facilitated the launching of a series of autonomous initiatives which were explicitly aimed at moving beyond the Cold War logic of bipolarism, and its own associated geography of threat, resulting in the remarkable dynamism which characterised Italian foreign policy in the early 1990s. Second, the geographic re-orientation of Italian foreign policy towards the Balkans, Africa and the Mediterranean shows the degree to which the new geopolitical landscape impacted upon the direction of its foreign policy.

However, an exclusively international account can only provide a very general frame of analysis. Consider, for instance, the interventions carried out in the Balkans in the 1990s and in the Middle East in the 2000s. It is doubtful that the way in which Italy took part in these operations was shaped exclusively by international pressures – it is much more plausible to argue that this also had something to do with domestic politics. In the case of Albania and Kosovo, for instance, the need to keep the coalition in government united and the presence of vocal left-wing minorities were both reflected in Italy's participation, such as by making the government extremely cautious on the issue of the use of ground troops or by explicitly limiting the use of the Italian air force to 'humanitarian' objectives. The same concerns have resurfaced in Iraq, Afghanistan and, most recently, Libya.

Thus, in the exercise of military force abroad Italy's conduct was not only influenced by international factors such as the need to participate in NATO's operations or the need to respond to a 'threat'. Domestic political concerns did play a role in shaping decisions on several foreign policy options. Further, if foreign policy really was externally driven, one would not be able to explain the frequent threat that domestic politics poses to the survival of governments (especially centre-left ones) and to the pursuit of their foreign policy, as they often struggle in maintaining majorities in Parliament. The debacle of the Prodi governments in Albania 1998 and again over Afghanistan in 2007 are cases in point. To borrow Alan Lamborn's terminology, therefore, Italy seems to be a classic case of 'policy' being hijacked by 'politics' (Lamborn 1991).

If one understands the primacy of the international to be about international institutions, then the revival of multilateralism of post-Wall international politics has certainly strengthened the validity of this outlook. In the context of Italian foreign policy international institutions such as the EU and the UN have equally constituted indispensable frameworks. In the 1990s, participation in 'Europe' was deemed such an imperative as to have arguably 'dictated' not only a certain macroeconomic policy to the Prodi government, but also a particular foreign policy (i.e. the 1997 operation in Albania, or the 2006 intervention in Lebanon, both of which were presumed to earn Italy credibility in Europe and in the international community at large).

However, the degree to which international institutions have constrained Italy's foreign policy has been, at best, variable. Consider, for instance, the different ways in which the centre-left and centre-right governments have approached the issue of European foreign policy, for instance in the case of Iraq. There is no doubt that instead of bridging gaps or mending the cracks within the European front, the centre-right government of Berlusconi has not only not felt constrained by any European solidarity, but it has marginally widened those cracks by siding resolutely with the US and legitimising the division between 'old' and 'new' Europe. Interestingly, and perhaps more surprisingly, it was when the centre-left government of D'Alema was in power that Italy intervened in Kosovo in the absence of the UN normative – i.e. at a time when the governing coalition was most expected to be susceptible to that normative constraint.

Can an exclusively domestic explanation make sense of the foreign policy of Italy of the last decade, as the primacy of the domestic would predict? How determining were domestic concerns in shaping Italy's external behaviour?

In answering these questions it is interesting to start by noting that the domestic political crisis which marked the years 1992–1994 did not translate directly into a 'crisis', or the neutralisation of Italian foreign policy, as a purely domestic account would tend to suggest (Romano 1992). Rather, it translated into its exact opposite, i.e. a remarkable dynamism. One interpretation could be that during the crisis of 1992–1994 foreign policy leadership played a crucial role, filling the void left by the implosion of an entire domestic political system (for example, contrast the very different but equally determining roles of the two Foreign Ministers De Michelis and Andreatta in shaping the foreign policy of Italy between 1990–1994).

There can be little doubt that domestic politics has played a rather central role in influencing the foreign policy strategies pursued by Italy in the 'Second Republic'. Humanitarian interventions are a case in point. In Kosovo, for instance, Italy was the only Western country to keep its embassy open in Belgrade while participating in the bombings against the Serbs – hardly a strategic necessity, but rather a policy dictated by preferences set domestically. More recently, as discussed earlier, a number of analysts have argued that the alternation of centre-left and centre-right governing coalitions has clearly impacted upon Italy's foreign policy vis-à-vis Europe, the Middle East, and the US, clearly offering a domestic reading of Italian foreign policy.

All this being said, however, and just as with the 'primacy of the international' explanations, it is important to question the exclusively domestic readings of Italy's foreign policy. The general problem with these readings, in fact, is that they are all dismissive of context. In the case of the changes brought about by the centre-right government of Berlusconi, for instance, the reading mentioned above fails to take into account the degree to which the restructuring of the international system post-9/11 created incentives for Italy to revamp its Atlanticism as well as revise its attitude towards Europe. In other words, the 'new course' could hardly have taken place in any international system, but rather required a set of specific international conditions to bring it about. Thus, domestic politics should be more clearly related to the international scenario and, in particular, the role of the US in it.

As for Italy's participation in humanitarian interventions, there is no doubt that domestic politics heavily constrained Italy's conduct and policies, as discussed above. Yet, this constraint did not prevent Italy from participating fully in the series of international military or humanitarian operations in Bosnia, Somalia, Albania and Kosovo (Davidson 2011). Despite all of its eccentricities, Italy complied with the strategic requirements of NATO operations and asserted its position within the multilateral frameworks of which it is part.

Dualist approaches

According to dualist/additive models, foreign policy results from the addition of domestic and international pressures; further, foreign policy is conceptualised as a 'balancing activity' between two equally pressing constraints. Can this view capture the way Italian foreign policy was influenced by domestic politics and international relations?

As discussed in Chapter 1, this view of foreign policy is extremely sound in descriptive terms, although it is lacking in terms of its explanatory power. Consider again the case of Kosovo, for instance. Doubtless, Italy's foreign policy during the crisis had to balance domestic and international constraints and unfold within this 'dual' constraint. Thus, a straightforward account of this particular case could be obtained by simply adding the number of influences – domestic and international – that have played a role in the crisis.

However, this would not provide an explanation in itself, but merely a list of relevant factors. First, no interaction between the variables would be accounted for; second, no idea as to their relative weight would be forthcoming. These two problems, however, are crucial in providing an explanation of foreign policy. Compare, for instance, the Kosovo intervention of 1999 to the intervention in Iraq of the 2000s: given the strength of the coalition and its political culture (i.e. more or less war-prone), the domestic constraint played a variable role, in one case heavily constraining the intervention in Kosovo, while in the case of Iraq providing a less sanctioning set of imperatives. Coalition politics, as variable, had a critical importance in 1999, while it became less central with the centre-right government between 2001–2006, and also to a degree between 2008–2011.

As for the interactions between the variables, consider the case of the intervention in Albania of 1997–1998 and, in particular, the extent to which the fall of the Prodi government in October 1998 resulted from the collapse of the domestic coalition supporting the government which, in turn, was significantly hastened by the intervention in Albania. In other words, Italy's foreign policy was the result of two 'games' – played on the domestic and international front – just as it was the result of the entanglements between the two 'games'. As this instance (among others) testifies, the assumption of the discreteness of foreign policy vis-à-vis domestic politics and international relations is empirically difficult to sustain. Just as with the inability to account for the varying degrees to which variables influence foreign policy, this feature seriously impairs the usefulness of additive approaches.

A second dualist approach that can be adopted to explain the foreign policy of Italy during the 'Second Republic' is that of 'nested games'. This approach assumes that international relations provide a 'first cut' explanation of foreign policy, leaving domestic politics to decide its specific details. How does such an approach fare when applied to the case of Italian foreign policy between 1992 and 2011?

Let us consider the revival of Atlanticism which characterised the foreign policy course pursued by the Berlusconi government between 2001 and 2006. Can the post-9/11 international relations account for this line of foreign policy, at least in its main features? To start with, if we take American hegemony to constitute the main tenet around which the international system currently revolves, then neo-realist approaches grounded in a 'nested games' framework would predict a balancing strategy, rather than a bandwagoning approach. Italy, in other words, should have been encouraged to join other European countries in balancing against rather than joining such a power.

Hence, Italy's decision to strengthen its ties with the US cannot but be explained by a recourse to domestic politics, and not merely to decide the 'details' of this strategy, but in relation to its very essence as well. In fact, in these accounts domestic politics ultimately seems to do most of the explanatory work. The leadership of Berlusconi and the ideology/political culture of the centre-right coalition in government were equally important in bringing about such a policy.

More generally, domestic politics exerted a constraining effect upon foreign policy which was just as important as that of international relations, if not even more so. Indeed, the relatively loose international system of the early 1990s was not only compatible with many foreign policies, the exact shape of which was decided by domestic politics; more crucially, this system was in itself largely indeterminate and could, as such, hardly provide a 'first cut' at anything. Hence, the hierarchy of causes typical of 'nested games' seems, once again, to be vulnerable to criticism.

Can the pendulum approach better capture the development of Italy's foreign policy over the last decade or so? Has foreign policy perhaps been swinging from one end to the other of the pendulum trajectory? Let us consider the various segments into which Italian foreign policy under the 'Second Republic' can be divided.

A reading of Italy's foreign policy in the 'Second Republic' would proceed as follows. Between 1989 and 1994 (t_1 in Figure 5.1) both domestic politics and international politics were in a state of flux caused by the end of bipolarism in the first case and the end of the 'First Republic' in the second. Foreign policy was influenced neither by strong international pressures nor by precise domestic stimuli; indeed, to borrow Romano's expression, Italian foreign policy as we knew it (i.e. the product of the particular pre-1989 combination of international and domestic constraints) was dead (Romano 1992). It was rather the initiative of particular personalities, or more generally the role of leadership, that 'kept it alive', so to speak, and actually determined a phase of relative dynamism in

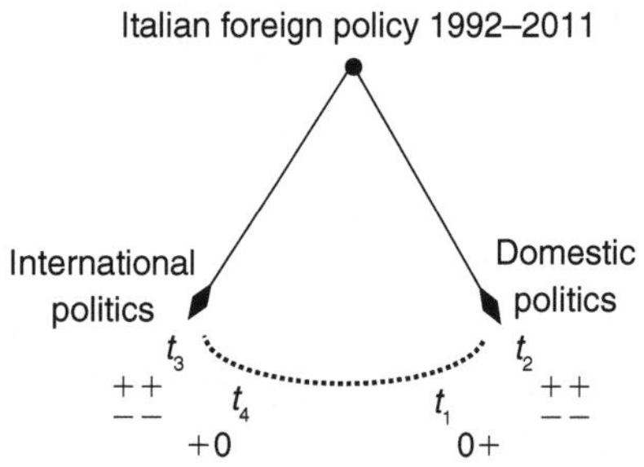

Figure 5.1 A 'pendulum' approach to Italian foreign policy 1992–2011. The application of the pendulum model to Italian foreign policy 1992–2011; with t_1: 1989–1994; t_2: 1994–2001; t_3: 2001–2006; t_4: 2006–2011.

foreign affairs: hence, Italy's activism in the nascent EU and in Central Europe in the early 1990s, but also its intervention in Somalia and its innovative proposal for a reform of the UN Security Council, between 1993 and 1994.

From 1994 until 2001 (t_2), with the restructuring of the domestic political system and the continued state of flux of international relations, domestic politics came to have a greater impact upon foreign policy than was the case in the previous phase. Variables such as ideology and political culture, the impact of party/political dynamics and the alternation in government all played a great role in determining Italy's attitude vis-à-vis some of the fundamental issues of its foreign policy – i.e. its participation in the process of European integration and, more generally, in the multilateral frameworks of which Italy is a part; the propensity to use of force; and the recourse to bilateralism. Even the instances of participation in international interventions, such as those in Bosnia, Albania and Kosovo, were motivated by domestic concerns (among others, immigration) and shaped by domestic factors (wrangling inside the governing coalition) relatively more than international ones.

With the events of 11 September 2001, however, the years of the relative primacy of domestic politics came to an end (t_3). The consequent intensification, or tightening up, of the international constraint – visible most of all in the further reaffirmation of US hegemony – inevitably changed the environment of Italian foreign policy, making it less 'permissive'. The 'imperatives' of the 'Global War on Terror' weighed significantly upon Italian foreign policy. Domestic politics did not disappeared altogether from the equation, although its relative stability between 2001 and 2006 rendered it less turbulent and potentially 'damaging' for foreign policy.

Last, the period between 2006 and 2011 (t_4) has seen foreign policy influenced by a less stringent international environment marked by the progressive disengagement from Iraq and Afghanistan as well as the more cooperative policies of the US under the democratic administration of Barack Obama. Domestically, instability has coupled with weaker coalitions and a relatively more fragmented party system, which has made the pendulum swing back towards the centre. Interestingly, differently from (t_1) when foreign policy was anything but dead, despite not being pulled by the pendulum in any clear directions, over the last few years and especially since the 'bipartisan' withdrawal from Iraq (2006) foreign policy seems to have become not only more consensual but essentially de-politicised and stagnant.

As usual with the pendulum approach, this model is descriptively rich but cannot account for the swings of foreign policy, i.e. cannot offer explanations as to why and when the pendulum swings in the first place. Those cases in which both international and domestic factors are relevant, or interrelated, become more difficult to account for, let alone explain.

Dialectical approaches

In the dialectic morphogenetic approach, foreign policy results from the sequential interplay of international relations and domestic politics; the former operates through a 'structural conditioning', the latter through the 'emergent properties' of the state. When played out, in turn, foreign policy can influence the international environment surrounding it, leading either to morphogenesis or morphostasis. Can such an approach explain the way in which Italian foreign policy developed in the 'Second Republic'? Can it provide an interesting conceptualisation of foreign policy for the period at hand?

Consider, for instance, the 'new course' initiated by the second Berlusconi government in 2001. One could argue that this has not come about simply through the working of the 'structural' features of international relations post-9/11, or exclusively as the result of domestic changes. Rather, it was the sequential interplay of such developments that crucially precipitated the new foreign policy course. However, four puzzles arise from such an account.

First, although the model conceptualises the relationship between foreign policy, international relations and domestic politics as sequential and dialectic, when empirically applied to foreign policy this mechanism too easily comes to resemble the logic of the 'additive' models reviewed above. Further, in this sequence international and domestic factors impact unproblematically upon foreign policy, as if no discursive/ideational mediation were in place. However, the fact that Berlusconi mobilised a particular, moderately nationalist discourse through which to understand Italy's place in the post-9/11 international relations did influence the final outcome. Had this mobilisation not taken place, the urge to follow Washington in its foreign policy agenda would have felt much less compelling.

Second and relatedly, from a tentative application of the morphogenetic model it is difficult to capture the degree to which the domestic politics and international relations of Italy since 2001 interrelated and interacted. Rather, one has the impression that each developed according to its own logic. This is probably proof of the ontological dualism discussed in Chapter 1.

Third, the fact that international relations and domestic politics reside, as the model suggests, in two 'different temporal domains' is difficult to justify in empirical terms because of their temporally co-extensive character in reality. In the particular instance of Italy's foreign policy after 9/11, the residual bias for structure that the morphogenetic model exhibits could not do justice to the fact that the restructuring of international relations followed and did not predate the domestic influences on foreign policy associated with the establishment of the second Berlusconi government. Hence, the sequence seems to be rather different.

Fourth, and last, despite its ambitions, this foreign policy course did not produce dramatic changes in the environment surrounding it, hence it is difficult to indicate any instances of morphogenesis which resulted from it. This, however, would indicate that Italian foreign policy has been simply the result of the sequential addition of 'structural conditioning' and 'emergent properties', leaving no scope for any feedback process.

Is a strategic-relational approach better equipped to deal with the foreign policy of Italy in the 'Second Republic'? Can the dialectic between a strategically-selective context, discourse and strategy account for the way in which foreign policy was produced over the last two decades? In order to answer these questions, let us first reconsider the foreign policy of Italy between 2001 and 2006.

In terms of context, there is no doubt that international relations post-9/11 provided a highly contoured environment for Italy. In particular, the further consolidation of American hegemony and the divisions in Europe have also meant a change in Italy's position in relation to its environment. In purely strategic terms, in fact, a relatively weak state such as Italy can maximise its relative power when placed between two countervailing groups or powers. When, however, one of the two blocs rises above the other, there is a high incentive to join, rather than oppose it. In more concrete terms, the rise of American hegemony following the events of 9/11 has brought with it an incentive to bandwagon rather than balance, and has influenced (but has not determined) Italian foreign policy in this direction.

In terms of strategy, as mentioned in Section 1 ('Losing a status and finding a role? Italy in search of a foreign policy'), the Berlusconi government has most of all attempted to enhance the profile and status of Italy, in multilateral and especially bilateral contexts. A more assertive direction for foreign affairs has coupled with the use of a number of foreign policy instruments, especially a greater ease in using military force.

Finally, in terms of discourse, the centre-right has broken with tradition and articulated a vision of foreign policy centred upon a moderate form of nationalism. The emergence of a distinct 'national interest' talk has coupled with an emphasis upon Italy's autonomy and freedom of action in choosing its foreign policy objectives.

Neither contextual factors, nor purely domestic pressures nor, finally, discourse alone, can account for the re-orienting of Italy's foreign policy between 2001 and 2006. Rather, this seems to be the result of the dialectical interplay between three interrelated elements: a strategically-selective context, Italy's own strategy and, finally, the prevailing discourse in matters of foreign affairs. The strategic-relational model suggests that had any of these elements been different, the dialectic would have likely produced a different outcome.

First, had the context of relations not been one of relative hegemony – had Italy been bigger, more powerful or, conversely, had the US not been so powerful – the strategic incentives to join the American wagon and forsake the European front on issues such as the war on Iraq would have been far less significant. Second, had the coalition in government expressed a different strategy, or had a different coalition (e.g. the centre-left) been in government, the result would presumably have been different. It would be hard to imagine Italy pursuing the same policy post-9/11 had, for instance, the centre-left of Romano Prodi been in government – it is reasonable to assume that divisions in European foreign policy would have not been exploited or exacerbated, and the sending of troops to Iraq (as opposed to Afghanistan) would have been less likely to start with. Had the strategy of the government in power been norm-oriented and not one of pure maximisation of power, or had it valued international institutions such as the EU or the UN more, the incentive to follow the American leadership in the war on Iraq, for instance, would have been less marked. Last, had the prevailing foreign policy discourse not been one of resurgent nationalism, but one of firm multilateralism, the opportunities to supposedly enhance the profile and status of the country would have been valued differently. Indeed, they would have probably not even been considered as opportunities.

It is interesting to note that the return of the centre-right to power between 2008 and 2011 has not produced a similarly stark re-orientation of Italian foreign policy. Domestically-driven accounts of foreign policy would, however, lead us to expect precisely that. The strategic-relational model, on the other hand, alerts us to the fact that even if strategy and discourse remained the same – which they did not, as I argue below – it would be enough for the context to change in order for foreign policy to be affected differently. And indeed this was the case in the period under consideration, when the unipolar and tense environment post-9/11 had given way to a more cooperative and less hegemonic system, influenced to some degree by the change in leadership and administration in the US.

On closer inspection, however, between 2008 and 2011 the centre-right government has not only operated in a different international context, but has also partly changed its outlook as to the perceived benefits of a strategy of bandwagoning, no doubt on the strength of previous experience, which included being 'entrapped' and dragged in unpopular military campaigns such as Iraq. Thus, the more predictable and traditional foreign policy pursued between 2008–2011 can be explained on the basis not only of a change in the strategically-selective context surrounding Italy, but also partly through adaptation and feedback from foreign policy to strategy, as the strategic-relational model predicts (f_1 in Figure 1.9).

That the strategically selective context may have changed the balance of opportunities and constraints for Italy post-2006, offering a more permissive environment in which to operate, is also testified by the foreign policy choices made since then, for instance concerning the recent intervention in Lebanon. This intervention would have hardly been possible only a few years earlier, between 2001 and 2006, for at least two different reasons. On the one hand, the centre-right would have not perceived this as a particularly desirable course, and indeed would have preferred to send more troops to Iraq than to send any contingent to Lebanon. On the other hand, in the tightly knit post-9/11 international environment the margins for autonomous initiatives such as this one would have been much narrower, while the pressures to conform to systemic incentives and transatlantic solidarity higher, even in the case of a centre-left government.

Thus, the strategic-relational model seems to be able to provide an intelligible yet complex account of the evolution of Italian foreign policy during the 'Second Republic' as well as of specific foreign policy choices made at this time. This account can reject the strictures of simple monocausal models, yet also offer a coherent and parsimonious framework that illustrates the dialectical interplay of foreign policy, domestic politics and international relations.

Conclusions

In this chapter I have examined the foreign policy of Italy's 'Second Republic'. As I argued in the first section, in the post-1989 era Italy has pursued a rather dynamic foreign policy, as if the end of the bipolar constraint had finally offered the opportunity to restructure foreign policy around a more confident assessment of Italy's national interests. Between 1992 and 2005, domestic instability and the restructuring of the country's entire political system has led to the emergence of two alternative understandings and discourses of Italy's foreign policy. Since 2005, however, substantive differences in the discourse over foreign policy have evaporated and foreign policy has become more 'consensual'.

By examining the overall trajectory of Italian foreign policy between 1992 and 2011 against the backdrop of the models and approaches illustrated in Chapter 1, I have attempted to provide a response to the stalemate which characterises the current academic and intellectual debate. As I have argued, mono-causal models are insufficiently equipped to deal with Italy's foreign policy during the period at hand. Dualist models are more promising, yet they fall short of examining the ways in which foreign policy, domestic politics and international relations interact. Dialectical models, and especially the strategically-relational model, can provide a complex yet manageable account of how Italian foreign policy has responded to pressures and influences coming from domestic politics and international relations, at a time of flux for both.

Conclusions

Foreign policy, domestic politics and international relations: the case of Italy

Despite being at the heart of FPA, the issue of how domestic and international factors combine to generate foreign policy has been subject to little explicit theorising and limited agreement. Its location on the boundary between disciplines and its ramifications into a host of ontological, epistemological and normative issues renders the task particularly complex. The low propensity towards theory and metatheory in FPA is also partially to blame, as is the framing of the question from which the existing approaches derive. Yet, this arguably remains one of the central questions – if not *the* central question – of FPA.

This state of affairs needs redressing and progress in this direction, I have argued, is realistically within the discipline's reach. Drawing on critical realism, I have offered a reconceptualisation of the puzzle centred upon the tripartition of monocausal, dualist and dialectical frameworks. In assessing the relative merits and limits of the frameworks thus generated, I have particularly emphasised the potential of a dialectical model – the strategic-relational. Because of the solution it offers to a number of seemingly intractable dichotomies – inside and outside, explaining and understanding, structure and agency, efficient and intentional causality, etc. – this model goes beyond the current interpretative impasse and towards a complex theory of foreign policy in its relations with domestic and international politics.

On the strength of these considerations I have moved on to examine the foreign policy of Italy over the last century, according to the following periodisation: the liberal age, the fascist era, the 'First Republic' and the 'Second Republic' (Chapters 2 to 5). The orthodoxy in matters of Italian foreign policy is rather unsatisfying. In the same way that FPA has failed to move confidently beyond monocausal theories and towards more complex accounts, so too has the literature on Italian foreign policy typically reinforced the confrontation between a structuralist, arch-realist interpretation of foreign policy and an inward-looking, ephemeral and often factionalist account of its diplomatic conduct.

The application of robust theoretical frameworks sketched out in Chapter 1 was designed precisely to expose the limits of traditional accounts, generate alternative, counterfactual viewpoints, liberate some space for more creative and balanced interventions, and test the frameworks against the empirical record. Naturally, the results yielded by this inquiry cannot but be considered partial and specific to the case of Italy, yet they are heuristically important in so far as they shed some light upon an admittedly complex process, help discern interesting general patterns, and suggest possible theoretical solutions.

Main findings

I now refer back to the research questions listed in Chapter 1 in order to assess the main findings of this research. Thus, starting from the first question:

> Q_1: Was Italian foreign policy *exclusively* a function of international relations? Or was it instead *exclusively* a function of domestic politics? In more theoretical terms, were monocausal theories (primacy of the international, primacy of the domestic) ever corroborated during each period? If so, under what conditions?

There is sufficient evidence to argue that in none of the four periods were monocausal approaches to Italian foreign policy entirely corroborated. On a first look this might of course appear to be a rather mundane result: after all, few would really endorse such extreme views of foreign policy. As I have tried to argue, however, this is a logically indispensable step for the remainder of my analysis in order to refute monologic arguments loosely inspired by such models, examples of which abound in the case of Italy.

Thus, in terms of the liberal period, exclusively international or purely domestic explanations are at a loss in explaining important episodes such as the Libyan intervention or the diplomatic wavering which Italy followed in the run-up to the First World War. Further, monocausal approaches are unsatisfactory even in those cases where one would expect them to be most plausible, i.e. at times of high international tension (First World War) in the case of the 'primacy of the international' or at times of particularly powerful domestic constraints (nationalism and the rise of the industrial-financial complex) for the 'primacy of the domestic'.

In the case of fascist foreign policy, monocausal approaches are equally lacking. Questions such as the troubled alliance with Germany or Italy's strategy in the run-up to the Second World War can hardly be explained by recurring to exclusively international or purely domestic explanations. In fact, these readings perform worst precisely under those conditions considered to be 'ideal' for the theory, i.e. in the case of high international tension (Second World War) and 'compelling' domestic circumstances (fascist ideology).

In the third period of Italy's foreign policy (that of the 'First Republic') no monocausal readings can make sense of the entire trajectory of the foreign policy pursued over almost five decades. Neither strong international constraints (such as the Cold War), nor an intense domestic political dynamic (of its party-political system) can in isolation account for trends such as Italy's 'pacifist Atlanticism', the phase of neutralisation of foreign policy around the mid-1970s, or episodes such as the Sigonella crisis of 1985.

Last, Italy's foreign policy during the 'Second Republic' also failed to respond unequivocally to either international or domestic pressures. Trends such as the new foreign policy course initiated by the Berlusconi government in 2001, Italy's participation in the military campaigns of the 'Global War on Terror', in Iraq and Afghanistan, and the humanitarian interventions of the 1990s and the recent intervention in Lebanon, cannot be explained by either international or domestic factors taken in isolation.

There is enough evidence, therefore, to refute monocausal approaches to foreign policy. Once again this may seem like an unsurprising and futile result. However, in itself it is significant. A large part of the appeal of monocausal models is their claim to be able to explain 'a lot with very little', i.e. their parsimony and wide applicability. Neither, however, sustains empirical scrutiny.

Turning to the second set of questions, let us consider the results concerning dualist approaches to foreign policy, namely

> Q_2 and Q_6: What was the 'relative weight' of international and domestic factors bearing on Italian foreign policy in each period? What was the relative weight of international and domestic factors bearing on Italian foreign policy over the four periods at hand? Did these vary or stay constant?
>
> Q_7: In theoretical terms, are dualist conceptualisations compatible with the way the relative weight of international and domestic factors have changed over time in the case of Italy? Can they provide a suitable account of it in terms of 'comparative static'?

My findings suggest that the plausibility of dualist models varies greatly. Additive approaches have proven to be the least useful in accounting for the foreign policy of Italy, in all of the cases examined. In fact, their claim that foreign policy is always the result of the simple addition of international and domestic factors is so general as to be unfalsifiable and, hence, of very limited use.

'Nested games' approaches, on the other hand, are both more promising and yet ultimately limited. In the case of liberal Italy, for example, the 'nested games' model is unable to account for instances when Italian foreign policy makers pursued a foreign policy clearly incompatible with the changing international relations of the time and mainly for domestic purposes, for instance, at the 1919 Paris Peace Conference. In the case of fascist Italy, it is doubtful whether international relations enjoyed a relative primacy throughout the period. In general, these approaches cannot accommodate the fact that fascist Italy was a distinctive national production which aimed at revolutionising the environment surrounding it, rather than being determined by it. Hence, international relations did not, almost by definition, provide a constantly prominent constraint, but rather a shifting influence. By contrast, throughout the 'First Republic', 'nested games' approaches seem to provide a more plausible interpretation of some phases within the overall trajectory of Italy's foreign policy post-1945 (e.g. the period 1947–1954), yet they fail to account for other phases (e.g. détente). Last, during the 'Second Republic' Italy's foreign policy has not always responded to international relations relatively more than to domestic politics, as these approaches assume. Neither the humanitarian interventions of the 1990s nor Italian foreign policy post-9/11 point in the direction expected by the model. It is unclear how the more uncertain, indeterminate environment of the post-Cold War can provide an accurate 'first cut' explanation of any foreign policy.

If we analyse the four periods comparatively, then, there is sufficient evidence to conclude that the relative weight of international and domestic factors has not been constantly skewed in favour of the former set of factors, as the theories of foreign policy grounded in the 'nested games' approach advance. Rather, the relative weights have tended to vary in each period and over the four periods at hand – however, the model is unable to account for this change and variance.

Moving on to the third and last dualist model, that of the 'pendulum', this has performed remarkably well in some periods, while less so in others. As to the latter group of cases, neither the liberal nor the fascist period seem to be clearly explainable through this model. In fact, in both periods, domestic politics and international relations seem to have *both* been important for the articulation of foreign policy at any given time. The foreign policies of liberal and fascist Italy, in other words, seem to constitute two examples of those cases that the 'pendulum' model cannot easily account for, as illustrated in Chapter 1. However, in both the 'First' and 'Second Republic' the 'pendulum' model has provided valuable accounts of the trajectory of foreign policy. In particular, the model can illuminate how foreign policy has served different 'functions' – domestic and international – at different times.

Comparing the four periods at hand, then, the general conclusion to be drawn is that the foreign policy of Italy has responded to a different combination of international and domestic factors at different times. The pendulum approach (Figure 1.7) is valid in those cases where the *difference of intensity* between the two constraints is *high* (t_1 and t_5), whereas it does not seem to be able to account for those instances where the *difference of intensity* between the two constraints is *low*, either because both constraints are permissive (t_3), or because both are intense (and escape the pictorial representation of Figure 1.7).

The third set of questions concerns the issue of foreign policy change, and refers to dialectical approaches:

> Q_3 and Q_8: What were the patterns of interaction between international relations, foreign policy and domestic politics during each period and over the four periods in question? How determining was this interplay in the construction of foreign policy and can dialectical approaches account for it?

> Q_4 and Q_9: Can the examination of the dialectic between strategy, context and discourse account for foreign policy change as the strategic-relational model suggests?

The morphogenetic approach has proved useful in accounting for foreign policy change in all four periods at hand, but especially during the liberal and fascist periods. This model was able to offer plausible explanations of episodes of Italian foreign policy as diverse as the Libyan intervention during the liberal period, or the Corfù crisis during the fascist period, stressing the interplay of domestic and international factors in determining the trajectory of foreign policy as well as its feedback on the system. In the last two periods under examination the morphogenetic model has, however, yielded less interesting results. In general terms, the model has proven to be limited in the way it deals with a few aspects of the subject matter: most of all, its unqualified view of 'structure' and its inability to take discourse into consideration.

A sophisticated treatment of the last two elements is offered, by contrast, by the strategic-relational model. Across all four periods this is the framework which provided the most generally valid account of how foreign policy responds to international and domestic influences. The analysis of how the context, strategy and discourse of Italy's foreign policy have interacted in each period under examination has yielded the most elaborate and plausible accounts of episodes such as fascist Italy's war in Ethiopia, the interventions in Libya of 1911 and 2011, as well as the big (and not so big) oscillations of Italy's foreign policy in the 2000s.

Before drawing some conclusions deriving from an overall assessment of these results, I address the last research question specified in Chapter 1, namely:

> Q_5: Did Italian foreign policy change with each change of domestic regime, or did it stay the same despite it? What patterns of continuity or discontinuity can be traced in the relations between foreign policy, domestic politics and international relations in the Italian case?

There is no doubt that changes in the domestic politics of Italy have affected its foreign policy over the last century. After all, the very fact that monocausal readings of Italian foreign policy centred upon the 'primacy of the international' are not substantiated by the empirical evidence necessarily implies two considerations: first, that the overall trajectory of Italian foreign policy cannot be simply understood as a long chain of continuities; and second, that domestic politics did play a role in shaping Italy's foreign policy during the four periods under consideration.

Yet, despite this rather general result, other issues need to be considered as well. Despite all of the discontinuity provided by changes in domestic politics, similar themes and tendencies have surfaced in many instances and at different stages of the development of the foreign policy of Italy over the last century. Consider, for instance, the atypical strategy of 'bandwagoning' which was pursued a number of times during the liberal, fascist and republican periods; or, again, the policy of 'determinant weight', which was frequently attempted over the four periods at hand; or, finally, the periodical recourse to (an albeit temporary) neutrality.

Are these issues to be considered as the final vindication of some overarching, natural 'law' of Italian foreign policy? Are these the supreme proof of the fundamental continuity of Italian foreign policy? I should like to argue that this need not be the case.

If one examines these issues through the lens of the strategic-relational model, in particular, it is possible to generate a few counter-explanations. As the model suggests, foreign policy results from the dialectical interaction of three elements: context, strategy and discourse. In the presence of changes in strategy (i.e. changes in domestic politics), continuities cannot be simply inferred from continuities of context (i.e. international relations). Rather, they have to also be considered in terms of continuities in the discourse, paradigms and visions of foreign policy, i.e. in the ways in which international relations (and the actor's role in it) are perceived, framed and understood in the political process.

Therefore, the tendency to bandwagon, or to play the determinant weight, or again to revert to neutrality in Italian foreign policy cannot only be associated with continuities in the context surrounding the country. These cannot be considered as the proof of the context's ability to direct Italy's behaviour according to some arcane and invisible external law, as proponents of monocausal approaches to international relations have it. Stanley Hoffmann's words (1968: 12) are instructive here:

> Nothing is more mistaken than to assume that the international system is a sort of monster with an implacable will of its own [...] that the participants' [moves] are either mere responses to its dictates or exercises in irrelevance or self-defeat when they go against the system's logic.
>
> (Hoffman 1968: 12)

Complicit in foreign policy choices are always perceptions of the environment as well as self-perceptions, i.e. ideas about Italy's place in the world and *relative to* the world. One can hypothesise that continuities in discourse and self-perceptions (or misperceptions: for instance, Italy's indomitable self- and misperception of weakness) were just as important as continuities in context. In no instance did Italy's relative position in the context of international relations simply dictate a foreign policy: as the strategic-relational model suggests, in all cases this position was in fact mediated by political discourse and intersected with different political strategies.

Thus, for instance, in the liberal period there were two competing visions of Italy's place in the international system of relations: the liberal vision stressing neutrality, and the nationalist vision stressing maximisation of power. Within the *same* context of relations, the fact that the latter discourse prevailed meant that Italy embarked upon a strategy of revisionism and bandwagoning, joining the victorious side in the hope of maximising gains. Again, during fascism the fact that Italy found itself once more between two blocs of powers opened up a number of foreign policy options – i.e. alliance with either bloc, neutrality, creation of a counterbalancing bloc – which were pursued actively or at the margins until the very end of the regime (i.e. until 1943). It was the prevailing of a particular understanding within fascist nationalism which inspired the gain-seeking strategy of bandwagoning – this was based on a self-perception of weakness and on the desire to avenge it vis-à-vis the rising hegemon. The context of relations can, of itself, hardly hold the key to these foreign policy predicaments.

Therefore, rather than dismissing ideational categories simply as 'constructivist' and hence irrelevant because they fail the arbitrary Humean standard of empirical regularity and observability – and in doing so, fundamentally misunderstanding the critical realist position (Kurki 2008) – analysts of Italian foreign policy should consider the extent to which ideas and discourses must be acknowledged as causes too, albeit not causes of the same, efficient kind. In particular, they should consider the extent to which foreign policy continuities are to be ascribed to the substantial continuity of the political discourse around foreign policy, loosely framed around an arch-realist and opportunistic consideration of international politics as power politics, which they themselves have contributed to strengthen. Continuities do not simply reflect the unproblematic dictates of the environment, but, rather, always result from the complex interplay of contextual factors, strategies and the way that these are interpreted in the foreign policy political process.

Summary

The conclusions to be drawn from an overall assessment of these results is that Italy's foreign policy over the last century cannot be accounted for in monocausal terms. More complex frameworks are needed to make sense of it: dualist, but especially dialectical models provide good starting points. In particular, an assessment of the dialectical interaction between context, strategy and discourse, just as the strategic-relational model suggests, can offer a particularly valuable framework of analysis.

More generally, dualist and dialectical models have proved to have different domains of applicability. While the dualist pendulum approach seems to be validated when the difference of intensity between the two constraints is high (namely, when one constraint is considerably more important than the other), the additive models work best when both constraints are either in a permissive or acute state. Finally, the strategic-relational approach seems to have the widest domain of applicability: the model is in fact applicable to all those circumstances in which foreign policy is influenced by both constraints, provided the distinction between the two is sufficiently marked.

This different domain of applicability of the models can, in turn, be accounted for as follows: when the difference between the two constraints is high, the dialectic around which the strategic-relational model revolves tends to be influenced more by the most intense set of factors, and hence the strategic-relational model tends to approximate to the pendulum approach. Naturally, this does not mean that the other two factors in the dialectic are unimportant – in the end, the result of the dialectic is always contingent. On the other hand, the weaker the distinction between the two constraints, the more the additive model resembles the strategic-relational framework, albeit without the important mediation of ideas. However, in all other cases the strategic-relational model is able to subsume and perform better than all of the other dialectical, dualist and, naturally, monocausal approaches. As this book has illustrated in the case of Italy, this model can provide, in other words, the default explanation of foreign policy in its relations with domestic politics and international politics.

Towards a strategic-relational theory of foreign policy

The findings of this research confirm the need for FPA to make progress towards the elaboration of more complex frameworks for the analysis of how foreign policy interacts with international relations and domestic politics. Despite general agreement on this point, no 'cumulation' has taken place over the last few decades.

This work has advanced a reconceptualisation of the issue that might bear some promise in this respect. In particular, the successful application of the strategic-relational model to the foreign policy of Italy leads to three main implications for a theory of foreign policy.

First, the model is able to suggest a way of overcoming the epistemological impasse between positivism and post-positivism and recuperate a fuller notion of causality. In fact, the dialectic between context, strategy and discourse on which the approach is predicated enables analysts to successfully combine a consideration of material and objective influences bearing upon foreign policy (context and strategy) with an account of the ideational and social processes through which foreign policy is articulated (discourse). Foreign policy thus becomes conceptualised as an activity upon which both material and ideational factors have an impact, and which needs to be both explained and understood.

The second implication is that FPA needs to elaborate the approaches to foreign policy which acknowledge the notion of complexity and, most of all, contingency. The strategic-relational model is one such approach. Its founding notion – that of dialectic – aims precisely at challenging linear understandings of the relation between foreign policy international relations and domestic politics. At the same time, it acknowledges that the result of the complex interplay between the three elements of context, strategy, and discourse is always historically contingent.

Third, the results of this research also have specific implications for a number of theories of foreign policy which currently have wide purchase in the field. One of these is the democratic peace theory. As seen above, the investigation of the foreign policy of fascist Italy has not validated monocausal theories of foreign policy grounded in the exclusive appreciation of domestic factors, to which the democratic peace theory belongs. In fact, fascist foreign policy was not exclusively the product of a particular ideology or institutional setting, but rather resulted from the interplay of three interrelated factors, namely the international relations of the time (and, more specifically, Italy's role in it), the prevailing foreign policy discourse, and the particular foreign policy strategy pursued by fascist Italy. An exclusively 'domestic' reading can explain Italy's foreign policy during this period no more than a purely 'international' one can. Both elements need to be taken into account together with the mediation of discourse.

More generally, all monocausal approaches to foreign policy, domestic politics and international relations (Figure 1.2: boxes 1, 2, 3, 4) should be treated with great scepticism on the basis of the evidence from the case of Italy. These include, for instance, neo-realist approaches to foreign policy. In fact, given its relatively small size and vulnerability, Italy could have perhaps be thought of as an 'easy' case for structural realist approaches. However, not even during the phases of most intense pressure from international relations has Italy simply conformed to the dictates of the system. This, in turn, points to the need for a theory of foreign policy and the international/domestic to always include an account of agency and, with it, choice.

Italian foreign policy, domestic politics and international relations

The results of this research have rather important implications for the study of Italian foreign policy, four of which stand out in particular. These become apparent as soon as one compares its main findings with the extant material on the subject.

First, the foreign policy of Italy cannot be simply taken for granted, or explained by recurring to stereotypical readings of the subject matter. In fact, it has proven to be far more complex and nuanced than is usually granted, and therefore in need of complex explanations. Further, to the extent that the case of Italy is representative of the larger group of Western, middle-sized, democratic political systems, this result implies that in these cases too foreign policy is to be considered as a complex political activity in need of complex explanations.

Second, as discussed throughout the book, traditional understandings of Italian foreign policy have usually tended to reinforce two alternative and largely monocausal readings of the subject matter in which Italy's foreign policy is either fatalistically portrayed as perennially crushed by overwhelming international pressures, or innocently depicted as entirely self-determined. The former has usually led to the belief that in matters of foreign policy 'there was not much that Italy could do', while the latter has often led to the conviction that it could do 'too much'. The political debate on Italy's foreign policy has, in other words, often oscillated between impotence and omnipotence. However, as Leopoldo Nuti recently stated in relation to Italy's foreign policy during the Cold War:

> there were many important decisions to be made, and there were also many different ways to interpret the adherence to the Western bloc [...]. They all deserve to be studied with great attention to understand all their [...] differences, and get a better grasp of the intricacies of Italian foreign relations.
>
> (Nuti 2011: 42)

One can add that a study more attentive to those differences may reveal not only nuances, but real choices and alternatives. As the strategic-relational approach suggests, foreign policy always contains an element of free will and a part of necessity; it stems from a particular and always contingent combination of autonomy and determinism, along the spectrum between impotence and omnipotence. To paraphrase Gaetano Salvemini, foreign policy is no 'monolithic block which moves solidly in a linear direction, as if pulled by a single force'; rather, it is an 'amalgam streaked and stressed by many different streams, which is not impossible to direct according to one's will, provided one has a clear vision as to where exactly to position oneself' (Salvemini quoted in Bracco 1998: 100). An acknowledgement of this result is, in the case of Italy, urgent for its political and normative implications.

Third, and relatedly, the results of this research imply that there is a need to investigate Italian foreign policy more critically and freely, and most of all to recover the notions of contingency, agency and responsibility. In this respect, the strategic-relational approach especially alerts us to the banal yet important consideration that things could have been different, or that there were possibilities which were not pursued alongside those that were, indeed, seized and acted upon. A more open-ended approach to Italian foreign policy would lead to a better assessment of its overall historical trajectory and would naturally benefit its future construction and investigation.

Fourth, and last, the results of this research lead to a particularly important policy recommendation for Italy in the field of foreign affairs. As the strategic-relational model suggests, three elements combine dialectically to produce foreign policy: context, strategy and discourse. In the case of Italy, it has often been the case that foreign policy has been formulated without a clear awareness of the strategy to adopt, without a thorough assessment of the context in which it was to be adopted, and without a conscious and pluralistic articulation of the foreign policy vision or paradigm through which it was expressed. The consequence of this state of affairs has often been a reactive foreign policy, often articulated around a default, clichéd realist paradigm. As this research has argued, however, this need not be the case.

Implications for further research

In this book I have skimmed over a variety of issues that would have deserved more careful treatment. In terms of theory, future research should concentrate on specifying the features of the strategic-relational model when applied to foreign policy more in detail. In particular, one should consider whether and to what extent strategy and discourse are overlapping notions, as well as investigate more thoroughly the relationship between discourse and context. Further, one should better probe the relationship between dialectical and systemic theorising in foreign policy, their similarities, respective merits and limits (e.g. whether these models genuinely explain or merely map reality). Finally, future research could pursue the opposite methodological strategy to the one adopted in this book – namely, embark upon a synchronic, comparative study of a single conceptual framework, i.e. the strategic-relational model, as applied to a range of cases or countries.

In terms of research on the particular case of Italian foreign policy, two issues seem particularly urgent. First, this research has not addressed the question of how different discourses become predominant, and how these come to interact with strategy and context in order to generate foreign policy. This question, however, is rather crucial and leads in the direction of a Gramscian inquiry into the 'economy of power' underlying foreign policy. This would shed light on the constellations of power that impacted upon the foreign policy domestic political process at different historical stages. Second, future research should better engage with the foreign policy traditions and discourses expressed by Italian political movements such as political parties. This would be a key step in rightfully acknowledging the rich legacy left by Italian political thinkers who were called, over the last 150 years of national history, to express their views of Italy's foreign policy, its possibilities, and its alternatives.

Notes

Introduction

1 Federico Chabod masterfully summarised them as follows:

> All united in the problem of *being* ... we were successful in that the constitution of Italy as a state, though going against a few interests, favoured some others. The collision between the imperial interest of France and that of Austria was the first great help; then, the second came from the collision between the interest of Prussia and that of Austria; and the third from that between Germany and France. And the prevailing liberalism in Europe, together with the anti-papal tendency [...] saw in the Italian revolution [...] a civic interest not to be antagonised, but rather to be favoured. Thus we became a state.

Taken from Chabod's *Storia della politica estera italiana dal 1870 al 1896* (Bari: Laterza, 1951), 552. Unless otherwise stated, all translations are my own.

2 This periodisation is widely accepted among scholars of Italian foreign policy (for two eminent examples, see Nuti 2002: 98 and Varsori 1998). The choice not to start my examination of the liberal period from 1861 – the date of the country's unification – but from 1901, however, needs to be motivated. On the one hand, the intention is to limit my study of Italian foreign policy to the twentieth and twenty-first century in the belief that this represents a discrete (and sufficiently complex) subject. On the other, I share the widely held belief (Vigezzi 1997a) that the *età giolittiana* (i.e. the era of Giovanni Giolitti, starting precisely in 1901) constitutes not only a distinctive phase within the long post-unitary liberal period, but its veritable climax and nemesis.

3 Given the timeframe under consideration, it was decided to rely primarily upon secondary sources, integrated with primary sources, such as memoirs and diaries, where available. To pursue systematic research into archival material would have led, at best, to selectivity, given also the mixed availability of sources (Nuti 2002; Vigezzi 1997b). While this in no way implies that I take the 'facts' of Italian foreign policy at face value, it nevertheless suggests that historiographical and theoretical interpretations remain my main concern.

1 Foreign policy, domestic politics and international relations: a strategic-relational analysis

1 Rather tellingly, FPA has often privileged the vaguer notion of 'source' over the more precise category of cause, at least since James Rosenau's seminal *The Domestic Sources of Foreign Policy* (1967).

2 It is important to note that this debate overlaps but cannot be subsumed under the umbrella of another popular confrontation, e.g. on the material/ideational divide. Structures can be of an ideational kind, just as agency can be understood in material

terms. Recent contributions, however, have unfortunately reiterated this misunderstanding (e.g. Eun 2012: 771, 776–7, 779).

3 This point has been questioned by Wendt and Dessler, among others, who argue that neo-realism actually relies upon a 'thoroughly individualistic ontology' consisting of states (Wendt 1991: 389). Cf. also Robert Keohane's remarks that 'the link between system structure and actor's behavior is forged by the rationality assumption [...]. Taking rationality as a constant permits one to attribute variations in state behaviour to various characteristics of the international system' (Keohane 1986: 167). Here, however, I follow the more 'orthodox' and structural reading of Waltz' neo-realism.

4 This is reminiscent of Hollis and Smith's comment that 'as the dance goes round and round the maypole the ribbons grow shorter, the circle closer and the bemused theorist is drawn to a centre where everything mediates everything and is mediated by everything' (Hollis and Smith 1991: 409).

5 The term is borrowed from George Tsebelis (1988, 1990). As will become clear in what follows, while I tend to reject the game-theoretical nature of the approach, I take on board and adapt the idea that 'the actor is involved in a network of games – [i.e.] nested games', and in particular in 'games in multiple arenas' (Tsebelis 1990: 7).

6 As Carlsnaes notes (1992: 266), this surely echoes Jon Elster's well-known solution to explaining human action, in which

> any single piece of human behaviour may be seen as the end product of two successive filtering devices. The first is defined by the set of structural constraints which cuts down upon the set of abstractly possible courses of action and reduces it to the (much smaller) subset of feasible actions. [...] The second filtering process is the mechanism that singles out which member of the feasible set shall be realized.
>
> (Elster 1979: 113)

For the only explicit conceptualisation of foreign policy drawing on Elster's philosophy, see Panebianco 1997: 133–56, esp. 134–35.

7 In his *Perception and Misperception* Jervis makes the argument that foreign policy is influenced by a variety of factors (international, domestic, cognitive) whose relative weight varies as follows: 'the impact of other variables decreases if the variables on one level are in extreme states' (Jervis 1976: 17; cf. also Greenstein 1969: 41; and Wolfers 1962: 11).

8 Because of its central place in historical materialism, the term 'dialectic' is, of course, heavily loaded. Two qualifications are therefore in order: first, the term will be used exclusively to indicate the process of interaction between foreign policy, international relations and domestic politics in which dialectical models are grounded. Second, I shall follow Jennifer Ring in claiming that it is possible to embark upon the dialectic train without taking the specific politics of Marxism or Hegelianism 'along with the ride' (Ring 1991: 50; for examples of dialectical thinking in political science, see Etzioni 1962; Cleggs 1989; in IR, see Alker and Biersteker 1984; Heine and Teschke 1996; Albert and Lapid 1997).

9 Interestingly, Hay's position resonates with and systematises the Sprouts' early intuitions on ecological possibilism:

> Neither milieu nor environed unit can be defined without reference to the other. [...] There is no concept of milieu in general [...] A milieu is invariably the milieu of some specified environed unit. [...] There are two parts to the relation: the environed unit and the milieu to which that unit is responsive or otherwise related.
>
> (Sprout and Sprout 1965: 204 and 31)

10 This too resonates with the Sprouts' argument on the importance of perceptions in apprehending the environment, as it is only 'in this way, and in this way alone [that] environmental factors can be said to "influence", or to "condition", or to otherwise "affect" human values and preferences, moods and attitudes, choices and decisions' (Sprout and

Sprout 1965: 11). Within the strategic-relational model, the notions of discourse and 'policy paradigms' also echo the Sprouts' proto-constructivist notion of 'images and ideas' that make up an actor's psycho-milieu (Sprout and Sprout 1965: 28).

11 The question resonates with issues discussed at length in the context of the 'agency-structure' debate. On the one hand are those who claim that '*structure-agency is not so much a problem as a language by which ontological differences between contending accounts might be registered*' (Hay 2002: 91, emphasis in original). As such, it follows that all the schemata presented in the previous section could not be adjudicated empirically because they merely register incommensurable ontological sensitivities. On the other hand are those who maintain instead that the problem is precisely the opposite, namely that 'the advocates of individualism, structuralism, and structuration theory have all done a poor job specifying the conditions under which their claims [...] would be falsified' (Wendt and Shapiro 1997: 181).

The position which I should like to defend here starts by acknowledging the Weberian difference between 'models' and 'empirical theories' (Weber 1968; Boudon 1984). If we accept that models are *conceptual* constructions delineating abstract and general relations between given observable phenomena, whereas theories are *empirical* constructions framed around specific relations between variables and with limited spatio-temporal applicability, then the difference between the positions of the proponents of the 'incommensurability thesis' and those of the 'falsifiability thesis' becomes more intelligible. In fact, the former are rightly arguing against treating models as empirical theories; the latter are arguing in favour of putting empirical theories to the empirical test. The crux of the matter, however, is that empirical theories are *always* derived from abstract models – hence the two counterparts of the debate risk talking past each other.

2 Italian foreign policy: the liberal age (1901–1922)

1 A detailed assessment of the Vatican's influence on Italian foreign is yet to be carried out and is well beyond the scope of this present book (for an overview see Pollard 1991; for the wider background, see Pollard 2008).

2 Emilio Visconti Venosta was the most eminent foreign minister of the *Destra Storica*, holding office for over fifteen years, in different governments. His prominence is at odds with the fact that no serious work has yet been dedicated to him as a diplomat (for a partial exception, see Halperin 1963).

3 The trade war initiated by Italy against France in 1887, which coincided with a generally protectionist turn in Italian foreign economic policy, was the beginning of a structural change in the thrust and direction of Italy's commercial relations. Briefly, while in 1886 44 per cent of Italian trade was directed towards only one country – France – by 1913 this figure had dropped to 9.2 per cent. The structure of Italy's commercial relations had now acquired a much more multipolar character, and Germany became Italy's privileged trading partner (Zamagni 1990; Tedesco 2002).

4 Between 1902 and 1909 Italy signed friendly agreements with all *Entente* powers: with France and Great Britain, as seen, on the Mediterranean, and with Russia on the status quo in the Balkans, mainly to contain Austria-Hungary's expansionism. For the international relations of the time see Taylor 1971; Joll 1992; Kehr 1977.

5 This speech was not just revelatory of German anxieties towards Italy's loyalty to the Triple Alliance, but also illustrated nicely the asymmetrical (and gendered) nature of the alliance Italy had joined. The full quote from von Bülow's passage is:

> In a happy marriage the husband must not get violent if his wife ventures to dance an innocent *extratour* with another. The main thing is that she doesn't run away from him, and she won't do that as long as she's better off with him than with anyone else.
> (quoted in Seton-Watson 1967: 327)

6 The renewal of the Triple Alliance was signed on 28 June 1902, and the Prinetti-Barrére accords between Italy and France on the 30 June 1902 – i.e. only two days later. Knowing that such a detail, in its simple truth, could reveal Italy's ambiguous diplomatic orientation, Prinetti and the King Vittorio Emanuele decided to have the Italo-French Accords bear a false date, that of November 1902 (Seton-Watson: 331).

7 The Tittoni-Aerenthal agreement of 1907, regarding the status quo in the Balkans, marked the highest point in Italo-Austrian relations before the First World War; however, the annexation of Bosnia by Austria, in the following year, ran precisely against the letter of this agreement. This irritated Italian counterparts enough to push them towards the Italo-Russian *rapprochement* of Racconigi (1909). Phases of particular tension also occurred at the Algeciras conference (1906) and with the Hohenloe decrees of 1913, with which Austria dismissed all Italians from public office in the city of Trieste.

8 Europe in general had very little sympathy for Italy's war in Libya: on the one hand, states such as Britain were particularly keen to see the Young Turks' attempt to modernise Turkey come to fruition; on the other hand, Austria and Germany were particularly afraid that a further weakening of Turkey would provoke more crises in the Balkans. Their prediction, as it turned out, was entirely correct (Croce 1929: 120).

9 A guerrilla war between the Italian army and the Senussi resistance led by Umar al Mukhtar carried on, however, until 1931, when fascist troops definitively 'pacified' Libya. Until then Italy's actual control over Libya was limited to the coastal areas and excluded much of the inland regions.

10 The January 1912 episode of the *Manouba* and *Carthage* (two French boats discovered carrying supplies for the Turkish resistance in Libya) determined a new and virulent wave of anti-French sentiment; relations with Britain and Russia had also cooled down, mainly due to Italy's reluctance to return the Dodecanese islands to Turkey, as well as its territorial ambitions in Asia Minor.

11 The elections of 1913 were the first elections in which Catholics participated *en masse*, finally ending the policy of *non expedit* which had kept them formally away from an active engagement in Italian politics.

12 The *sacro egoismo* speech was pronounced by Salandra when he assumed the interim position of Foreign Minister after di San Giuliano's death, on the 18 October 1914. As Salvemini noted, the speech was remarkable for its Machiavellian character, at a time when Europe was plunging into an unprecedented conflict; for the quote and comment, see Salvemini 1970: 423–4.

13 On the nature and consequences of the *giornate radiose*, much as been written, including the views that the anti-Giolittian campaign of the *Corriere della Sera* had the decisive effect of shifting public opinion to the interventionists' side; that Mussolini and his *Il Popolo d'Italia*, perhaps the most fervent organ of the interventionist party, received funds from both *Entente* powers – a weekly 'salary' from the British and 'French gold' – to sway public opinion in favour of the intervention; and that the government itself had engineered the demonstrations to prove the pro-war attitude of the country (Vigezzi 1997a: 129–78; Seton-Watson 1967: 436–45; and, most recently, Andrew 2009: 104–5).

14 The term *vittoria mutilata* was coined by Gabriele D'Annunzio – the nationalist and soon-to-be poet of fascism – in a poem published in *Il Corriere della Sera* on 24 October 1918. Another nationalist and soon-to-be fascist intellectual, Gioacchino Volpe, compared Italy's frustration at the end of the First World War to

> a thick and heavy fog. Disappointment, resentment, undefined discontent. All the sufferings and pain of the war slowly emerged into conscience. Arrogance of the newly rich; irritation and bitterness of the newly poor. Painfully and with malicious joy people cried out at the failure of war.
>
> (Volpe quoted in De Rosa 2003: 42)

3 Italian foreign policy: the fascist 'ventennio' (1922–1943)

1 One of Mussolini's first decrees was to relocate the Ministry from the Palazzo della Consulta (hence the shorthand), to Palazzo Chigi, in Rome. Except for the years of the Second World War, this is where the Ministry remained until 1959, when it was moved to its current location at the Palazzo della Farnesina.

2 In the words of US diplomat Henri Stimson: '[Mussolini] was in those years, in his foreign policy, a sound and useful leader, no more aggressive in his nationalism than many a democratic statesman' (Stimson and Bundy 1948: 270).

3 In fact, responsibility for the assassination of Gen. Tellini was never ascertained. Even the 'incident' of his assassination worked out so conveniently as to make more than a few wonder whether it had not been deliberately planned in Rome with the aim of precipitating the crisis (Lowe and Marzari 1975: 195; Cassels 1970: 126; Di Nolfo 1960: 82–6; Moscati 1963: 84–87; and most, recently, Giannasi 2008).

4 The 1926 Treaty of Rome, which granted Italy a de facto protectorate over Albania, was the first step in this direction. Then followed the 1927 agreement with the revisionist Hungary. In 1928, finally, Italy also signed agreements with Turkey and Greece. As a reaction to Italy's encircling strategy in the Balkans, France and Yugoslavia signed a treaty of friendship in November 1927.

5 Mussolini accompanied Grandi's dismissal in uncharitable and typically gendered terms:

> In three years Grandi got everything wrong, everything: he allowed the League of Nations to imprison him, he practised a pacifist and collective policy, he behaved as an ultra-democratic and a super-Swiss [...] 'he went to bed with England and France, and since those were the males Italy got pregnant with disarmament' and our foreign policy was by that time deprived of any freedom of action.
>
> (Mussolini quoted in Grispo 1963: 119)

6 Mussolini had already officially expressed a concrete interest in what was then called Abyssinia in the early 1920s. Further, in December 1925 Mussolini had spoken about the possibility of pursuing a 'definitive violent solution' to the issue, before entering into negotiations with Britain over the issue of the Tsana region (Kallis 2000; Carocci 1969: 237; cf. also Gramsci 1955: 198). The Stresa Conference had also failed to discuss the dispute of the Wal-Wal (5 December 1934) between Italy and Ethiopia, which would later escalate during the war (for a particularly sharp comment, see Carr 1947: 223–4).

7 The anti-war 'Peace Ballot' was published in Britain in June 1935 and public condemnation of the war grew only stronger after Haile Selassie's stirring speech at League of Nations in June 1936. Britain's growing apprehensions about the war in Ethiopia (and a possible Anglo-Italian naval rivalry as a result) were possibly also due to British vulnerability in the area (Quartararo 1977).

8 This episode reveals what Mario Toscano (1968a: 190) described as the abyss of intentions between the typical 'insincerity of the Nazis and the acquiescence or superficiality of the Italians'.

9 At this time, Italy's temporising was predicated upon Mussolini's conviction that a victory for either would be disastrous. In Ciano's words:

> In fact the *Duce* prefers that the European giants fight bitterly against one another, and, in spite of all that is said about our will to peace, he prefers that, if with some measure of restraint, I throw some kerosene on the flames.
>
> (Ciano 1963: 4 October 1939)

10 Later in the war, Ciano supported the idea of a separate peace with Russia and with the Anglo-American forces (Kallis 2000: 160–74; Toscano 1968a: 254). For these views he was dismissed from the post of Foreign Minister on 19 January 1943, condemned to death by a fascist court, and executed on 11 January 1944.

11 This passage is strikingly reminiscent of E.H. Carr's invective against 'morality' in international politics (Carr 1947: 63).
12 Grandi had made his famous 'determinant weight' speech on 2 October 1931, famously attributing Italy's pivotal role to no less than 'destiny' (Grandi 1930: 64). In the 1980s De Felice edited various works on Grandi himself (e.g. Grandi 1985). In the apparent attempt to re-legitimise Grandi's figure, Knox has noted, De Felice's editing of these documents has included 'textual adjustments' of dubious value (Knox 1987; see also Mack Smith 2000).
13 Indeed, the debate originated from one fundamental contradiction at the heart of Salvemini's argument: despite the hegemonic role of Mussolini in fascist foreign policy, Salvemini in the end attributed little responsibility to *il Duce* regarding the outbreak of the Second World War (for Salvemini's famous 'arithmetic of the blame', see Salvemini 1967: 689).

4 Italian foreign policy: the 'First Republic' (1943–1992)

1 While these initiatives mark the apex of De Gasperi's Europeanism, the traditional historiographical interpretation of De Gasperi as one of the 'founding fathers' of the European project is admittedly somewhat exaggerated (Pastorelli 1987: 145–208, esp. 200–8).
2 Italy's firm Atlanticism, in fact, was confirmed in 1957, with the installation of NATO's *Jupiter* and *Thor* missiles (Ilari 1994: 69ff.; Nuti 1996–1997: 97ff.).
3 In June 1961 Foreign Minister Fanfani and Head of Government Segni had visited the US and openly discussed the possibility with President Kennedy. Besides, Saragat's appointment as Foreign Minister in June 1963 had already reassured Washington, given the Minister's renowned Atlanticism (Schlesinger jr., 1968; Nuti 1999).
4 Italy's acceptance provided crucial support to Germany, in particular. It also had positive effects upon Italo-American relations, after the tense years of the 'historic compromise'. The adoption of the so-called *clausola di dissolvenza* ('zero clause') was the only concession made to the opposition by the Cossiga government.
5 The greater dynamism and assertiveness of Italian foreign policy in the 1980s was also the result of a greater continuity at the lead of the Foreign Ministry. Only three Foreign Ministers occupied this post in a decade – Emilio Colombo, Giulio Andreotti, and Gianni De Michelis – compared to the five of the 1970s and the six of the 1960s.
6 In a 1985 parliamentary debate Craxi went so far as to compare Arafat with Mazzini – both using violence as a legitimate tool towards national liberation. On Italy's relations with the PLO between the 1970s and 1980s – the role of the Foreign Ministry, that of the Secret Service (*Servizio per le Informazioni e la Sicurezza Militare*, SISMI), of individual political figures such as Andreotti and of the Vatican – a full story is yet to be written (Ferraris 1996: 383 n222).
7 Italy's participation in the multinational force led by the US and France to Lebanon from June 1982 had provided a partial occasion to strengthen Italy's relations with the US (Davidson 2011: 48–51), despite Italy's highly critical stance regarding the management of the mission (Tana 1985). Relations with Libya, on the other hand, were much more ambiguous. Italy insisted on keeping a political dialogue open throughout the 1980s, even during the bombings of Tripoli and Bengasi in the aftermath of the terrorist attacks in West Germany of April 1986 (Cremasco 1995; Silvestri 1999).
8 Panebianco points out, however, that during the formative years, international and domestic determinants of foreign policy worked in synergy (Panebianco 1977: 877 n37; see also Panebianco 1982). He later argued, however, that 'l'Italia [è nell'età della guerra fredda] un sistema politico modellato sulla guerra fredda ed *eterodiretto.* La politica estera e della sicurezza [...] sarà il terreno principale su cui tale influenza esterna si manifesterà' ('During the Cold War Italy had a political system modelled after the Cold War and as such externally-driven. Foreign and security policy was the

terrain where this external influence would be most visible') (Panebianco 1997: 228, emphasis added).

5 Italian foreign policy: the 'Second Republic' (1992–2011)

1 The Schäuble/Lamer proposal – excluding Italy from the hard core of EMU/EU – had been publicised in September 1994 and was met with stiff criticism in Italy. In March 1995, Dini lifted Italy's veto on EU negotiations with Slovenia, thus ending the *querelle*.

2 Washington on the other hand perceived Italy's proneness to compromise as deeply suspect: the State Department's Chief Spokesman James Rubin went so far as to openly accuse Italy of collusion with the Serbs (Rubin 2000; for the ensuing polemic, see *La Repubblica* 2001a; *La Repubblica* 2001b).

3 Thus, in its various denominations the centre-right included FI, AN, and the CCD/UDC at its core and the LN at its margins. The centre-left, on the other hand, had a more variable geometry: at its core, it has grouped the DS and the PPI/Margherita; at its margins, the Greens, the PDCI, PRC and other minor political formations such as the *Italia dei Valori* (IdV) led by former *Mani Pulite* prosecutor Antonio di Pietro.

4 These guidelines form the common denominator foreign policy agenda of the parties comprising the coalition. One should add, however, that the LN's foreign policy agenda has diverged significantly from the rest of the coalition, most notably regarding European affairs but also, during the crises in Kosovo and most recently Libya, regarding NATO (see Lega Nord 2004).

5 This represents the common denominator position among the centre-left. However, this position contrasts significantly from that of the PRC, which has at times been part of the centre-left coalition. PRC's foreign policy vision is articulated around the firm rejection of NATO, a primacy granted to the UN, and a pacifist/'neutralist' understanding of Italy's foreign policy (see IAI 1994c: 237–40).

Bibliography

Adler, F. H. (1995) *Italian Industrialists from Liberalism to Fascism: The Political Development of the Italian Bourgeoisie, 1906–1934*, Cambridge: Cambridge University Press.

Aga-Rossi, E. (1985) *L'Italia nella sconfitta: politica interna e situazione internazionale durante la seconda guerra mondiale*, Napoli: Edizioni Scientifiche Italiane.

Albert, M. and Lapid, Y. (1997) 'On Dialectic and IR Theory: Hazards of a Proposed Marriage', *Millennium: Journal of International Studies* 26(2): 403–15.

Albertini, L. (1952–57) *The Origins of the War of 1914*, trans. I. M. Massey, London: Oxford University Press.

Aliboni, R. (1985) 'Italy and the new international context: an emerging foreign policy profile', *The International Spectator* 21(1): 3–17.

Aliboni, R. (1999) 'Italy and the Mediterranean in the 1990s', in Stavridis, S., Couloumbis, T., Veremis, T. and Watts, N. (eds) *The Foreign Policies of the European Union's Mediterranean States and Applicant Countries in the 1990s*, Basingstoke: Macmillan.

Aliboni, R. (2004) 'La politica estera del governo Berlusconi', in Colombo, A. and Ronzitti, N. (eds) *L'Italia e la politica internazionale: Edizione 2003*, Bologna: il Mulino.

Aliboni, R. and Greco, E. (1996) 'Foreign Policy Re-nationalization and Internationalism in the Italian Debate', *International Affairs* 72(1): 43–51.

Aliboni, R. and Pioppi, D. (2000) 'Il caso Öcalan, l'Italia e i rapporti euro-turchi', in Aliboni, R., Bruni, F., Colombo, A., and Greco, E. (eds) *L'Italia e la politica internazionale: Edizione 2000*, Bologna: il Mulino.

Alker, H. and Biersteker, T. (1984) 'The Dialectics of World Order: Notes for a Future Archeologist of International Savoir Faire', *International Studies Quarterly* 28(2): 121–42.

Allison, G. and Zelikow, P. (1999) *Essence of Decision: Explaining the Cuban Missile Crisis*, New York: Longman.

Almond, G. with Genco, S. (1990) 'Clouds, Clocks, and the Study of Politics', in Almond, G. (ed.) *A Discipline Divided: Schools and Sects in Political Science*, Newbury Park, CA: Sage.

André, G. (1963) 'L'Italia nella seconda guerra mondiale fino all'intervento degli Stati Uniti nel conflitto', in Torre, A. (ed) *La politica estera Italiana dal 1914 al 1943*, Torino: Eri, Edizioni Rai Radiotelevisione Italiana.

Andreatta, F. (2000) *Istituzioni per la pace: teoria e pratica della sicurezza collettiva da Versailles alla ex-Jugoslavia*, Bologna: il Mulino.

Andreatta, F. (2001) 'Italy at the crossroad: the foreign policy of a medium power after the Cold War', *Daedalus* 130: 45–66.

Andreatta, F. (2008a) 'Le uniche scelte bipartisan possibili? In politica estera', *Il Corriere della Sera*, 5 March.

Andreatta, F. (2008b), 'La politica estera Italiana: "policy analysis" di una media potenza' in Capano, G. (ed) *Non solo potere: le altre facce della politica. Saggi in onore di Giorgio Freddi*, Bologna: Il Mulino.

Andreatta, F. (2008c) 'Italian Foreign Policy: Domestic Politics, International Requirements and the European Dimension', *Journal of European Integration* 30(1): 169–81.

Andreatta, F. and Brighi, E. (2003) 'The Berlusconi Government's Foreign Policy: The First 18 Months', in Blondel, J. and Segatti, P. (eds) *Italian Politics: The Second Berlusconi Government*, New York: Berghahn Books.

Andreatta, F. and Hill, C. (2000) 'Struggling to Change: The Italian State and the New Order', in Wallace, W. and Niblett, R. (eds) *Rethinking the European Order: West European Responses, 1989–1997*, Oxford: St Martin's Press.

Andreatta, N. (1993a) 'Una nuova architettura Europea', *Affari Esteri* 25(10): 659–63, reprinted in *Per un'Italia moderna: questioni di politica e di economia* (Bologna: il Mulino, 2002), 167–72.

Andreatta, N. (1993b) 'Una politica estera per l'Italia', *il Mulino* 43(5): 881–91, reprinted in *Per un'Italia moderna: questioni di politica e di economia* (Bologna: il Mulino, 2002), 173–90.

Andreatta, N. (1997) 'Conclusioni del ministro della Difesa, Beniamino Andreatta', in Corsico, F. (ed.) *Interessi nazionali e identità Italiana*, Milano: FrancoAngeli.

Andreatta, N. (2002) *Per un'Italia moderna: questioni di politica e di economia*, Bologna: il Mulino.

Andreotti, G. (1988) *L'URSS vista da vicino*, Milano: Rizzoli.

Andreotti, G. (1995) *Cosa loro: mai visti da vicino*, Milano: Rizzoli.

Andrew, C. (2009) *The defence of the realm: the authorized history of MI5*, London: Allen Lane.

Angelini, M. (2010) 'Confronting the present: fascist foreign policy and war', *Storia della Storiografia* 28: 110–37.

Aquarone, A. (1965) *L'organizzazione dello stato totalitario*, Torino: Einaudi.

Aquarone, A. (1981) *L'Italia giolittiana 1896–1915*, Bologna: Il Mulino.

Aran, A. (2009) *Israel's Foreign Policy towards the PLO: The Impact of Globalization*, Brighton: Sussex Academic Press.

Archer, M. (1988) *Culture and Agency: The Place of Culture in Social Theory*, Cambridge: Cambridge University Press.

Archer, M. (1995) *Realist Social Theory: The Morphogenetic Approach*, Cambridge: Cambridge University Press.

Archer, M. (1998) *Critical Realism: Essential Readings*, London: Routledge.

Archer, M., Bhaskar, R., Collier, A., Lawson, T. and Norrie, A. (eds) (1998) *Critical Realism: Essential Readings*, London: Routledge.

Arcidiacono, B. (1990) 'L'Italia fra sovietici e anglo-americani: la missione di Pietro Quaroni a Mosca, 1944–1946', in Di Nolfo, E., Rainero, R. H. and Vigezzi, B. (eds) *L'Italia e la politica di potenza in Europa, 1945–1950*, Milano: Marzorati.

Aron, R. (1964) *Dimensions de la conscience historique*, Paris: Plon.

Artom, I. and Artom, E. (1954) *Iniziative neutralistiche della diplomazia Italiana nel 1870 e nel 1915*, Torino: Giulio Einaudi Editore.

Aruffo, A. (2003) *Storia del colonialismo Italiano: da Crispi a Mussolini*, Roma: Datanews.

Attinà, F. (1998) 'La partnership Euro-mediterranea: politica e sicurezza', in *Italia fra Europa e Mediterraneo: il bivio che non c'è più* (Bologna: il Mulino, 1998): 112–15.

Auerswald, D. P. (1999) 'Inward Bound: Domestic Institutions and Military Conflicts', *International Organization* 53(3): 469–504.

Auerswald, D. P. (2000) *Disarmed Democracies: Domestic Institutions and the Use of Force*, Ann Arbor, Michigan: University of Michigan Press.

Azzi, S. C. (1993) 'The Historiography of Fascist Foreign Policy', *The Historical Journal* 36(1): 187–203.

Bachelard, G. (1964) *The Poetics of Space*, Boston: Beacon Press.

Baer, G. W. (1967) *The coming of the Italo-Ethiopian war*, Cambridge, MA: Harvard University Press.

Balfour, R., Menotti, R. and de Biase, G. M. (1999) 'Italy's Crisis Diplomacy in Kosovo, March-June 1999', *The International Spectator* 34(3): 55–66.

Battaglia, R. (2000) *Gaetano Martino e la politica estera Italiana 1954–1964*, Messina: Confcommercio EDAS.

Baumann, R., Rittberger, V. and Wagner, W. (2001) 'Neorealist foreign policy theory', in Rittberger, V. (ed.) *German Foreign Policy since Unification: Theories and Case-Studies*, Manchester: Manchester University Press.

Beard, C. (1940) *A Foreign Policy for America*, New York: Alfred Knopf.

Bedeschi Magrini, A. (1992) 'Spunti revisionistici nella politica estera di Giovanni Gronchi Presidente della Repubblica', in Di Nolfo, E., Rainero, R. H., Vigezzi, B. (eds) *L'Italia e la politica di potenza in Europa, 1950–1960*, Milano: Marzorati.

Bellucci, P. (1997) 'Italian Intervention in Bosnia and the (Slow) Redefinition of Defense Policy', in D'Alimonte, R. and Nelken, D. (eds) *Italian Politics: The Centre-Left in Power*, Boulder, CO: Westview Press.

Benzoni, A. (1967) 'I Socialisti e la politica estera', in Bonanni, M. (ed.) *La politica estera della repubblica Italiana*, Milano: Edizioni di Comunità.

Benzoni, A., Gritti, R. and Landolfi, A. (1993) *La dimensione internazionale del socialismo Italiano: 100 anni di politica estera del PSI*, Roma: Edizioni Associate.

Berlusconi, S. (2002) 'Discorso del Presidente del Consiglio e Ministro degli Affari Esteri *ad interim* Berlusconi alla Camera dei Deputati', Rome, 14 January.

Bernstein, S., Lebow, R., Gross Stein, J. and Weber, S. (2000) 'God Gave Physics the Easy Problems: Adapting Social Science to an Unpredictable World', *European Journal of International Relations* 6(1): 43–76.

Bhaskar, R. (1979) *The Possibility of Naturalism: A Philosophical Critique of Contemporary Human Sciences*, Brighton: Harvester Press.

Bhaskar, R. (1986) *Scientific Realism and Human Emancipation*, London: Verso

Bhaskar, R. (1989) *Reclaiming Reality*, London: Verso.

Bieler, A. and Morton, D. A. (2001) 'The Gordian Knot of Agency-Structure in International Relations: A Neo-Gramscian Perspective', *European Journal of International Relations* 7(1): 5–35.

Bloomfield, L. (1982) *The Foreign Policy Process: A Modern Primer*, New York: Prentice Hall.

Boekle, H., Rittberger, V. and Wagner, W. (2001) 'Constructivist Foreign Policy Theory', in Rittberger, V. (ed.) *German Foreign Policy since Unification*, Manchester: Manchester University Press, 105–37.

Bonanate, L. (1978) 'L'Eurocomunismo ovvero: "il gioco delle parti"', in *Scientia: Rivista internazionale di sintesi scientifica* 72: 133–50.

Bonanate, L. (1997) 'Qualche argomento contro l'interesse nazionale', *Limes: rivista Italiana di geopolitica* 2: 305–13.

Bonvicini, G. (1983) 'Italy: An Integrationist Perspective', in Hill, C. (ed.) *National Foreign Policies and European Political Cooperation*, London: Allen & Unwin.

Bonvicini, G. (1996) 'Regional reassertion: The Dilemmas of Italy', in Hill, C. (1996) *The Actors in Europe's Foreign Policy*, London: Routledge.

Bosworth, R. J. B. (1979) *Italy the Least of the Great Powers: Italian Foreign Policy Before the First World War*, London: Cambridge University Press.

Bosworth, R. J. B. (1983a) *Italy and the approach of the First World War*, London: Macmillan.

Bosworth, R. J. B. (1983b) 'Italian Foreign Policy and its Historiography', in Bosworth R. J. B. and Rizzo G. (eds) *Altro Polo: Intellectuals and Their Ideas in Contemporary Italy*, Sydney: Fredrick May Foundation for Italian Studies.

Bosworth, R. J. B. (1996) *Italy and the Wider World*, 1860–1960, London: Routledge.

Bosworth, R. J. B. (1998) 'Fascist Foreign and Racial Policies: "One Man Alone"?', in *The Italian Dictatorship: Problems, Perspectives in the Interpretation of Mussolini*, London: Arnold.

Boudon, R. (1984) *La place du desordre: critiques des théories du changement sociale*, Paris: Presses Universitaires de France.

Bova, S. and Rochat, G. (1974) 'Le forze armate', *Inchesta* 1: 3–21.

Bracco, B. (1998) *Storici Italiani e politica estera: tra Salvemini e Volpe 1917–1925*, Milano: Franco Angeli.

Braudel, F. (1972) 'History and the Social Sciences', in Burke, P. (ed) *Economy and Society in Early Modern Europe: Essays from the Annales*, New York: Harper, pp. 11–42.

Brecher, M. (1972) *The Foreign Policy System of Israel: Setting, Images, Process*, London: Oxford University Press.

Brighi, E. (2006) '"One Man Alone?" A *Longue Durée* Approach to Italy's Foreign Policy under Berlusconi', *Government and Opposition* 41(2): 278–97.

Brighi, E. (2007a) 'How to Change Your Foreign Policy in 100 Days: A New Course for the New Prodi Government? *The International Spectator* 42(1): 129–40.

Brighi, E. (2007b) 'La politica estera dell'Italia', in Colombo, A. and Ronzitti, N. (eds) *L'Italia e la politica internazionale 2006*, Bologna: il Mulino.

Brighi, E. (2007c) 'Europe, the USA, and the 'policy of the pendulum': the importance of foreign policy paradigms in the foreign policy of Italy (1989–2005)', *Journal of Southern Europe and the Balkans*, vol. 9(2): 99–115.

Brighi, E. (2011) 'Resisting Europe? The Case of Italy's Foreign Policy', in Wong, R. And Hill, C. (eds.) *National and European Foreign Policies: Towards Europeanization*, New York: Routledge.

Brighi, E. and Hill, C. (2012) 'Implementation and Behaviour', in Smith, S., Hadfield, A. and Dunne, T. (eds.) *Foreign Policy: Theories, Actors, Cases*, Oxford: Oxford University Press.

Brighi, E. and Petito, F. (2012) 'Geopolitics in the "Land of the Prince": A *Passe-Partout* to Global Power Politics?' in Guzzini, S. (ed.) *The Return of Geopolitics in Europe?* Cambridge, CUP.

Brown, M. (1996) *Debating the Democratic Peace*, Cambridge, MA: MIT Press.

Bryant, C. (1985) *Positivism in Social Theory and Research*, Basingstoke: Macmillan.

Burgwyn, H. J. (1997) *Italian Foreign Policy in the Interwar Period, 1918–1940*, Westport, CONN: Praeger.

Butterfield, H. (1975) *Raison d'Etat: The Relations Between Morality and Government*, Brighton: University of Sussex.

Buzan, B. (1985) 'The Levels of Analysis Problems in International Relations Reconsidered', in Booth, K. and Smith, S. (eds) *International Relations Theory Today*, Cambridge: Polity Press.

Cameron Watt, D. (2001) *How War Came: The Immediate Origins of the Second World War, 1938–1939*, rev. edn, London: Pimlico.

Cammarano, F. (1999) *Storia politica dell'Italia liberale 1861–1901*, Bari: Laterza.

Campbell, D. (1998) *Writing Security: United States Foreign Policy and the Politics of Identity*, Minnesota: Minnesota University Press.

Canavero, A. (1990) 'Nenni, i socialisti e la politica estera', in Di Nolfo, E., Rainero, R. H. and Vigezzi, B. (eds) *L'Italia e la politica di potenza in Europa, 1945–1950*, Milano: Marzorati.

Caporaso, J. (1997) 'Across the Great Divide: Integrating Comparative and International Politics', *International Studies Quarterly* 41(4): 563–92.

Caracciolo, L. (2001) *Terra incognita: le radici geopolitiche della crisi Italiana*, Roma-Bari: Laterza.

Carbone, M. (2007) 'The domestic foundations of Italy's foreign and development policies', *West European Politics* 30(4): 903–23.

Carbone, M. (2008) 'Russia's Trojan Horse in Europe? Italy and the War in Georgia', in Baldini, G. and Cento Bull, A. (eds.) *Governing Fear: Italian Politics 2008*, Berghahn Books, New York.

Carbone, M. and Quaglia, L. (2011) 'Italy in the EU: Seeking Visibility, Fearing Exclusion', in Carbone, M. (ed.) *Italy in the Post-Cold War: Adaptation, Bipartisanship and Visibiity*, Lanham: Lexington Books.

Carbone, M., Coralluzzo, V., Del Sarto, R. and Tocci, N. (2011) 'Italy in the Mediterranean: Between Europeanism and Atlanticism', in Carbone, M. (ed.) *Italy in the Post-Cold War: Adaptation, Bipartisanship and Visibiity*, Lanham: Lexington Books.

Carlsnaes, W. (1986) *Ideology and Foreign Policy: Problems of Comparative Conceptualisation*, Oxford: Oxford University Press.

Carlsnaes, W. (1992) 'The Agency-Structure Problem in Foreign Policy Analysis', *International Studies Quarterly* 36(3): 245–70.

Carlsnaes, W. (1993) 'On Analysing the Dynamics of Foreign Policy Change', *Cooperation and Conflict* 28(1): 5–30.

Carlsnaes, W. (1994) 'In Lieu of a Conclusion: Compatibility and the Agency-Structure Issue in Foreign Policy Analysis', in Carlsnaes, W. and Smith, S. (eds) *European Foreign Policy: The EC and Changing Perspectives in Europe*, London: Sage.

Carlsnaes, W. (2004) 'Where is the Analysis of European Foreign Policy Going?' *Journal of European Union Politics* 5(4): 495–508.

Carlsnaes, W. (2012) 'Actors, Structures, and Foreign Policy Analysis', in Smith, S., Hadfield, A. and Dunne, T. (eds) *Foreign Policy: Theories, Actors, Cases*, Oxford: Oxford University Press.

Carlsnaes, W. (2013) 'Foreign Policy' in Carlsnaes, W., Simmons, B. and Risse-Kappen, T. (eds) *Handbook of International Relations*, London: Sage.

Carocci, G. (1963) *Giolitti e l'età giolittiana*, Torino: Einaudi.

Carocci, G. (1969) *La politica estera dell'Italia fascista*, Bari: Laterza.

Carocci, G. (1985) *L'Età contemporanea*, vol. 3 of *Corso di Storia*, Bologna: Zanichelli.

Carr, E. H. (1947) *The Twenty Years' Crisis: International Relations Between the Two World Wars*, London: Macmillan.

Cassels, A. (1968) *Fascist Italy*, New York: Crowell.

Cassels, A. (1970) *Mussolini's Early Diplomacy*, Princeton, NJ: Princeton University Press.

Cassese, A. (1987) *Il Caso 'Achille Lauro': terrorismo, politica e diritto nella comunità internazionale*, Roma: Editori Riuniti.

Catalano, F. (1967) 'La politica estera del CLN', in Bonanni, M. (ed.) *La politica estera della repubblica Italiana*, Milano: Comunità.

Catalano, F. (1969) *L'economia Italiana di guerra*, Milano: Movimento di Liberazione in Italia.

Ceccarini, L., Diamanti, I. and Lazar, M. (2013) 'End of an Era: The Disintegration of the Italian Party System', in *Italian Politics 2012*, New York: Berghan Books, forthcoming.

CeMiSS (1997) *Il Sistema Italia: gli interessi nazionali Italiani nel nuovo scenario internazionale*, Milano: FrancoAngeli.

Chabod, F. (1951) *Storia della politica estera Italiana dal 1870 al 1896*, Bari: Laterza, trans. (1998) *The Statecraft of the Founders*, Princeton, NJ: Princeton University Press.

Checkel, J. T. (2012) 'Constructivism and Foreign Policy', in Smith, S., Hadfield, A. and Dunne, T. (eds) *Foreign Policy: Theories, Actors, Cases*, Oxford: Oxford University Press, 2nd edn.

Chiesa, G. and Medvedev, R. (1989) *La rivoluzione di Gorbaciov: cronaca della perestrojka*, Milano: Garzanti.

Cialdea, B. (1967) 'L'Italia e il Trattato di Pace', in Bonanni M. (ed.) *La politica estera della repubblica Italiana*, Milano: Edizioni di Comunità.

Ciano, G. (1963) *Diario 1939–1943*, Milano: Rizzoli.

Ciano, G. (1980) *Diario 1937–1940*, ed. Felice, F., Milano: Rizzoli.

Cladi, L. and Webber, M. (2011) 'Italian foreign policy in the post-cold war period: a neoclassical realist approach', *European Security* 20(2): 205–19.

Cleggs, S. (1989) *Frameworks of Power*, London: Sage, 1989.

Collier, A. (1994) *Critical Realism: An Introduction to Roy Bhaskar's Philosophy*, London: Verso.

Collotti, E. (1977) *La collocazione internazionale dell'Italia dall'armistizio alle premesse dell'alleanza atlantica, 1943–1945*, in Istituto nazionale per la storia del movimento di liberazione in Italia (ed.) *L'Italia dalla liberazione alla repubblica*, Milano: Feltrinelli.

Collotti, E. (1998) 'Il razzismo negato', *Italia contemporanea*, 212: 557–87.

Collotti, E. (2000) *Fascismo e politica di potenza: politica estera 1922–1939*, Milano: La Nuova Italia.

Coralluzzo, V. (1991) 'La politica mediterranea dell'Italia: le immagini dei decision-makers', in Santoro, C. M. *Il mosaico del Mediterraneo*, Bologna: il Mulino.

Coralluzzo, V. (2000) *La politica estera dell'Italia repubblicana, 1946–1992: modello di analisi e studio di casi*, Milano: FrancoAngeli.

Corner, P. (2012) *The Fascist Party and Popular Opinion in Mussolini's Italy*, Oxford: Oxford University Press.

Corsico, F. (ed.) (1998) *Interessi nazionali e identità Italiana*, Milano: FrancoAngeli.

Coticchia, F. and Giacomello, G. (2011) 'All Together Now: Military Operations Abroad as "Bipartisan" Instrument of Italian Foreign Policy', in Giacomello, G. And Verbeek, B. (eds) *Italy's Foreign Policy in the Twenty-First Century*, Lanham: Lexington Books.

Coverdale, J. F. (1977) *I fascisti Italiani alla guerra di Spagna*, Roma: Laterza.

Cremasco, M. (1984) 'The Political Debate on the Development of Euromissiles: Italy', *The International Spectator* 20(1): 115–21.

Cremasco, M. (1995) *Libya*, Rome: Istituto Affari Internazionali.

Cremasco, M. (2000) 'Italy and the Management of International Crises', in Martin, P. and Brawley, M. R. (eds) *Alliance Politics: Kosovo, and NATO's War: Allied Force or Forced Allies?*, New York: Palgrave.

Croce, B. (1929) *A History of Italy, 1871–1915*, Oxford: Clarendon Press.

Croci, O. (1995) 'The Italian Intervention in Somalia: A New Foreign Policy?', in *L'Italia nella politica internazionale, 1994*, Roma: Editore SIPI.

Croci, O. (2000) 'Forced Ally? Italy and the "Operation Allied Force"', in Gilbert, M. and Pasquino, G. (eds) *Italian Politics: the Faltering Transition*, New York: Berghahn Books.

Croci, O. (2005) 'Much Ado about Little: The Foreign Policy of the Second Berlusconi Government', *Modern Italy* 10(1): 59–74.

Croci, O. (2008) 'The Second Prodi Government and Italian Foreign Policy: New and Improved or the Same and Wrapped up Differently?', *Modern Italy* 13(3): 137–55.

Czempiel, E. O. (1963) 'Der Primat der auswärtigen Politik', *Politische Vierteljarhess-chirft*, 4: 266–87.

D'Alema, M. (1999a) *Kosovo: gli Italiani e la guerra*, Milano: Mondadori.

D'Alema, M. (1999b) 'Intervento alla Camera dei Deputati del Presidente del Consiglio On. Massimo D'Alema sull'incidente della funivia del Cermis', Rome, 19 March.

D'Amoja, F. (1961) *La politica estera dell'impero: storia della politica estera fascista dalla conquista dell'Etiopia all'Anschluss*, Padova: Cedam.

Dalby, S. and O' Tuathail, G. (eds) (1998) *Rethinking Geopolitics*, New York: Routledge.

Dallmayr, F. and McCarthy, T. A. (eds) (1977) *Understanding and Explaining Social Enquiry*, Notre Dame, IN: University of Notre Dame Press.

Daniels, P. (1997) 'The Italian Presidency of the European Union', in D'Alimonte, R. and Nelken, D. (eds) *Italian Politics: The Centre-Left in Power*, Boulder, CO: Westview Press.

Dassù, M. and Menotti, R. (1997) 'Italy and NATO Enlargement', *The International Spectator* 32(3/4): 65–86.

Davidson, J. W. (2011) *America's Allies and War: Kosovo, Afghanistan, and Iraq*, New York: Palgrave.

De Felice, R. (1973) 'Sulla politica estera mussoliniana', in De Felice, R. (ed.) *L'Italia fra tedeschi e alleati: la politica estera fascista e la seconda guerra mondiale*, Bologna: Il Mulino.

De Felice, R. (1974) *Mussolini il Duce, vol. 1: Gli anni del consenso*, Torino: Einaudi.

De Felice, R. (1998) *Il fascismo e l'Oriente: arabi, ebrei e indiani nella politica di Mussolini*, Bologna: Il Mulino.

De Leonardis, M. (1990) 'Manlio Brosio a Mosca e la scelta occidentale', in Di Nolfo, E., Rainero, R. H. and Vigezzi, B. (eds) *L'Italia e la politica di potenza in Europa, 1945–1950*, Milano: Marzorati.

De Michelis, G. (1996) 'La vera storia di Maastricht', *Limes* 3: 137–44.

De Michelis, G. (2003) *La lunga ombra di Yalta: la specificità della politica Italiana, conversazione con Francesco Kostner*, Venezia: Marsilio Editori.

De Rosa, G. (2003) 'La Conferenza di pace di Parigi', in Scottà, A. (ed.) *La Conferenza di pace di Parigi tra ieri e domani, 1919–1920*, Catanzaro: Rubbettino.

Decleva, E. (1987) *L'incerto alleato: ricerche sugli orientamenti internazionali dell'Italia unita*, Milano: Franco Angeli.

Del Boca, A. (1991) 'I crimini del colonialismo fascista', in Del Boca, A. (ed.) *Le guerre coloniali del fascismo*, Roma: Laterza.

Del Boca, A. (1993) *Una sconfitta dell'intelligenza: Italia e Somalia*, Roma: Laterza.

Del Pero, M. (2001) *L'alleato scomodo. Gli USA e la DC negli anni del centrismo (1948–1955)*, Roma: Carocci.

Del Pero, M. (2003) 'Containing Containment: Rethinking Itay's Experience during the Cold War', *Journal of Modern Italian Studies* 8(4): 532–55.

Del Sarto, R. and Tocci, N. (2008) 'Italy's Politics without Policy: Balancing Atlanticism and Europeanism in the Middle East', *Modern Italy* 13(2): 135–53.

Dessler, D. (1989) 'What's at Stake in the Agent-Structure Debate?', *International Organization* 43: 441–73.

Di Nolfo, E. (1960) *Mussolini e la politica estera Italiana*, Padova: Cedam.

Di Nolfo, E. (1978) *Vaticano e Stati Uniti 1939–1952: dalle carte di Myron C. Taylor*, Milano: Franco Angeli.

Di Nolfo, E. (1985) 'La svolta di Salerno come problema internazionale', in *Storia delle Relazioni Internazionali* 1(1): 5–28.

Di Nolfo, E. (1986) 'The Shaping of Italian Foreign Policy during the Formation of the East-West blocs: Italy between the Superpowers', in Becker, J. and Knipping, F. (eds) *Power in Europe? Great Britain, France, Italy and Germany in a Postwar World 1945–1950*, Berlin: Walter de Gruyter.

Dini, L. (2001) *Fra Casa Bianca e Bottheghe Oscure: fatti e retroscena di una stagione alla Farnesina*, Milano: Guerini e Associati.

Dodds, K. and Atkinson, D. (2000) *Geopolitical Traditions: A Century of Geopolitical Thought*, London: Routledge.

Donatucci, P. and Lucarelli, S. (1998) *Il contributo Italiano all'intervento internazionale per la pacificazione e la ricostruzione della Bosnia-Erzegovina*, Roma: IAI.

Doty, R. L. (1997) 'Aporia: A Critical Examination of the Agency-Structure Problematique in International Relations', *European Journal of International Relations* 5(3): 365–92.

Doyle, M. (1983) 'Kant, liberal legacies and foreign affairs', *Philosophy and Public Affairs* 12(3): 205–35.

Duggan, C. (2012) *Fascist Voices: An Intimate History of Mussolini's Italy*, London: Bodley Head.

Dunne, T. (1998) *Inventing International Society: A History of the English School*, New York: Palgrave Macmillan.

Dunne, T. and Wheeler, N. (1999) *Human Rights in Global Politics*, Cambridge: Cambridge University Press.

Eade, C. (ed.) (1951) *The War Speeches of Winston S. Churchill*, London: Cassels & Company.

Eckstein, H. (1975) 'Case Study and Theory in Political Science', in Greenstein, F. and Polsby, N. (eds) *Handbook of Political Science, vol. 6: Policies and Policy-making*, Reading, MASS: Addison Wesley.

Ellwood, D. W. (1977) *L'alleato nemico: la politica dell'occupazione Anglo-Americana in Italia, 1943–46*, Milano: Feltrinelli.

Ellwood, D. W. (1985) *Italy 1943–1945*, Leicester: Leicester University Press.

Elman, C. (1996a) 'Horses for Courses: Why Not Neorealist Theories of Foreign Policy?', *Security Studies* 6(1): 7–53.

Elman, C. (1996b) 'Cause, Effect, and Consistency: A Response to Kenneth Waltz', *Security Studies* 6(1): 58–63.

Elster, J. (1979) *Ulysses and the Sirens: Studies in Rationality and Irrationality*, Cambridge: Cambridge University Press.

Ercolessi, M. C. (1994) 'L'Italia e l'intervento dell'ONU in Somalia', in *L'Italia nella politica internazionale, 1994*, Roma: Editore SIPI.

Etzioni, A. (1962) 'The Dialectics of Supranational Unification', *American Political Science Review* 56: 927–35.

Eun, Y. (2012) 'Why and how should we go for a multicausal analysis in the study of foreign policy? (Meta-)theoretical rationales and methodological rules', *Review of International Studies* 38: 763–83.

Evangelista, M. (1997) 'Domestic Structure and International Change', in Doyle, M. W. and Ikenberry, G. J. (eds) *New Thinking in International Relations*, Boulder, CO: Westview.

Evans, P., Jacobson, H. and Putnam, R. D. (eds) (1993) *Double-edged Diplomacy: International Bargaining and Domestic Politics*, Berkeley, CA: University of California Press.

Fanfani, A. (1978) *Giorgio La Pira: un profilo e 24 lettere inedite*, Milano: Rusconi.

Farrell, R. B. (ed.) (1966) *Approaches to Comparative and International Politics*, Evanston, IL: Northwestern University Press.

Favaretto, T. and Greco, E. (1997) *Il confine riscoperto: beni degli esuli, minoranze e cooperazione economica nei rapporti dell'Italia con Slovenia e Croazia*, Milano: Franco Angeli.

Ferraris, L. V. (1993) 'Dal Tevere al Danubio: L'Italia riscopre la geopolitica a tavolino', in *Limes: rivista Italiana di geopolitica* no. 1.

Ferraris, L. V. (1996) *Manuale della politica estera, 1947–1993*, Roma: Laterza.

Ferraris, L. V. (1997) 'Diario di una missione a Tirana', *Limes: rivista Italiana di geopolitica: Quaderno Speciale, Albania Emergenza Italiana*, 1.

Fischer, F. (1961) Krieg der Illusionen: die duetsche Politik 1911 bis 1914, Düsseldorf: Droste Verlag, trans. (1975) *War of Illusions: German Policies from 1911 to 1914*, New York: Chatto and Windus.

Fisichella, D. (1997) 'Interessi nazionali Italiani e forze politiche Italiane', in CeMiSS (ed.) *Il sistema Italia: gli interessi nazionali nel nuovo scenario internazionale*, Milano: FrancoAngeli.

Follini, M. (1994) *C'era una volta la DC*, Bologna: il Mulino, 1994.

Forza Italia (2004) 'Il governo Berlusconi sta cambiando l'Italia'.

Frankel, P. H. (1960) *Mattei, Oil and Power Politics*, London: Faber.

Frattini, F. (2004) 'Discorso di apertura della Conferenza degli Ambasciatori del Ministro Frattini', Rome, 27 July.

Frattini, F. and Panella, C. (2004) *Cambiamo rotta*, Casale Monferrato: Edizioni Piemme.

Fubini, F. (1999) 'Il Bacio di Madeleine: ovvero come (non) negoziammo a Rambouillet', *Limes: rivista Italiana di geopolitica* 2: 17–34.

Fulci, F. P. (1997a) 'Tre scenari per la battaglia alle Nazioni unite', *Limes: rivista Italiana di geopolitica* 4: 251–58.

Fulci, F. P. (1997b) 'La riforma del Consiglio di Sicurezza: un nostro interesse vitale', *Limes: rivista Italiana di geopolitica* 4: 263–74.

Fulci, F. P. (1999) 'Italy and the Reform of the UN Security Council', *The International Spectator* 34(2): 7–16.

Gaja, R. (1995) *L'Italia nel mondo bipolare*, Bologna: Il Mulino.

Galante, S. (1978) 'La scelta Americana della DC', in Isneghi, M. and Lanaro, S. (eds) *La Democrazia Cristiana dal fascismo al 18 Aprile*, Padova: Marsilio Editori.

Galante, S. (1980) *La fine di un compromesso storico: PCI e DC nella crisi del 1947*, Milano: Franco Angeli Editore.

Galante, S. (1990) 'Il PCI e la genesi della politica d'impotenza, 1941–1949', in Di Nolfo, E., Rainero, R. H. and Vigezzi, B. (eds) *L'Italia e la politica di potenza in Europa, 1945–1950*, Milano: Marzorati.

Galli, G. (1967) 'La politica internazionale del PCI', in Bonanni, M. (ed.) *La politica estera della repubblica Italiana*, Milano: Comunità.

Galli, G. (1977) 'Il sistema politico Italiano e la politica estera', in Ronzitti, N. (ed.) *La politica estera Italiana: autonomia, interdipendenza, integrazione e sicurezza*, Milano: Comunità.

Galli della Loggia, E. (1993) 'Tavola rotonda: alla ricerca dell'interesse nazionale', *Limes: rivista Italiana di geopolitica* 1–2.

Galli della Loggia, E. (1996) *La morte della patria*, Roma: Laterza.

Galli della Loggia, E. (1998) *L'identità nazionale*, Bologna: il Mulino.

Garosci, A. (1967) 'L'Italia e il patto Atlantico', in Bonanni M. (ed.) *La politica estera della repubblica Italiana*, Milano: Edizioni di Comunità.

George, A. (1969) 'The "Operational Code": A Neglected Approach to the Study of Political Leaders and Decision-Making', *International Studies Quarterly* 13(2): 190–222.

George, A. (1979) 'Case Studies and Theory Development: The Method of Structured, Focused Comparison', in Loren, P. G. (ed.) *Diplomacy: New Approaches in History, Theory and Policy*, New York: Free Press.

Giannasi, A. (2008) *L'eccidio Tellini. Da Giannina all'occupazione di Corfù (agosto-settembre 1923)*, Prospettiva editrice, Civitavecchia.

Giddens, A. (1979) *Central Problems in Social Inquiry*, London: Macmillan.

Giddens, A. (1984) *The Constitution of Society*, Cambridge: Polity.

Giddens, A. (1999) *The Runaway World*, London: Profile Books.

Ginsborg, P. (1994) *Modern Italy*, London: Routledge.

Gordon, P. (1993) *A Certain Idea of France: French Security Policy and the Gaullist Legacy*, Princeton, NJ: Princeton University Press.

Gourevitch, P. (1978) 'The second image reversed: international sources of domestic politics', *International Organization* 32(4): 881–911.

Gramsci, A. (1955) *Note sul Machiavelli, sulla politica e sullo stato moderno*, Torino: Giulio Einaudi Editore.

Gramsci, A. (1975) *Quaderni dal carcere*, Gerratana, V. (ed.), Torino: Einaudi.

Grandi, D. (1930) *L'Italia fascista nella politica internazionale*, Rome: Libreria del Littorio.

Grandi, D. (1985) *Il mio paese: ricordi autobiografici*, De Felice, R. (ed.), Bologna: Il Mulino.

Grange, D. J. (1994) *L'Italie et la Mediterranée (1896–1911): les fondaments d'une politique étrangère*, Roma: École française de Rome.

Gray, C. (1988) *The Geopolitics of Super Power*, Lexington: University Press of Kentucky.

Greco, E. (1994) 'L'Italia e la crisi balcanica', in *L'Italia nella politica internazionale, 1994*, Roma: Editore SIPI.

Greco, E. (2000) 'La politica Italiana durante il conflitto del Kosovo', in Aliboni, R., Bruni, F., Colombo, A., and Greco, E. (eds) *L'Italia e la politica internazionale: Edizione 2000*, Bologna: il Mulino.

Greenstein, F. I. (1969) *Personality and Politics: Problems of Evidence, Inference and Conceptualisation*, Chicago: Markham Publishing Company.

Grispo, R. (1963) 'Il Patto a Quattro, la questione austriaca, il fronte di Stresa', Torre, A. (1963) *La politica estera Italiana dal 1914 al 1943*, Torino: Eri, Edizioni Rai Radiotelevisione Italiana.

Guazzone, L. (1992) 'Italy and the Gulf War: the European dimension and domestic politics', in Gnesotto, N. and Roper, J. (eds) *Western Europe and the Gulf: A Study of West European Reactions to the Gulf War*, Paris: ISS.

Guazzone, L. (2000) 'Le iniziative diplomatiche verso Iran, Iraq e Libia', in Aliboni, R., Bruni, F., Colombo, A., and Greco, E. (eds) *L'Italia e la politica internazionale: Edizione 2000*, Bologna: il Mulino.

Guzzini, S. (1994) 'The Implosion of Clientelistic Italy in the 1990s: A Study of "Peaceful Change" in Comparative Political Economy', Florence: EUI Working Paper SPS 94/12.

Guzzini, S. (ed.) (2012) *The Return of Geopolitics in Europe? Social Mechanisms and Foreign Policy Identity Crises*, Cambridge: Cambridge University Press.

Halliday, F. (1994) *Rethinking International Relations*, London: Macmillan.

Halperin, S. W. (1963) *Diplomat under stress: Visconti Venosta and the crisis of July 1870*, Chicago: University of Chicago Press.

Halperin, S. W. (1964) *Mussolini and Italian Fascism*, Princeton: Princeton University Press.

Hanrieder, W. (1971) 'Compatibility and Consensus', in Hanrieder, W. (ed.) *Comparative Foreign Policy*, New York: MacKay.

Hanrieder, W. (1980) 'West German Foreign Policy, 1949–1979: Necessities and Choices', in Hanrieder, W. (ed.) *West German Foreign Policy: 1949–1979*, Boulder, CO: Westview Press.

Hardt, M. and Negri, A. (2000) *Empire*, Cambridge, MA: Harvard University Press.

Harper, J. L. (1987) *L'America e la ricostruzione dell'Italia, 1945–1948*, Bologna: Il Mulino.

Hassner, P. (1975) 'The Political Evolution of Italy and the International Context: A Personal View', unpublished paper.

Hawthorn, G. (1991) *'Plausible Worlds': Possibility and Understanding in History and the Social Sciences*, Cambridge: Cambridge University Press.

Hay, C. (1995) 'Structure and Agency', in Marsh, D. and Stoker, G. (eds) *Theory and Methods in Political Science*, London: Macmillan.

Hay, C. (1999) 'What Place for Ideas in the Agency-Structure Debate? Globalisation as a Process without a Subject', paper presented at BISA Annual Conference, Manchester, December, available at: http://www.criticalrealism.com/archive/cshay_wpisad.html.

Hay, C. (2000) 'Willing Executioners of Hitler's Will? The Goldhagen Controversy, Political Analysis and the Holocaust', *Politics* 20(3): 119–28.

Hay, C. (2002) *Political Analysis: A Critical Introduction*, Basingstoke: Palgrave.

Hay, C. (2005) 'Ever Diminishing Expectations? Or, Why Politics Is Not All That It Was Once Cracked Up to Be', paper presented at the General Seminar of the Department of International Relations at LSE, London, January.

Hay, C. and Marsh, D. (eds) (2000) *Demystifying Globalization*, Basingstoke: Macmillan in association with POLSIS.

Hay, C. and Rosamond, B. (2002) 'Globalisation, European Integration and the Discursive Construction of Economic Imperatives', *Journal of European Public Policy* 9(2): 147–67.

Heine, C. and Teschke, B. (1996) 'Sleeping Beauty and the Dialectical Awakening: On the Potential of Dialectic for International Relations', *Millennium: Journal of International Studies* 25(2): 399–424.

Hellman, S. and Pasquino, G. (eds) (1992) *Italian Politics: A Review, Volume 7*, London: Pinter.

Hill, C. (2000) 'What is left of the domestic? A reverse angle view of foreign policy', in Ebata, M. and Neufeld, B. (eds) *Confronting the Political in International Relations*, London: Palgrave Macmillan.

Hill, C. (2003) *The Changing Politics of Foreign Policy*, Basingstoke: Palgrave Macmillan.

Hill, C. and Stavridis, S. (1996) *Domestic Sources of Foreign Policy: West European Reactions to the Falklands Conflict*, Oxford: Berg.

Hillgruber, A. (1987) 'Le discussioni sul "primato della politica estera" e la storia delle relazioni internationali nellla storiografia tedesca dal 1945 ad oggi', in Pizzetti, S. (ed.) *La storia delle relazioni internazionali*, Milano: Jaca Book.

Hine, D. (1992) 'Italy and Europe: The Italian Presidency and the Domestic Management of the European Community', in Leonardi, R. and Anderlini, F. (eds) *Italian Politics: A Review, Volume 6*, London: Pinter.

Hintze, O. (1962 [1906]) *Staat und Verfassung: Gesammelte Abhandlungen zur allgemeinen Verfassungsgeschichte*, Göttingen: Vandenhoeck und Ruprecht.

Hoffmann, S. (1968) *Gulliver's Troubles, or the Setting of American Foreign Policy*, New York: McGraw-Hill.

Hoffmann, S. (1974a) 'Foreword', in Vannicelli, P. *Italy, NATO, and the European Community: The Interplay of Foreign Policy and Domestic Politics*, Harvard: Center for International Affairs.

Hoffmann, S. (1974b) 'Pranzo a tre sulla politica estera Italiana', in Cavazza, F. L. and Graubard, S. R. (eds) *Il caso Italiano*, Milano: Garzanti.

Hollis, M. and Smith, S. (1986) 'Roles and Reasons in Foreign Policy Decision Making', *British Journal of Political Science* 16(3): 269–86.

Hollis, M. and Smith, S. (1990) *Explaining and Understanding International Relations*, Oxford: Clarendon Press.

Hollis, M. and Smith, S. (1991) 'Beware of Gurus: Structure and Action in International Relations', *Review of International Studies* 17(4): 393–410.

Hollis, M. and Smith, S. (1992) 'Structure and Action: Further Comment', *Review of International Studies* 18(2): 187–8.

Ignazi, P. (2004) 'Al di là dell'Atlantico, al di qua dell'Europa', *il Mulino* 53(2): 267–76.

Il Corriere della Sera (2001), 'Berlusconi: "Occidente, civiltà superiore" ', 27 September.

Il Mulino (1998) 'L'Europa e l'Italia nella moneta unica', 47(3).

Ilari, V. (1994) *Storia militare della Prima Repubblica*, Ancona: Nuove ricerche.

International Herald Tribune (1999) 'Italy Proves Equal to the Task', 12 June.

Istituto Affari Internazionali (1991) *L'Italia nella politica internazionale: 1989–1990*, Milano: Franco Angeli.

Istituto Affari Internazionali (1992) *L'Italia nella politica internazionale, 1990–1991*, Milano: Franco Angeli.

Istituto Affari Internazionali (1993) 'The Dual Crisis', *The International Spectator* 28(1): 5–30.

Istituto Affari Internazionali (1994a) 'I programmi di politica estera dei principali partiti per le elezioni politiche del 27–28 Marzo 1994: Forza Italia', in *L'Italia nella politica internazionale: Edizione 1994*, Roma: Editore Sipi.

Istituto Affari Internazionali (1994b) 'I programmi di politica estera dei principali partiti per le elezioni politiche del 27–28 Marzo 1994: Partito democratico della Sinistra', in *L'Italia nella politica internazionale: Edizione 1994*, Roma: Editore Sipi.

Istituto Affari Internazionali (1994c) 'I programmi di politica estera dei principali partiti per le elezioni politiche del 27–28 Marzo 1994: Partito della Rifondazione Comunista' in *L'Italia nella politica internazionale: Edizione 1994*, Roma: Editore Sipi.

Jackson, P. T. (2004) 'Forum: The State as Person', *Review of International Studies* 30(2): 255–316.

Janis, I. L. (1972). *Victims of groupthink: A psychological study of foreign policy decisions andfiascoes*. Boston: Houghton Mifflin Company.

Jean, C. (1995) *Geopolitica*, Roma: Laterza.

Jervis, R. (1970) *The Logic of Images in International Relations*, New York: Columbia University Press.

Jervis, R. (1976) *Perception and Misperception in International Politics*, Princeton, NJ: Princeton University Press.

Jervis, R. (1997) *Systems Effects: Complexity in Political and Social Life*, Princeton, NJ: Princeton University Press.

Jessop, B. (1990) *State Theory: Putting Capitalist States in Their Place*, Cambridge: Polity Press.

Jessop, B. (1996) 'Interpretative Sociology and the Dialectic of Structure and Agency', *Theory, Culture and Society* 13(1): 119–28.

Joll, J. (1992) *The Origins of the First World War*, London: Longman.

Joseph, J. and C. Wight (2010) *Scientific Realism and International Relations*, New York: Palgrave.

Kahler, M. (1997) *Liberalization and foreign policy*, New York: Columbia University Press.

Kallis, A. (2000) *Fascist Ideology: Territory and Expansionism in Italy and Germany, 1922–1945*, London: Routledge.

Katz, R. S. and Ignazi, P. (1996) *Italian Politics: The Year of the Tycoon*, Boulder, CO: Westview Press.

Katzenstein, P. J. (ed.) (1978) *Between Power and Plenty: the Foreign Economic Policies of the Advanced Industrial States*, Madison: University of Wisconsin Press.

Katzenstein, P. J. (ed.) (1996) *The Culture of National Security: Norms and Identity in World Politics*, New York: Columbia University Press.

Kaufman, R. (1992) 'To Balance or to Bandwagon? Alignment Decisions in 1930s Europe', *Security Studies* 1(3): 417–47.

Kehr, E. (1977) *Economic Interest, Militarism, and Foreign Policy: Essays on German History*, Berkeley: University of California Press.

Kennedy, P. (1982) 'The Kaiser and German Weltpolitik: Reflexions on Wilhelm II's Place in the Making of German Foreign Policy', in Röhl, J. C. and Sombart, N. (eds) *Kaiser Wilhelm II: New Interpretations*, Cambridge: Cambridge University Press.

Kennedy, P. (1986) 'A. J. P. Taylor and "Profound Forces" in History', in C. Wrigley (ed.) *Warfare Diplomacy and Politics: Essays in Honour of A. J. P.Taylor*, London: Hamish Hamilton.

Kennedy, P. (1988) *The Rise and Fall of the Great Powers*, London: Unwin Hyman.

Keohane, R. O. (1986) 'Theory of World Politics', in Keohane, R. O. (ed.) *Neorealism and its Critics*, New York: Columbia University Press.

King, A. (1999) 'Against Structure: A Critique of Morphogenetic Social Theory', *Sociological Review* 47(2): 199–227.

Kirkpatrick, I. (1964) *Mussolini: A Study in Power*, London: Odhams.

Kissinger, H. (1957) *A World Restored: Castelreagh, Metternich and the Restoration of Peace, 1812–1822*, Boston: Houghton Mifflin.

Kissinger, H. (1968) 'Domestic Structure and Foreign Policy', *Daedalus* 95(2): 503–29.

Knox, M. (1987) 'I testi aggiustati dei discorsi segreti di Grandi', *Passato e Presente* 13(2): 97–117.

Knox, M. (1991) 'Il fascismo e la politica estera Italiana', in Bosworth, R. J. B. and Romano, S. (eds) *La politica estera Italiana: 1860–1985*, Milano: 1991.

Knox, M. (2000) *Common Destiny: Dictatorship, Foreign Policy and War in Fascist Italy and Nazi Germany*, New York: Cambridge University Press.

Knox, M. (2002) 'Fascism, Ideology, Foreign Policy and War', in Lyttelton, A. (ed.) *Liberal and Fascist Italy*, Oxford: Oxford University Press.

Knudsen, O. F. (1989) 'Book Review of Ideology and Foreign Policy', *Conflict and Cooperation* 24: 99–102.

Kogan, N. (1963) *The Politics of Italian Foreign Policy*, New York: Praeger.

Krasner, S. (1978) *Defining the National Interest: Raw Materials Investments and US Foreign Policy*, Princeton, NJ: Princeton University Press.

Kubálková, V. (ed.) (2001) *Foreign Policy in a Constructed World*, Armonk, NY: M. E. Sharpe.

Kurki, M. (2006) 'Causes of A Divided Discipline: Rethinking the Concept of Cause in International Relations Theory', *Review of International Studies* 32 (2): 189–216.

Kurki, M. (2008) *Causation in International Relations: Reclaiming Causal Analysis*, Cambridge: Cambridge University Press.

L' Ulivo (2001) 'Rinnoviamo l'Italia, insieme: il programma dell'Ulivo per il governo 2001/2006 presentato da Francesco Rutelli'.

L' Ulivo (2004) 'Prefazione: l'Europa contro le nostre paure – Il Programma della Lista Uniti nell'Ulivo'.

La Pira, G. (1971) *Unità, disarmo e pace*, Firenze: Cultura editrice.

La Repubblica (1999) 'Cermis, nessun colpevole: assolto anche il navigatore', 16 March.

La Repubblica (2001a) ' "A Rambouillet tutti ne parlavano" ', 17 February.

La Repubblica (2001b) 'Dini, bufera con gli USA', 4 March.

La Repubblica (2002) 'Berlusconi soddisfatto: "Riconosciuto il nostro ruolo" ', 14 May.

La Repubblica (2005) 'Berlusconi rifiutò la trattativa sull'Iran', 4 April.

La Stampa (1994) 'Il migliore resta Mussolini', 1 April.

Labs, E. J. (1992) 'Do Weak States Bandwagon?, *Security Studies* 1(3): 383–416.

Lagorio, L. (1998) *L'ultima sfida degli Euromissili*, Firenze: Loggia de' Lanzi.

Lamb, R. (1999) *Mussolini as a Diplomat: Il Duce's Italy on the World Stage*, New York: Fromm International.

Lamborn, A. C. (1991) *The Price of Power: Risk and Foreign Policy in Britain, France and Germany*, Boston: Unwin Hyman.

Larsen, H. (1997) *Foreign Policy and Discourse Analysis: France, Britain and Europe*, London: Routledge.

Lebow, R. N. (2001) 'Contingency, Catalysts and International System Change', *Political Science Quarterly* 115(4): 591–616.

Lega Nord per l'indipendenza della Padania (2000) 'Programma per le elezioni Europee 2004'.

Leonardi, R. and Anderlini, F. (1992) 'Introduction', in Leonardi R. and Anderlini, F. (eds) *Italian Politics: A Review, Volume 6*, London: Pinter.

Letta, E. (1997) *Euro sì. Morire per Maastricht*, Bari-Roma: Laterza.

Limes: rivista Italiana di geopolitica (1997) 'Euro o Non Euro', no. 2.

Linklater, A. and Suganami, H. (2006) *The English School of International Relations: A Contemporary Reassessment*, Cambridge: CUP.

Loi, B. (2004) *Peace-keeping, pace o guerra? Una risposta Italiana: l'operazione IBIS in Somalia*, Roma: Vallecchi.

Lombardi, B. (2011) 'The Berlusconi Government and Intervention in Libya', *The International Spectator* 46(4): 31–44.

Lowe, C. J. and Marzari, F. (1975) *Italian Foreign Policy 1870–1940*, London: Routledge and Kegan Paul.

Lucarelli, S. and Menotti, R. (2002) 'No Constructivists' Land: International Relations in Italy in the 1990s', *Journal of International Relations and Development* 5(2): 114–42.

Lucarelli, S. and Radaelli, C. M. (2004) 'Italy: Think Tanks and the Political System', in Stone, D., Garnett, M. and Denham, A. (eds) *Think Tanks in Comparative Perspective: Insiders or Outsiders?*, Manchaster: MUP.

Lyttelton, A. (2002) *Liberal and Fascist Italy*, Oxford: Oxford University Press.

Mack Smith, D. (1975) 'A Monument for the Duce', *Times Literary Supplement*, 31 October.

Mack Smith, D. (1976) *Le guerre del duce*, Bari: Laterza, trans. *Mussolini's Roman Empire*, London: Longman.

Mack Smith, D. (1981) *Mussolini*, London: Weidenfeld and Nicolson.

Mack Smith, D. (2000) 'Mussolini: Reservations about De Felice's Biography', *Modern Italy* 5(2): 193–210.

Mallet, R. (2003) *Mussolini and the Origins of the Second World War*, London: Palgrave.

Manners, I. and Whitman, R. (eds) (2000) *The Foreign Policy of European Member States*, Manchester: MUP.

Martini, F. (1999) *Nome in codice Ulisse: trent'anni di storia Italiana nelle memorie di un protagonista dei servizi segreti*, Milano: Feltrinelli.

Mastny, V. (ed.) (1995) *Italy and East-Central Europe: Dimensions of the Regional Relationship*, Boulder, CO: Westview Press.

McAnulla, S. (1998) 'The Structure-Agency debate and its Historiographical Utility', paper presented at the Annual Political Science Association Conference, Newcastle, April 1998.

McAnulla, S. (2002) 'Structure and Agency', in Marsh, D. and Stoker, G. (eds) *Theory and methods in political science*, London: Palgrave Macmillan.

McCarthy, P. (1996) '*Forza Italia:* The Overwhelming Success and the Consequent Problems of a Virtual Party', in Katz, R. S. and Ignazi, P. (eds) *Italian Politics: The Year of the Tycoon*, Boulder, CO: Westview Press.

Mearsheimer, J. (1990) 'Back to the Future: Instability in Europe after Cold War', *International Security* 15(1): 5–56.

Mengozzi Rostagni, C. (1990) 'La Santa Sede e la politica estera Italiana, 1945–1949', in Di Nolfo, E., Rainero, R. H. and Vigezzi, B. (eds) *L'Italia e la politica di potenza in Europa, 1945–1950*, Milano: Marzorati.

Menotti, R. (2007) 'Italy's Growing Burden of Choice in Security Policy', *The International Spectator* 42(3): 431–44.

Merlini, C. (1993) 'Six Proposals for Italian Foreign Policy', *The International Spectator* 28(3): 5–21.

Merlini, C. (1994) 'Cinque punti sul nazionalismo Italiano', *il Mulino* 43(2).

Mershon, C. and Pasquino, G. (eds) (1995) *Italian Politics: Ending the First Republic*, Boulder, CO: Westview Press.

Michel, T. (2012) 'In Heidegger's Shadow: A Phenomenological Critique of Critical Realism', *Review of International Studies* 38: 209–22.

Milner, H. (1997) *Interests, Institutions and Information: Domestic Politics and International Relations*, Princeton, NJ: Princeton University Press.

Milner, H. V. (1998) 'Rationalizing Politics: The Emerging Synthesis of International, American and Comparative Politics', *International Organization* 52(4): 759–86.

Missiroli, A. (1997) 'La PESC e la politica estera Italiana: vincoli, problemi e scenari', in Bonvicini, G. (ed.) *Italia senza Europa: il costo della non partecipazione Italiana*, Milano: Franco Angeli.

Missiroli, A. (2004) 'Dopo Berlusconi: la presidenza Italiana e l'Europa', *ItalianiEuropei* 1: 108–16.

Missiroli, A. (2007) 'Italy's security and defence policy: between EU and US, or just Prodi and Berlusconi?', *Journal of Southern Europe and the Balkans* 9(2): 149–168.

Mola, A. A. (1980) *L'imperialismo industriale Italiano: la politica estera dall'Unità al fascismo*, Roma: Editori Riuniti.

Molinari, M. (2011) 'Roman Ruins: How Muammar al-Qaddafi hoodwinked Italy for decades', *Foreign Policy*, 3 March.

Mombelli, G. (1967) 'La politica estera nella stampa Italiana', in Bonanni, M. (ed.) *La politica estera Italiana*, Milano: Comunità.

Moravcsik, A. (1993a) 'Introduction: Integrating International and Domestic Theories of International Bargaining', in Evans, P., Jacobson, H. K. and Putnam R. D. (eds) *Double-Edged Diplomacy: International Bargaining and Domestic Politics, Berkeley*, CA: University of California Press.

Moravcsik, A. (1993b) 'Preferences and Power in the European Community: a Liberal Intergovernmentalist Approach', *Journal of Common Market Studies* 31(4): 473–524.

Moravcsik, A. (2003) 'Liberal International Relations Theory: A Scientific Assessment', in Elman, C. and Elman, M. F. (eds) *Progress in International Relations Theory: Appraising the Field*, Cambridge, MASS: MIT Press.

Mori, R. (1963) 'L'impresa Etiopica e le sue ripercussioni internazionali', in Torre, A. (ed.) *La politica estera Italiana dal 1914 al 1943*, Torino: Eri.

Moscati, R. (1963) 'Gli esordi della politica estera fascista, il periodo Contarini, Corfù', in *La politica estera italiana dal 1914 al 1943*, Torre, A. (ed.) Torino: Eri, Edizioni Rai Radiotelevisione italiana.

Mouritzen, H. (1996) 'Kenneth Waltz: A Critical Rationalist Between International Politics and Foreign Policy', in Neumann, I. B. and Wæver, O. (eds) *The Future of International Relations: Masters in the Making?*, London: Routledge.

Müller, H. and Risse-Kappen, T. (1993) 'From the Outside In and from the Inside Out', in Skidmore, D. and Hudson, V. (eds) *The Limits of State Autonomy*, Boulder, CA: Westview Press.

Mussolini, B. (1932) 'La dottrina del fascismo', in *Enciclopedia Italiana*, Rome: Treccani, pp. 847–51, reprinted in Oakeshott, M. (1942) *The Social and Political Doctrines of Contemporary Europe*, Cambridge: Cambridge University Press, pp. 170–71.

Mussolini, B. (1934) *L'inizio della nuova politica*, vol. 3 of *Scritti e Discorsi di Benito Mussolini*, Milano: Ulrico Hoepli Editore.

Mussolini, B. (1956–1980) *Opera Omnia*, Firenze: La Fenice.

Neal, P. N. (1996) 'The New Foreign Policy', in in Katz, R. S. and Ignazi, P. (eds) *Italian Politics: The Year of the Tycoon*, Boulder, CO: Westview Press.

Neumann, I. (1998) *Uses of the 'Other': the 'East' in European Identity Formation*, Minneapolis, MN: Minnesota University Press.

Newell, J. (2011) 'Italian Politics after the Cold War: The Continuation of a Two-Level Game', in Carbone, M. (ed.) *Italy in the Post-Cold War: Adaptation, Bipartisanship and Visibiity*, Lanham: Lexington Books.

Nexon, D. (2009) 'The Balance of Power in the Balance', *World Politics* 61(2): 330–59.

Nicolson, H. (1934) *Curzon: The Last Phase, 1919–1925*, London.

Novak, B. C. (1970) *Trieste, 1941–1954: The Ethnic, Political and Ideological Struggle*, Chicago: University of Chicago Press.

Nuti, L. (1996/7) 'Dall'operazione *Deep Rock* all'operazione *Pot Pie*: una storia documentata dei missili SM 78 Jupiter in Italia', *Storia delle relazioni internazionali* 11–12(1), 12(2): 95–138 and 105–49.

Nuti, L. (1999) *Gli Stati Uniti e l'apertura a sinistra, 1953–1963. Importanza e limiti della presenza Americana in Italia*, Roma-Bari, Laterza.

Nuti, L. (2002) 'Sources for the Study of Italian Foreign Policy, 1861–1999', *Cold War History* 2(3): 93–110.

Nuti, L. (2005) 'The richest and farthest master is always best: US–Italian relations in historical perspective', in Andrews, D. M. (ed.) *The Atlantic Alliance Under Stress: US-European Relations after Iraq*, Cambridge: Cambridge University Press.

Nuti, L. (2011) 'Italian Foreign Policy in the Cold War: A Constant Search for Status', in Carbone, M. (ed.) *Italy in the Post-Cold War: Adaptation, Bipartisanship and Visibility*, Lanham: Lexington Books.

Oakeshott, M (1942) *The Social and Political Doctrines of Contemporary Europe*, Cambridge, MA: Cambridge University Press.

Olivi, B. (1978) *Carter e l'Italia: la politica estera Americana, l'Europa e i comunisti Italiani*, Milano: Longanesi.

Olivi, B. (1993) *L'Europa difficile: storia politica della Comunità Europea*, Bologna: Il Mulino.

Ortona, E. (1986) *Anni d'America: la diplomazia 1953–1961*, Bologna: il Mulino.

O' Tuathail, G. (1996) *Critical Geopolitics: The Politics of Writing Global Space*, London: Routledge.

Panebianco, A. (1977) 'La politica estera Italiana: un modello interpretativo', *il Mulino* 254: 845–79.

Panebianco, A. (1982) 'Le cause interne del "basso profilo"', *Politica Internazionale* 10(2): 15–21.

Panebianco, A. (1997) *Guerrieri democratici: la democrazia e la politica di Potenza*, Bologna: Il Mulino.

Parker, G. (1998) *Geopolitics: Past, Present and Future*, London: Pinter.

Pasquino, G. (1974) 'Pesi internazionali e contrappesi nazionali', in Cavazza, F. L. and Graubard, S. R. (eds) *Il caso Italiano*, Milano: Garzanti.

Pasquino, G. and McCarthy, P. (1993) *The End of Post-War Politics in Italy: The Landmark 1992 Elections*, Boulder, CO: Westview Press.

Pastorelli, P. (1963) 'Dalla dichiarazione di guerra agli Stati Uniti all'armistizio', in Torre, A. (ed.) *La politica estera Italiana dal 1914 al 1943*, Torino: Eri.

Pastorelli, P. (1971) 'La storiografia Italiana del dopoguerra sulla politica estera fascista', *Storia e Politica* 10(4): 603–49.

Pastorelli, P. (1987) *La politica estera Italiana del dopoguerra*, Bologna: il Mulino.

Pastorelli, P. (1998) *Dalla prima alla seconda guerra mondiale: momenti e problemi della politica estera Italiana, 1914–1943*, Milano: LED Edizioni.

Perlmutter, T. (1998) 'The Politics of Proximity: The Italian Response to the Albanian Crisis', *International Migration Review* 32(1): 203–22.

Perrone, N. (1989) *Mattei nemico Italiano. Politica e morte del presidente dell'ENI attraverso i documenti segreti 1945–1965*, Milano: Leonardo.

Petersen, J. (1973) 'La politica estera del fascismo come problema storiografico', in De Felice, R. (ed.) *L'Italia fra tedeschi e alleati: la politica estera fascista e la seconda guerra mondiale*, Bologna: Il Mulino.

Petricciolі, M. (1983) *L'Italia in Asia Minore: equilibrio mediterraneo e ambizioni imperialistiche alla vigilia della prima guerra mondiale*, Firenze, Sansoni.

Petrignani, R. (1987) *Neutralità e Alleanza: le scelte di politica estera dell'Italia dopo l'Unità*, Bologna: Il Mulino.

Pioppi, D. (2002) 'Protagonista o comparsa? Il ruolo dell'Italia nel processo di normalizzazione della Libia', *Afriche e Orienti* 3: 50–56.

Pistone, S. (1989) *Altiero Spinelli: una strategia per gli Stati Uniti d'Europa*, Bologna: Il Mulino.

Poggiolini, I. (1990) *Diplomazia della transizione: gli alleati e il problema del trattato di pace, 1945–1947*, Firenze: Ponte alle grazie.

Pollard, J. (1991) 'Il Vaticano e la politica estera Italiana', in Bosworth, R. J. B. and Romano, S. (eds) *La politica estera Italiana, 1860–1985* Bologna: Il Mulino.

Pollard, J. (2008) *Catholicism in modern Italy: Religion, society and politics since 1861*, Abingdon–New York: Routledge.

Putnam, R. D. (1977) 'Italian Foreign Policy: The Emergent Consensus', in Penniman H. B. (ed.) *Italy at the Polls: The Parliamentary Elections of 1976*, Washington, DC: American Enterprise Institute for Public Policy Research.

Putnam, R. D. (1988) 'Diplomacy and Domestic Politics: The Logic of Two-Level Games', International Organization 43(3): 427–60.

Quartararo, R. (1977) 'Imperial Defence in the Mediterranean on the Eve of the Ethiopian Crisis (July-October 1935)', *The Historical Journal* 20(1): 185–220.

Quartararo, R. (1980) *Roma tra Londra e Berlino: la politica estera fascista dal 1931 al 1940*, Roma: Bonacci.

Quartararo, R. (1986) *Italia e Stati Uniti: gli anni difficili*, Napoli: Edizioni Scientifiche Italiane.

Ranieri, U. (1999) 'Italy Proves Equal to the Task', *International Herald Tribune/Italy Daily*, 12 June.

Ratti, L. (2011) 'Italy as a Multilateral Actor', in Carbone, M. (ed.) *Italy in the Post-Cold War: Adaptation, Bipartisanship and Visibility*, Lanham: Lexington Books.

Ratti, L. (2012) 'All aboard the bandwagon? Structural Realism and Italy's international role', *Diplomacy & Statecraft* 23(1): 87–109.

Ring, J. (1991) *Modern Political Theory and Contemporary Feminism: A Dialectical Analysis*, Albany, NY: State University of New York Press.

Rittberger, V. (1993) *Regime Theory and International Relations*, Oxford: Clarendon.

Rizzo, A. (1977) *La frontiera dell'eurocomunismo*, Bari: Laterza.

Robertson, E. M. (1971) *The Origins of the Second World War: Historical Interpretations*, London: Macmillan.

Robertson, E. M. (1979) *Mussolini as Empire-Builder: Italy and Africa, 1932–1936*, London: Palgrave.

Rochat, G. (1971) *Militari e politici nella preparazione della campagna d'Etiopia: studi e documenti*, Milano: Franco Angeli.

Romano, S. (1992) 'Com'è morta la politica estera Italiana', *il Mulino* 41(4): 714–20.

Romano, S. (1995) 'La politica estera Italiana: un bilancio e qualche prospettiva', *il Mulino* 44(1): 63–70.

Romano, S. (1996) 'Rinegoziamo le basi Americane', *Limes: rivista Italiana di geopolitica* 4: 249–53.

Romano, S. (2002) *Guida alla politica estera Italiana: da Badoglio a Berlusconi*, Milano: Rizzoli.

Romano, S. (2006) 'Berlusconi's foreign policy: Inverting traditional priorities', *The International Spectator* 41(2): 101–7.

Romeo, G. (2000) *La politica estera Italiana nell'era Andreotti*, Napoli: Rubbettino.

Rose, G. (1998) 'Neoclassical Realism and Theories of Foreign Policy', *World Politics* 51(1): 144–72.

Rosecrance, R. and Stein, A. (1993) *The Domestic Bases of Grand Strategy*, Ithaca, NY: Cornell University Press.

Rosenau, J. (1967), *The Domestic Sources of Foreign Policy*, NY: Free Press.

Rosenau, J. (1969) *Linkage Politics: Essays on the Convergence of the National and International System*, London: The Free Press.

Rosenau, J. (1971) *The Scientific Study of Foreign Policy*, New York: Free Press.

Rosenau, J. (1987) 'Introduction', in Kegley Jr, C. W., Hermann, C. and Rosenau, J. (1987) *New Directions in the Study of Foreign Policy*, Boston: Allen & Unwin.

Rosenberg, J. (2000) *The Follies of Globalisation Theory*, London: Verso.

Rosselli, N. (1954) *Inghilterra e Regno di Sardegna dal 1815 al 1847*, Torino: Einaudi.

Rossi, L. S. (2002) 'New Trends in Italy's European Policy', *The International Spectator* 37(1): 97–106.

Rossini, G. (1963) 'Introduzione', in Torre, A. (ed.) *La politica estera Italiana dal 1914 al 1943*, Torino: Eri.

Rowe, T. (2002) 'Italy in the International System', in Lyttelton, A. (ed.) *Liberal and Fascist Italy*, Oxford: Oxford University Press.

Rubin, J. (2000) 'Countdown to a Very Personal War', *Financial Times*, 30 September.

Ruggie, J. (1997) 'The Past as Prologue? Interests, Identity, and American Foreign Policy', *International Security* 21(4): 89–125.

Rumi, G. (1963) '"Revisionismo fascista" ed espansione coloniale', in *Il Movimento di Liberazione in Italia* 71: 37–73.

Rumi, G. (1968) *Alle origini della politica estera fascista*, Bari: Laterza.

Rusconi, G. E. (1993) *Se cessiamo di essere una nazione*, Bologna: il Mulino.

Sabbatucci, G. (1990) 'La soluzione trasformista: Appunti sulla vicenda del sistema politico Italiano', *Il Mulino* 39(2): 171–196.

Salvatorelli, L. (1923) *Nazionalfascismo*, Torino: Gobetti.

Salvemini, G. (1953) *Prelude to World War II*, London: Gollancz, 1953.

Salvemini, G. (1955) *Scritti sulla Questione Meridionale 1896–1955*, Torino: Einaudi.

Salvemini, G. (1964) *Dalla guerra mondiale alla dittature (1916–1925)*, Milano: Feltrinelli.

Salvemini, G. (1967) *Preludio alla seconda guerra mondiale*, Milano: Feltrinelli.

Salvemini, G. (1970) *La politica estera Italiana dal 1871 al 1915*, Milano: Feltrinelli.

Samuels, R. J. (2003) *Machiavelli's Children: Leaders and Their Legacies in Italy and Japan*, Ithaca, NY: Cornell University Press.

Santoro, C. M. (1991) *La politica estera di una media potenza: l'Italia dall'Unità ad oggi*, Bologna: Il Mulino.

Santoro, C. M. (1996) 'Le ambiguità di Limes e la vera geopolitica: elogio della teoria', *Limes: rivista Italiana di geopolitica* 4.

Santoro, C. M. (2001) 'Politica estera e identità nazionale', *Ideazione* 6.

Santoro, I. (1977) 'Le scelte economiche nella politica estera Italiana', in Ronzitti, N. (ed.) *La politica estera Italiana: autonomia, interdipendenza, integrazione e sicurezza*, Milano: Comunità.

Sassoon, D. (1976) 'The Italian Communist Party's European Strategy', *The Political Quarterly* 47(3): 253–75.

Sassoon, D. (1978) 'The Making of Italian Foreign Policy', in Wallace, W. and Paterson, W. E. (eds), *Foreign Policy-Making in Western Europe: A Comparative Approach*, Hants: Saxon House.

Sassoon, D. (1981) *The Strategy of the Italian Communist Party: From the Resistance to the Historic Compromise*, London: Pimlico.

Sayer, A. (2000) *Realism and Social Science*, London: Sage.

Sbragia, A. (2001) 'Italy Pays for Europe: Political Leadership, Political Choice, and

Institutional Adaptation', in Green Cowles, M., Caporaso, J. and Risse, T. (eds) *Transforming Europe: Europeanisation and Domestic Change*, Ithaca, NY: Cornell University Press, 2001.

Schlesinger Jr., A. M. (1968) *I mille giorni di John F. Kennedy alla Casa Bianca*, Milano: Rizzoli.

Schulin, E. (1987) 'L'eredità di Ranke e i problemi della storia delle relazioni internazionali', in Pizzetti, S. (ed.) *La storia delle relazioni internazionali nella Germania contemporanea*, Milano: Jaca Book.

Schweller, R. (1998) *Deadly Imbalances: Tripolarity and Hitler's Strategy of World Conquest*, Columbia, NY: Columbia University Press.

Schweller, R. (2006) *Unanswered Threats: Political Constraints on the Balance of Power*, Princeton: Princeton University Press.

Schweller, R. L. (1994) 'Bandwagoning for Profit: Bringing the Revisionist State Back In', *International Security* 19(1): 72–107.

Sciortino, G. (1998) 'The Albanian Crisis: Social Panic and Italian Foreign Policy', in Bardi, L. and Rhodes, M. (eds) *Italian Politics: Mapping the Future* (Boulder, CO: Westview Press, 1998).

Scoppola, P. (1977) *La proposta politica di De Gasperi*, Bologna: il Mulino.

Scoppola, P. (1997) *La Repubblica dei partiti: evoluzione e crisi di un sistema*, Bologna: Il Mulino.

Scottà, A. (ed) (2003) *La Conferenza di pace di Parigi tra ieri e domani, 1919-1920*, Catanzaro: Rubbettino.

Senghass, D. (1992) 'Weltinnenpolitik' – Ansätze für ein Konzept', *Europa-Archiv* 47(22): 643–52.

Serra, E. and Duroselle, J. B. (eds) (1984) *Italia e Francia 1946–1954*, Milano: Franco Angeli.

Serra, E. and Seton-Watson, C. (eds) (1990) *Italia e Inghilterra nell'età dell'imperialismo*, Milano: Francoangeli.

Seton-Watson, C. (1967) *Italy from Liberalism to Fascism 1870–1925*, London: Methuen & Co.

Sforza, C. (1952) *Cinque anni a Palazzo Chigi: la politica estera Italiana dal 1947 al 1951*, Roma: Atlante.

Sica, M. (1991) *Marigold non forì: il contributo Italiano alla pace in Vietnam*, Firenze: Ponte alle grazie.

Sica, M. (1994) *Operazione Somalia: la dittatura, l'opposizione, la guerra civile*, Venezia: Marsilio.

Silj, A. (ed.) (1998) *L'alleato scomodo: i rapporti tra Roma e Washington nel Mediterraneo: Sigonella e Gheddafi*, Milano: Corbaccio.

Silvestri, S. (1999) 'Libya and Transatlantic Relations: An Italian View', in Haas, R. N. (ed.) *Transatlantic Tensions: The United States, Europe, and Problem Countries*, Washington, DC: Brookings Institution Press.

Silvestri, S. (2007) 'Il Grande Fratello, sei ambasciatori e Veronica Lario', *Affari Internazionali*, 8 February 2007, available at www.affarinternazionali.it/articolo.asp?ID=450 (15 March 2013).

Simms, B. (2003) 'The Return of the Primacy of Foreign Policy', *German History* 21(3): 275–91.

Singer, J. D. (1961) 'The Level-of-Analysis Problem in International Relations', in Knorr, K. and Verba, S. (eds) *The International System: Theoretical Essays, Princeton*, NJ: Princeton University Press.

Smith, K. and Light, M. (2001) *Ethics and Foreign Policy*, Cambridge: CUP.

Smith, S. (1981) *Foreign Policy Adaptation*, Aldershot: Gower Publishing.

Smith, S., Hadfield, A. and Dunne, T. (eds) (2012) *Foreign Policy: Theories, Actors, Cases*, Oxford: Oxford University Press, 2nd edn.

Smith, T. W. (1999) *History and International Relations*, London: Routledge.

Snyder, J. (1991) *Myths of Empire: Domestic Politics and International Ambition*, Ithaca, NY: Cornell University Press.

Sørensen, G. (2001) *Changes in Statehood: The Transformation of International Relations*, Houndmills: Palgrave.

Spadolini, G. (1960) *Giolitti e i cattolici, 1901–1914*, Firenze: Le Monnier.

Spadolini, G. (1987) 'Prefazione', in Petrignani, R. *Neutralità e Alleanza: le scelte di politica estera dell'Italia dopo l'Unità*, Bologna: Il Mulino.

Spadolini, G. (ed.) (1994) *Nazione e Nazionalità in Italia: dall'alba del secolo ai nostri giorni*, Bari: Laterza.

Spinelli, A. (1967) 'Problemi e prospettive della politica estera Italiana', in Bonanni, M. (ed) *La politica estera della repubblica Italiana*, Milano: Edizioni di Comunità.

Spinelli, A. (2000) *Europa terza forza: politica estera e difesa comune negli anni della guerra fredda: scritti 1947–1954*, Graglia, P. S. (ed.), Bologna: Il Mulino.

Sprout, H. and Sprout, M. (1965) *The Ecological Perspective on Human Affairs: With Special Reference to International Politics*, Princeton: Princeton University Press.

Stephanson, A. (1994) 'The United States', in Reynolds, D. (ed.) *The Origins of the Cold War in Europe: International Perspectives*, New Haven, NJ: Yale University Press.

Sterpellone, A. (1967) 'Vent'anni di politica estera', in Bonanni, M. (1967) *La politica estera della repubblica Italiana*, Milano: Edizioni di Comunità.

Stimson, H and Bundy, M. (1948) *On Active Service in Peace and War*, New York: Harper.

Strange, S. (1988) *States and Markets*, London: Pinter.

Stuart Hughes, H. (1953) *The United States and Italy*, Cambridge, MA: Harvard University Press.

Suganami, H. (1996) *On the Causes of War*, Oxford: Clarendon Press.

Suganami, H. (1999) 'Agents, Structures, Narratives', *European Journal of International Relations* 5(3): 365–86.

Tamburrano, G. (1973) *Storia e cronaca del centro-sinistra*, Milano: Feltrinelli.

Tana, F. (1985) *La lezione del Libano: la missione della forza multinazionale e la politica estera Italiana*, Milano: Angeli.

Tarchiani, A. (1955) *Dieci anni tra Roma e Washington*, Milano: Mondadori.

Taylor, A. J. P (1964) *The Origins of the Second World War*, Harmonsworth: Penguin.

Taylor, A. J. P (1971) *The Struggle for Mastery in Europe, 1848–1918*, Oxford: Oxford University Press.

Taylor, C. (1985) *Philosophy and the Human Sciences*, Cambridge: Cambridge University Press.

Taylor, M. (1989) 'Structure, Culture and Action in the Explanation of Social Change', *Politics and Society* 17(2): 115–62.

Tedesco, L. (2002) *L'alternativa liberista in Italia: crisi di fine secolo, antiprotezionismo e finanza democratica nei liberali radicali, 1898–1904*, Catanzaro: Rubbettino.

Tetlock, P. and Belkin, A. (eds) (1996) *Counterfactual Thought Experiments in World Politics: Logical, Methodological and Psychological Perspectives*, Princeton, NJ: Princeton University Press.

The Economist (1994) 'Mussolini is Dead – For the Moment', 11 June.

The Wall Street Journal (2003), 'United We Stand: Eight European Leaders are as One with President Bush', 30 January.

Tilly, C. (1975) *The Formation of National States in Western Europe*, Princeton, NJ: Princeton University Press, 1975.

Togliatti, P. (1964) 'Per comprendere la politica estera del fascismo Italiano', in *Lo Stato operaio*, Rome: Editori Riuniti.

Torre, A. (1959) *La politica estera dell'Italia dal 1870 al 1896*, Bologna: R. Pàtron.

Torre, A. (1963a) *La politica estera Italiana dal 1914 al 1943*, Torino: Eri

Torre, A. (1963b) 'Prefazione', in Torre, A. (ed.) *La politica estera Italiana dal 1914 al 1943*, Torino: Eri.

Toscano, M. (1963a) 'L'Asse Roma-Berlino, Il Patto Comintern, La guerra civile in Spagna, l'Anschluss, Monaco', in Torre, A. (ed.) *La politica estera Italiana dal 1914 al 1943*, Torino: Eri.

Toscano, M. (1963b) 'Il Patto d'Acciaio, la seconda guerra mondiale, la "non belligeranza" dell'Italia', in Torre, A. (ed.) *La politica estera Italiana dal 1914 al 1943*, Torino: Eri.

Tripodi, P. (1999) *The Colonial Legacy in Somalia: Rome and Mogadishu from Colonial Administration to Operation Restore Hope*, Basingstoke: Macmillan.

Tripodi, P. (2002) 'Operation *Alba*: A Necessary and Successful Preventive Deployment', *International Peacekeeping* 9(4): 89–104.

Tsebelis, G. (1988) 'Nested Games: The Cohesion of French Coalitions', *British Journal of Political Science* 18(2): 145–70.

Tsebelis, G. (1990) *Nested Games: Rational Choice in Comparative Politics*, Berkley, CA: University of California Press.

Tunander, O., Baev, P. and Einagel, V. I. (eds) (1997) *Geopolitics in Post-Wall Europe Security, Territory and Identity*, London: Sage.

Urbinati, N. (2012) 'La fine della Seconda Repubblica scrita nell'epilogo della prima', *La Repubblica*, 8 April.

Vannicelli, P. (1974) *Italy, NATO, and the European Community: The Interplay of Foreign Policy and Domestic Politics*, Harvard: Center for International Affairs.

Varsori, A. (1998) *L'Italia nelle relazioni internazionali dal 1943 al 1992*, Roma: Laterza.

Varsori, A. (1990) 'De Gasperi, Nenni, Sforza e il loro ruolo nella politica estera Italiana del dopoguerra', in Di Nolfo, E., Rainero, R. H. and Vigezzi, B. (eds) *L'Italia e la politica di potenza in Europa, 1945–1950*, Milano: Marzorati.

Vasile, A. (1967) 'La politica estera della DC', in Bonanni, M. (ed.) *La politica estera della repubblica Italiana*, Milano: Comunità.

Vezzosi, E. (1990) 'La sinistra democristiana tra neutralismo e Patto Atlantico (1947–1949)', in Di Nolfo, E., Rainero, R. H. and Vigezzi, B. (eds) *L'Italia e la politica di potenza in Europa, 1945–1950*, Milano: Marzorati.

Vigezzi, B. (1969) *Da Giolitti a Salandra*, Firenze: Vallecchi.

Vigezzi, B. (1990) 'De Gasperi, Sforza, la diplomazia Italiana', in Di Nolfo, E., Rainero, R. H. and Vigezzi, B. (eds) *L'Italia e la politica di potenza in Europa, 1945–1950*, Milano: Marzorati.

Vigezzi, B. (1991) *Politica estera e opinione pubblica in Italia dall'Unità ai giorni nostri: orientamenti degli studi e prospettive della ricerca*, Milano: Jaca Book.

Vigezzi, B. (1992) 'L'Italia e i problemi della "politica di potenza"', in Di Nolfo, E., Rainero, R. H. and Vigezzi, B. (eds) *L'Italia e la politica di potenza in Europa, 1950-1960*, Milano: Marzorati.

Vigezzi, B. (1997a) *L'Italia Unita e le sfide della politica estera*, Milano: Unicopli.

Vigezzi, B. (1997b) *Repertorio bibliografico della politica estera Italiana dall'Unità ad oggi: guida agli studi apparsi dal 1980 al 1990*, Milano: ISPI-SPAI.

Von Ranke, L. (1950) 'A Dialogue on Politics', in von Laue, T. (ed.) *Leopold von Ranke: The Formative Years*, Princeton: Princeton University Press.

Wæver, O. (1994) 'Resisting the Temptation of Post Foreign Policy Analysis', in Carlsnaes. W. and Smith, S. (eds) *European Foreign Policy: The EC and Changing Perspectives in Europe*, London: Sage.

Wæver, O. (1996) 'The Rise and Fall of the Inter-paradigm Debate', in Smith, S., Booth, K. and Zalewski, M. (eds) *International Theory: Positivism and Beyond*, Cambridge: Cambridge University Press.

Waley, D. (1975) *British Public Opinion and the Abyssinian War, 1935–6*, London: London School of Economics, 1975.

Walker, R. B. J. (1993) *Inside/Outside: International Relations as Political Theory*, Cambridge: Cambridge University Press.

Wallace, W. (1971) *Foreign Policy and the Political Process*, London: Macmillan.

Walston, J. (2004) 'Italian Foreign Policy: Light and Shade in the Second Berlusconi Government', paper presented at the Annual Conference of the Association for the Study of Modern Italy (ASMI), London, 26–27 November.

Walston, J. (2007) 'Italian Foreign Policy in the "Second Republic". Changes of Form and Substance', *Modern Italy* 12(1): 91–104.

Walston, J. (2008) 'Foreign policy: the difficult pursuit of influence' in Donovan, M. and Onofri, P. (eds) *Italian Politics: Frustrated Aspirations for Change*, New York: Berghan.

Waltz, K. (1959) *Man, the State and War: A Theoretical Analysis*, New York: Columbia University Press.

Waltz, K. (1968) *Foreign Policy and the Democratic Politics: The American and British Experience*, London: Longmans.

Waltz, K. (1979) *Theory of International Politics*, Reading, MA: Addison Wesley.

Waltz, K. (1986) 'A Response to My Critics', in Keohane, R. O. (ed.) *Neorealism and its Critics*, New York: Columbia University Press.

Waltz, K. (1996) 'International Politics Is Not Foreign Policy', *Security Studies* 6(1): 54–7.

Watson, A. (1992) *The Evolution of International Society: A Comparative and Historical Analysis*, London: Routledge.

Watson, D. and Hay, C. (2003) 'The Discourse of Globalisation and the Logic of No Alternative: Rendering the Contingent Necessary in the Political Economy of the New Labour', *Policy and Politics* 31(3): 289–305.

Watt, D. C. (2001) *How War Came: The Immediate Origins of the Second World War, 1938–1939*, rev. edn., London: Pimlico.

Weber, M. (1949) *On the Methodology of the Social Sciences*, New York: The Free Press.

Weber, M. (1968) *Economy and Society: An Outline of Interpretative Sociology*, New York: Bedminster Press.

Webster, R. A. (1974) *L'imperialismo industriale Italiano, 1908–1915: studio sul prefascismo*, Torino: Einaudi.

Wehler, H. U. (1973) *Das deutsche Kaiserreich, 1871–1918*, Göttingen: Vandenhoeck & Ruprecht.

Wehler, H. U. (1984) *Bismarck und der Imperialismus*, 5th edn, Verlag: Suhrkamp.

Weitsman, P. (2004) *Dangerous Alliances: Proponents of Peace, Weapons of War*, Stanford: Stanford University Press.

Wendt, A. (1987) 'The Agency-Structure Problem in International Relations', *International Organisation* 41(2): 335–70.

Wendt, A. (1991) 'Bridging the theory/metatheory gap in international relations', *Review of International Studies* 17(4): 383–92.

Wendt, A. (1992) 'Levels of Analysis vs. Agents and Structures: Part III', *Review of International Studies* 18(2): 181–5.

Wendt, A. (1999) *Social Theory of International Politics*, Cambridge: Cambridge University Press.

Wendt, A. and Shapiro, I. (1997) 'The Misunderstood Promise of Realist Social Theory', in Monroe, K. R. (ed.) *Contemporary Empirical Political Theory*, Berkeley, CA: University of California Press.

White, B. (1999) 'The European Challenge to Foreign Policy Analysis', *European Journal of International Relations* 5(1): 37–66.

Wight, C. (1999) 'They Shoot Dead Horses Don't They? Locating Agency in the Agent Structure Problematique', *European Journal of International Relations* 5(1): 109–42.

Wight, C. (2006) *Agents, Structures and International Relations: Politics as Ontology*, Cambridge: Cambridge University Press.

Wight, C. (2012) 'Philosophy of Social Science and International Relations' in Carlsnaes, W., Simmons, B. and Risse-Kappen, T. (eds) *Handbook of International Relations*, London: Sage.

Wight, M (1952) 'The Balance of Power', in Toynbee, A. and Ashton-Gwatink, F. T. (eds) *Survey of International Affairs: The World in March 1939*, London: Oxford University Press.

Wolfers, A. (1962) *Discord and Collaboration: Essays on International Politics*, Baltimore, MD: The Johns Hopkins Press.

Wollemborg, L. (1983) *Stelle, strisce e tricolore: trent'anni di vicende politiche tra Roma e Washington*, Milano: Mondadori.

Zakaria, F. (1992) 'Realism and Domestic Politics', *International Security* 17(1): 177–98.

Zakaria, F. (1998) *From Wealth to Power: The Unusual Origins of America's World Role*, Princeton, NJ: Princeton University Press.

Zamagni, V. (1990), *Dalla periferia al centro: la seconda rinascita economica dell'Italia 1861–1981*, Bologna: Il Mulino.

Zannoni, F. (1997) *La logica del disordine: la politica di sicurezza Italiana nell'era post-bipolare*, Milano: Franco Angeli.

Index